D0074965

WILLIAM F. MAAG LIBRARY
YOUNGSTOWN STATE UNIVERSITY

An Epoch of Miracles

The Texas Pan American Series

Alonzo Gonzales Mó,
Ticul, Yucatán

Pascual May and his family, X-cacal, Quintana Roo

An Epoch of Miracles

ORAL LITERATURE OF THE YUCATEC MAYA

Translated with commentaries by ALLAN F. BURNS
Foreword by Dennis Tedlock

{WITHDRAWN}

Paulino Yamá, Señor, Quintana Roo

 UNIVERSITY OF TEXAS PRESS, AUSTIN

Copyright © 1983 by the University of Texas Press
All rights reserved
Printed in the United States of America
First Edition, 1983

Requests for permission to reproduce material from this work should be
sent to Permissions, University of Texas Press, Box 7819, Austin, Texas
78712.

Library of Congress Cataloging in Publication Data
Burns, Allan F. (Allan Frank), 1945–
  An epoch of miracles.

  (The Texas Pan American series)
  Bibliography: p.
  1. Maya literature—Translations into English.
2. Mayas—Folklore. 3. Indians of Mexico—Folklore.
I. Title. II. Series.
PM3968.55.E55 1982   398.2'08997   82-8508
ISBN 0-292-72037-8   AACR2

The drawings at the beginning of each chapter in this book are from *A
Study of Maya Art: Its Subject Matter and Historical Development*, by
Herbert J. Spinden, Memoirs of the Peabody Museum of American Ar-
chaeology and Ethnology, Harvard University, vol. 6 (Cambridge, Mass.:
Peabody Museum, 1913), figs. 8, 22, 24, 102i, 115c, 123d, 135, 207, 232.

*The Texas Pan American Series is published with the assistance of a
revolving publication fund established by the Pan American Sulphur
Company. Publication of this book was also assisted by a grant from
the National Endowment for the Humanities, an independent federal
agency whose mission is to award grants to support education, scholar-
ship, media programming, libraries, and museums in order to bring the
results of cultural activities to the general public.*

PM
3968.55
·E5
/1983

THIS BOOK IS DEDICATED
TO THE MEMORY OF MELVILLE JACOBS

WILLIAM F. MAAG LIBRARY
YOUNGSTOWN STATE UNIVERSITY

CONTENTS

FOREWORD

FOREWORD

BY DENNIS TEDLOCK

"Mr. Allan Burns, I am here to tell you an example, the example of the Hunchbacks." That's what Paulino Yamá, traditionalist and storyteller, said to Allan Burns, anthropologist and linguist, in the process of beginning a story that found its way into this book. The event itself is remarkable enough—that the person who asked for the story, Mr. Allan Burns, should become part of the text of that story. But what is more remarkable still is that Mr. Allan Burns, instead of acting, in these pages, as if he had been the invisible and mute observer of Maya who were simply going about their usual business, has chosen to drop the onlooker's mask and let us see plainly that these Maya took full account of his presence among them. In so doing, he has placed himself in the service of the Mayan notion that a person who asks for a verbal performance should participate in the event, rather than in the service of the traditional scholarly notion that verbal art is an object that should be collected without creating any disturbance.

There may be no people anywhere more reluctant than the Maya—in Yucatán and in general—to suspend or abridge the fundamentally dialogical nature of speech in favor of the demands of one single voice pronouncing the Word into a passive ear. In this they could scarcely be more different from missionaries—and, yes, from anthropologists too, who tend to produce certain books in which only anthropologists speak and other, quite separate books in which only natives speak. For the Yucatec Maya, even an asymmetrical genre such as narrative formally requires performance not only by "the person who knows the stories" but by "the person who knows how to answer," the latter being much more than a mere member of an audience. And (as we learn here for the first time), when the scene shifts to the gathering of an entire community for readings from a Chilam Balam book (the Mayan equivalent of Scripture), dialogue is preserved by having two readers, speaking antiphonally. At the opposite extreme, as when Alonzo Gonzales Mó sits down alone to write in a notebook for Allan Burns (see the "Definitions" in chapter 7), dialogue is kept alive through the use of the first and second persons, and questions are addressed to the reader.

Burns has brought the Mayan spirit of dialogue even to his task as a translator. Not only does he face some of his English pages with Mayan ones, but he eases our way into the Mayan language by introducing us to some of its general features early on, and he even gives us a glimpse of how Mayan speakers chose to teach him that language when he was in the field. He is also true to the spirit of dialogue when he lets us in on "experimental" discourses that go beyond Mayan generic boundaries, taking forms that developed specifically within the intersubjective, intercultural world created by and during field work. One of these experiments, "The Story of the Milpa," is a remarkably rich tapestry of Mayan self-description, the kind of text Paul Radin would have greatly admired, complete with its own internal storytelling interlude in a day in the life of a *milpero*, a story within a story.

In dealing with content, as with form, Burns does not allow himself to be limited by the standards of the antiquarian, who is always overanxious to learn what the Maya may have preserved from that mythic age before Europeans first arrived. In these pages we will find more from that age than we might have expected, especially when the Feathered Serpent and the Owners of Rain make their appearances, but we are also treated to the likes of Fidel Castro and Richard Nixon. Here, too, is Sylvanus G. Morley, who, if he were still with us, would finally learn just what the Maya were saying to him on a memorable public occasion down in Yucatán. At the very same time, it is abundantly clear that the Mayan "epoch of miracles" never really ends. We learn that, in Quintana Roo, the Caste War is still on, and Mexico "is so far away"! At home with the Maya, even a dark story about secrets can end with the narrator's remark that he recently walked by the very house where the survivors of that story still live.

This book not only deals with events but itself becomes an event in the process, an event for all those who study the Maya and for all those—be they linguists, anthropologists, or folklorists—who treat the verbal arts as performing arts. Here are not only texts and translations, words and sentences, but sounds and intervening silences, shouts and whispers, passages in which performers sneak up on things and others in which they take things by storm. And we can clearly see that there is much more to Mayan phrasing than the ceaseless milling of the couplets we have heard so much about, couplets though there may be.

There is no other book for all of Mesoamerica that so brings the verbal arts to life, that lets them breathe, the way this one does. We should all be thankful to Alonzo Gonzales Mó, Paulino Yamá, Pascual May, and Santiago Chan for sharing their ancient conversations, their counsels and secrets, their riddles and jokes with Allan Burns. And to Allan Burns, for sharing these with us, thanks again.

ACKNOWLEDGMENTS

I owe the greatest debt of gratitude to Julie Gray Burns and our children, Jessica and Christopher, for their help in writing this book. They assisted with the research in Yucatán, the frequent trips back to see friends and check on ideas, and the editing of the book. Our "other family" in Yucatán, the Tuyubs, were most gracious in the hospitality which they extended to us over the years. Doña Severina and Don Elias Orozco, their children, Manuela, Teresa, Luis Fernando, Mario, Arturo, and Manuel, and all of the grandchildren have always made our visits to Yucatán completely enjoyable. Our compadres Don Luis and Doña Julia and Don Mario and Doña Manuela remain our special friends, even though time and distance have put a strain on our relationship.

Each of the narrators included in this book taught me something of the style and grace that mark Yucatec Mayan culture and language. My master teacher was Alonzo Gonzales Mó. Alonzo introduced me to the bittersweet historic sense of the Yucatec Mayan world view, made highly personal by the complicated pattern of Alonzo's own life. He was patient in teaching me to talk in Mayan, to listen to the sounds and rhythms of the jungle and the milpa, and to see the ironic humor in many of the events of our lives. Paulino Yamá wanted to have his own words about the history and the contemporary life of Yucatec Mayan people become available to a wide audience beyond the Yucatán Peninsula. I hope that these translations have been a step in that direction. Pascual May and Santiago Chan were the other two performers who shared their stories with me. To all of them I owe a great debt of gratitude for their assistance in creating this book.

I would also like to acknowledge the intellectual stimulation of Dennis Tedlock and Melville Jacobs, who introduced me to oral literature as the most effective way to bring about a cultural dialogue between our way of life and that of others. Pat and Terry Hays, Keats Garman, and Carol Eastman have shown keen interest in this project and provided many hours of discussion, help, and other support during its preparation.

Institutional support for the first field work in Yucatán was provided through a National Science Foundation grant, "Yucatec Studies" (GS 3022), under the direction of Michael Owen at the University of Washington. Subsequent support was provided by the University of Washington Department of Anthropology and the University of Florida Department of Anthropology and Center for Latin

American Studies. I would like to thank Carol Shaffer for her excellent typing of the manuscript and Mary Fearn, who assisted her with some of the chapters.

Finally, I would like to thank two editors from the University of Texas Press, Scott Lubeck and Holly Carver. Without their interest in these stories, encouragement of the project, and careful readings of each page, this book would not have been possible. It has been a pleasure to work with such fine counselors.

An Epoch of Miracles

1. INTRODUCTION

One of the remarkable things about the Maya today is their keen interest in verbal art. Puns, plays on words, formal greetings and farewells, and folk narratives add an oral quality to Mayan life and give Mayan conversations a distinctive style. "Where do you come from?" someone might ask. "The town of Ticul" is one appropriate answer. "Oh, *ti-culcabah* or 'at that place they sat themselves down'" might be another reply, a reply which extends the sound and meaning of the place-name Ticul into a little play on words.[1]

The brief exchanges at the marketplace, the greetings on the street, the stories told on the park benches at dusk, and the secret myths told late at night make up a rich tapestry of oral literature that is as strong today among the Maya as it has been in the past. The Maya are well attuned to the soundscape of their culture. Theirs is a culture which pays close attention to the sounds that surround them, the sounds of unseen birds in the jungle, the sounds of the winds that bring rain, and the sounds of animals in the night. The folklorist Alan Dundes (1972) has shown how North Americans focus much of their attention on the sense of sight. The Maya, in contrast, are more aware of the aural side of perception. The importance of the spoken word was constantly reinforced during the two years my family and I lived in Yucatán learning about Mayan culture. For example, we were told never to say the word *chho* or "mouse" around our baby. If we saw a mouse and wanted to talk about it, we were told to call it a *ceh* or "deer." Saying *chho* out loud could cause our child to have colic. I later learned that deer are allies,

1. The alphabet I have used for Yucatec Mayan is given later in this chapter.

guardians who live in the deep forest as alter egos to people in villages and towns. Saying *chho* might upset the relationship between our child and her deer guardian. This connection between deer and small children was noted by Fray Diego de Landa in 1566 as he was describing the Maya at the time of the Spanish arrival. He relates that deer were so domesticated that Mayan women were seen "even offering their breast to the deer, which they have so tamed that they never run away into the woods" (1978: 55).

The myths, stories, and other forms of Yucatec Mayan verbal art in this book were collected in two villages, one a large town of more than fourteen thousand people, Ticul, Yucatán, the other a small village of four hundred people, Señor, Quintana Roo. The storytellers were modern Mayan people who live with radio, television, and rapid transportation. The narrators told many of the stories specifically so that their words and ideas would become known beyond the Mayan world. Their stories are the beginnings of a dialogue between the oral culture of the Maya and the literate culture of modern Mexico and the United States. Many of the themes and characters in the stories are found in our own tradition as well as that of the Maya. In this way the narrators attempted to make their own experiences comprehensible to the wider world. When one orator learned that I was an anthropologist, he created a narrative about the first time he had met the famous Mayan archaeologist Sylvanus Morley in the early part of this century. Other stories began with a greeting to the president of the United States or, in one case, with a greeting to my own father. Biblical characters such as Noah and Jesus Christ appear in many narratives, as do such folk heroes as Aladdin. Fidel Castro even makes an appearance in one narrative.

Since my family and I began work in Yucatán in 1970 and through the visits we have made back there every year, the storytellers and their families have taken pride in the fact that their oral literature, so central to their present-day culture, was being brought to a wider audience. Mayan oral literature has a sense of majesty that is complemented by both mirth and mysticism. The material I have translated here is only a small sample of the poetic repertoire of voices and images that Yucatec Mayan people use to give meaning to their lives.

The Mayan Tradition

Today there are over two million Mayan people living in Central America. The Maya constitute the largest group of indigenous people in the New World north of Peru (Coe 1966: 17). They continue to inhabit the lowlands and highlands of southern Mexico, Guatemala, Belize, El Salvador, and Honduras just as they have for the past two thousand years. The Maya of today are heirs to a long cultural tradition, one which has been recognizably Mayan in places like Tikal in the Petén of Guatemala since 600 B.C. Over the centuries the Mayan civilization has developed cultural patterns and artifacts which have had a great impact on the world.

The Maya built remarkable ceremonial centers which even today have not all been discovered and mapped. These monumental cities contained intricately designed temples, raised stages for ceremonial enactments of comedies and tragedies, and carefully constructed ball courts for ritual games. The Maya invented a system of writing to keep account of ritual and secular activities; this invention represents an event which has taken place only three other times in human history. Mayan astronomers and mathematicians developed calendars for the earth, the moon, Venus, and other heavenly bodies by basing their calculations on a number system which included place value and the concept of zero. This mathematical precision predated the European use of the concept of zero by a thousand years. It is possible that the Mayan concept of zero was diffused from the New World to the Orient and ultimately became the basis for modern science in Europe.

Important crops domesticated by the Maya included cacao, the beans of which were used as currency. The Maya learned to draw latex from sapodilla trees and gave the world chewing gum and rubber balls. Important food crops domesticated by Mayan farmers and now in general use include avocados, papayas, several types of beans and squashes, as well as several varieties of corn and tomatoes. The slash-and-burn or milpa system of shifting cultivation, still used by the Maya today, is an ecologically sound and productive system of multiple cropping which has sustained the Maya through their long history.

The rich heritage of the Maya was augmented by an equally rich but less understood system of thought. From pictographic and glyphic evidence, archaeologists have interpreted the Maya before European colonization as a people given to very elaborate religious traditions which supported the power of a political and managerial elite (Coe 1966; Stuart and Stuart 1977). Religious knowledge was highly valued, and an important function of religious specialists was divination. These specialists gave practical advice to peasants about meteorological changes in the wet and dry seasons and used their calendrical knowledge to predict which days would be auspicious for planting, harvesting, or preparing agricultural plots. In addition, more esoteric knowledge of how to interpret people's dreams, the supernatural winds and beings of the night, and the future of political intrigue gave the ancient Mayan philosopher-priests authority over the emotional and social lives of both the elite and the peasantry.

Our knowledge of ancient Mayan thought is slight in comparison to what is known of their physical lives. The few notions that have been gleaned from intense efforts to decode the three remaining Mayan hieroglyphic books or codices, from the study of the archaeology of the ceremonial centers, and from the few scattered accounts of the Maya written soon after European contact provide only a glimpse into the Mayan mind. One archaeologist, Richard Adams (1977: 5), has calculated that the past one hundred years of archaeological excavation have yielded only about 5 percent of what can be learned of pre-Columbian Mayan life. Our knowledge of Mayan thought probably amounts to less than 1 percent of what could be learned.

It is their system of thought that has sustained the Maya from their migration into the area in the first millennium before Christ, through the building of the elaborate ceremonial centers of Tikal, Uxmal, and Palenque, through the conquest of the New World in the sixteenth century, and into the petroleum age of today. Like the dramatic changes that have occurred in the past, such as the collapse of Classic Mayan society, new oil reserves that have been discovered off the coast of Yucatán and international tourism are effecting great changes in Mayan life today. But, while contemporary Mayan people have learned to speak Spanish and have become articulated with the rest of the world through trade and politics, they have remained true to their traditional way of life and way of looking at and understanding the universe. Although a modern petroleum age Mayan person may manufacture women's shoes in a small shop and sell wares to the European market, the thought of retiring to the countryside to make a small corn garden remains as a dream of the ideal life. The guardians of the forest, the helpers of the rain god Chac, and Yum Sun, otherwise known as Jesus Christ, still inhabit the Mayan cosmos today as they have in the past.

The myths, stories, jokes, and wordplay of the Mayan oral tradition provide a pathway into Mayan thought, a pathway which leads not just to the ancient Maya of archaeological interest but to the modern Maya as well. The Maya today do not view the myth age or the "epoch of miracles" as having ended. Instead the Feathered Serpent of pre-Columbian times is still talked about and has been reported to have landed in several cemeteries lately. Mayan oral literature today combines such images as the Feathered Serpent with famous people of the wider world like Fidel Castro. Mayan thought today, as illustrated by this collection of oral literature, embraces pre-Columbian and modern themes. The Maya living in the last quarter of this twentieth century are not antiquarian holdouts from a previous age, nor have they shed their cultural heritage in the process of becoming modern. Their culture is intact and full of internal strength, although as always it is changing, adapting, and integrating features from other cultural worlds.

The Yucatec Maya

The oral literature presented in this book is a product of the Yucatec Maya, a group of three hundred thousand people living in the Mexican states of Yucatán, Quintana Roo, and Campeche and in the lowlands of Guatemala and Belize. The Yucatec Maya speak one of the twenty-four Mayan languages of Central America, each of which is as different from the others as the Romance languages of Europe. The Yucatec Maya live in the lowlands of the Yucatán Peninsula, a hot, flat land. Compared to the highlands of Chiapas and Guatemala, the lowland environment of the peninsula is quite uniform. Few rivers or lakes are found on the limestone shelf which makes up the peninsula, and most settlements have historically been found around such natural water sources as the cenotes or sinkholes created by the collapse of the limestone into underground aquifers. The average annual temperature of the lowlands is seventy-eight degrees Fahrenheit, and the rainfall averages between twenty and ninety inches a year as one travels from the extreme northwest of the peninsula to the extreme southeast (Villa Rojas 1969).

This uniformity in environment is mirrored in a uniformity of culture in the Yucatec Mayan lowlands. Unlike the colorful highlands of Chiapas and Guatemala, where each mountain valley contains villages and towns which differ remarkably in dress, language, and craft specialization, the lowlands of Yucatán contain villages with little craft specialization, very few dialect differences, and an overall similarity in dress and house form. Local identity and distinctiveness are present in the lowlands, but the symbols used to express identity are not as dramatic as in the highlands. Yucatec Mayan people look for such subtle differences as the cut of a man's *arpagatas* or sandals, the stitching of his hat, or the particular flower design on a woman's huipil to learn someone's identity. Further insight is gained by listening to speech patterns. A preponderance of Spanish loanwords in a Mayan conversation signals the urban way of

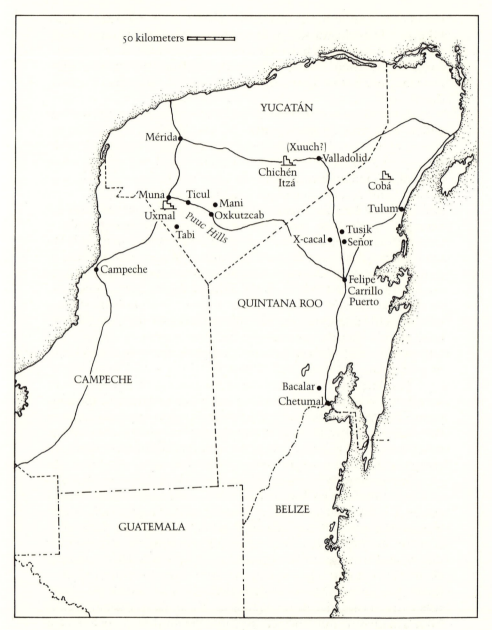

The Yucatán Peninsula, with the principal places mentioned in the text

life of someone living in the only major city of Yucatán, Mérida. Likewise, fewer loanwords from Spanish and topical themes of independence and strong religiosity in conversation might identify someone as coming from Quintana Roo, where rebel Maya set up an independent government during the Caste War of the nineteenth century (Reed 1964).

All place-names in Yucatán are Mayan, except for a few cities which were given Spanish names after the conquest. Even these cities are known unofficially by their Mayan names, though. Mérida, the capital of the state of Yucatán, is known in Mayan as Ti-Ho. The town of Valladolid, located near the ruins of Chichén Itzá, is known as Saci. Some recollection of preconquest ceremonial center identity still exists in Yucatán. Many Mayan people in the town of Ticul, for example, continue to take their identity from the nearby ruins of Uxmal. I was warned by Ticuleños that, if one visits Uxmal on his or her birthday, the voices of one's ancestral family members would be heard. In the isolated areas of Quintana Roo, some Mayan villages are centered around the ruins of Tulum. Villagers in that area refer to the ruins by the word meaning "town," *cah*. Another village where we lived in Quintana Roo, Señor, is one of the cluster of villages which identify themselves with the present-day ceremonial village of X-cacal (Villa Rojas 1945). Villagers there refer to the ceremonial village as "town" or *cah* as well.

The differences between Yucatec Mayan people are more those of region and history than those of community as found in the highlands of Chiapas and Guatemala. When Yucatán was conquered by the Spaniards in 1542, the area was already broken into a number of rival states, each ruled by a local noble family. In the years since the conquest, Yucatán has been the site of several native rebellions, the most recent of which was the Caste War, which began in 1848 and continues, in dormant form, even today. In the areas where Spanish control has been strongest, Mayan farmland has been replaced with plantations, which first produced sugarcane in the early nineteenth century and later switched to the cultivation of henequen, from which sisal is made. This change in land use has made Yucatán an area which exhibits a gradation from towns that are very Spanish to those that are very Mayan. Robert Redfield (1941) found the peninsula to be a classic locale for examining the process of acculturation from a native or folk society to a modern European society. The northern part of the peninsula, including the capital city of Mérida, has borne the brunt of European domination in culture, land use, and language. Beyond this zone of commercial henequen production is a middle zone of small corn farmers and commercial artisans, in

WILLIAM F. MAAG LIBRARY
YOUNGSTOWN STATE UNIVERSITY

towns like Ticul, who are bilingual and bicultural in Mayan and Spanish. Further south, in the rain forest of Quintana Roo, are Mayan people who still will have little to do with the national culture of Mexico, people who have built a boundary around their way of life by vividly remembering the events and causes of the Caste War. These historical differences, on top of the earlier regional differences which existed in Yucatán at the time of Spanish colonialism, are the basis for differences in Yucatecan communities. Beneath these differences is a common Mayan substrate, involving a set of common actions and beliefs surrounding corn, a system of social relationships, and the continued use of the Yucatec Mayan language.

The most significant social division in the Yucatán Peninsula is that between Mayan people and non-Mayan people. Many Maya would phrase this difference as being one between people who make a milpa or corn garden and those who do not. Preparing the forest for a milpa, harvesting the ears, transforming the kernels of corn into dough for tortillas, and eating the light, good-tasting food with every meal define one as Mayan. Even in towns and cities where forms of artistry such as pottery making or shoemaking have become full-time occupations, the fact that one can claim that relatives still are "of the milpa" is a symbol of Mayan identity. Corn farming is not a mere commercial activity for Mayan people but is a way of life based on a sacred and fulfilling tradition. Each year when new areas of the forest or jungle are mapped out, cut, burned, fenced, and planted with corn and other crops, Mayan people revitalize their common heritage. Simple corn, transformed from seeds to human food, changes its name in this cultural process. It is no longer plain *ixi'im* or "corn"—it becomes *santo gracia,* the "sacred grace" of life. Kernels of corn provide a basis for metaphor. Children are talked about as "little kernels," some of them good, some of them bad, suggesting that life is made up of the good and the bad. The corn garden provides a Mayan family with a great many other vegetables: pole beans climb up the cornstalks, squashes and watermelons grow along the ground in the shade of the corn leaves, and yams, jicamas, and manioc grow among the roots of the corn plants. Animals such as small deer, wild pigs, and wild turkeys are attracted to the corn fields, where they can be successfully hunted to supplement the Mayan diet with animal protein.

When Mayan women soak corn kernels overnight in a bucket to prepare dough, they infuse important minerals into the corn. The commercially prepared chalk or locally manufactured ashes and lime mixture which is put in to soak with the corn first loosens the outer shells of the kernels and second adds calcium to the Mayan diet. The ability to make corn dough into delicate tortillas is a characteristic of a true Mayan woman. Only during the harvest celebration, the *haanli col*, do men make tortillas, and then they purposely make them thick and odd-shaped to the laughter and enjoyment of both men and women.

Corn is a common topic of conversation. Whether in cities, where the price of corn is an indicator of the world economy, or in small villages, where arguments are made about the relative success of planting a short- or a long-term variety, talking about corn is equivalent to talking about life. One story included in this book about the pursuit of Jesus Christ by his enemies describes how Christ traveled through several gardens, only one of which was claimed to be a corn garden by an honest person. As a result of his honesty, this corn farmer has the only garden that flourishes while the other gardens grow only rock and thistle. One of the ways the rebel Maya of Quintana Roo dramatically communicated their plight was to describe the Mexican government as "eating" Yucatán, leaving the Maya without corn.

The growing of corn in the milpa, preparing corn for food, and the imagery of corn provide a common set of social relationships among Yucatec Mayan people today. Corn unites men and women: while men tend the milpas away from the villages and reap the benefits of their success in growing corn, women transform it into food. Yucatec Mayan men and women complement each other through this basic division of labor. Mayan women keep the money they make from the domestic sale of chickens, turkeys, pigs, and the produce of their house gardens, while men may keep the surplus money they earn from the milpa or from other opportunities away from villages, such as harvesting the rubber latex from sapodilla trees or raising cattle. Domestic decisions involving money are made together.

Yucatec Mayan families are made up of parents, children, and elderly grandparents residing in the household or *solar*. The oblong, rounded houses of the Maya are relatively small (ten feet by twenty feet), so family life is by necessity very close. Furniture is sparse so as to keep the living area open for hammocks, which are unrolled each night and suspended from walls and rafters. Some houses have cloth curtains which separate the parents' sleeping area from the children's area. If a room is added to a Mayan house, it is usually a kitchen and washing room. Within Mayan families elder siblings are accorded special respect and are even called by different terms. An elder sister, *ciic*, is thought to be more responsible than a younger brother or sister, *itzin*. This is true also for elder brothers, *sucu'u-*

no'ob. Soon after a child is born, she or he is baptized either in a Spanish Catholic ceremony or in a Mayan ceremony, the *hetz mec*. The Mayan ceremony is carried out by family members when the child is two or three months old. At this time small gifts are given to the child, a miniature machete and water gourd if it is a boy or a needle and thread if it is a girl. Whether a child goes through a Catholic baptism or a *hetz mec* or even both, new, fictive kin are added to the family through the sponsoring of these ceremonies. In remote villages these ritual sponsors or godparents are chosen from the parents and grandparents of the child. Villagers told me that choosing an immediate family member as a compadre or godparent gives the child a better chance of getting into heaven, since a parent or grandparent would presumably already be there. In more highly populated areas such as Ticul, sponsors are often nonrelatives who are chosen either out of friendship, *amistad*, or for future benefit, *interés* (Thompson 1974: 43).

After marriage, a Mayan husband and wife ideally live by themselves, although this is often not economically feasible. In remote villages newlyweds live for a time with the wife's parents and then move to the neighborhood of the husband's relatives. In villages around such shrine centers as X-cacal, each neighborhood forms a political unit under a village leader or *comandante*. During the year each political unit is responsible for spending a month at the ceremonial center as guards. In larger towns such as Ticul, new craft specialization since the Second World War has changed the nature of neighborhoods, which had previously been territorial and religious units. New trade associations are becoming more important in Ticul for personal and family identity than geographic neighborhoods (Thompson 1974).

In Mayan terminology, there are two kinds of people in the world: *otzi maaco'ob*, "poor people," and *dzulo'ob*, "rich people." Mayan people sometimes refer to themselves as *masehwalo'ob*, an Aztec word which means "people," but this term is sometimes used with derision, so the more neutral term *otzi maaco'ob* is more widespread. When Spanish is used to describe social divisions, several more categories are used. Out in the far-off jungle are the *indios* (*wi'itho'ob* in Mayan), who use bows and arrows and dress in loincloths. At home are *mestizos*, the people who wear Mayan clothing and speak Mayan, and *catrines*, descendants of Europeans who speak any non-Mayan language and dress in Western clothing. Within each of these two categories are several levels of wealth. There are "very poor" *mestizos*, "poor" *mestizos*, and *mestizos* of wealth (*de categoría*). Likewise, there are "poor" *catrines*, but none "very poor," and *catrines de categoría*. In villages like Ticul and in Mérida, more and more distinctions based on wealth and occupation are being made between people. While a family in a shrine village cluster like X-cacal can gain prestige and status by sponsoring one of the fiestas or ceremonies performed each year, status and prestige in larger towns are accorded those people with high-paying occupations. In small towns the straightness of rows of corn in the milpa is an indication of a good person; in larger towns being a worker or *obrero* is much more important than being a farmer or *milpero*.

Outside of family and occupational identities, the status of a person of knowledge or *hmen* is important. The *hmen* is a shaman who solves community problems. If insufficient rain has come to the corn gardens, a *hmen* is called to carry out a rain ceremony or *chachac*. *Hmeno'ob* are also important orators at the opening of wells, at bee-keeping ceremonies, and at the harvest festival of *haanli col*. *Hmeno'ob* can also be curers who use knowledge of plants and human pathology to alleviate physical illnesses, although being a curer and being a *hmen* are not always synonymous. One is called to be a *hmen* through dreams. One curer told me that he was called for three nights straight to become a *hmen*. He awoke each morning after dreaming of the prayers and supernatural beings with a small crystal in his hammock, a *saastun*. This crystal is used for divining. Each morning he threw the crystal out of his door because he did not want to become a *hmen*. When he did not have any dreams on the fourth night and the *saastun* did not return, he knew he did not have to become a *hmen*. He is, however, a very successful curer who uses plants and herbs as well as purchased pharmaceuticals in his work. Curers can be men or women; they specialize in herbal medicine, bone setting, massage, and midwifery. There are people who practice sorcery and black magic, including astral flight, bewitchment, and murder, but such activities do not give a person public identity or status.

The Yucatec Maya are under the national political system of Mexico. Each state in the peninsula is divided into *municipios*, similar in size and function to counties in the United States. Each *municipio* has a head town or *cabezera* where administrative and judicial offices are located. Smaller villages in *municipios* have local leaders who are often young men bilingual in Spanish and Mayan. In remote villages like those around X-cacal, this official governmental system exists along with a Mayan system developed during the Caste War. In this Mayan system, each village is divided up into *compañías* under an elder leader. These units carry out guard service, as I have mentioned, and sponsor different fiestas during the year at the ceremonial center. They are all under the command of two religious-secular leaders who live in X-cacal (Villa Rojas 1945). Most towns and villages in the peninsula are officially designated ejidos, community units where land is held in common by all community members.

This ethnographic sketch of Yucatec Mayan people today can be supplemented by consulting several of the fine studies that have been carried out in the peninsula. The several works by Robert Redfield and Alfonso Villa Rojas (1934, 1962) and Redfield's *The Folk Culture of Yucatan* (1941) are particularly complete in their ethnographic detail. Mary Elmendorf's restudy of a village first described by Redfield, Chan Kom, *Nine Mayan Women* (1976), is an excellent presentation of the role of women today in Yucatán. Richard Thompson's study of Ticul, *The Winds of Tomorrow* (1974), portrays the social changes that have occurred in the community where much of the material for this book was collected.

Speaking Mayan

All the oral literature presented in this book was first told in Yucatec Mayan. In the translation process that I have followed, I have been concerned first of all with correctly rendering the vocal style of the original performances. This required that I learn Yucatec Mayan so that I would have a command of the meaning of the speech and also so that I could participate as an interlocutor and as a narrator in the verbal art tradition. Yucatec Mayan oral literature arises out of conversation and requires a second person to listen and respond to the speech during performance. I used many of the techniques of descriptive linguistics (Gleason 1961) to learn Mayan, and within a year and a half I was able to speak it well enough to understand and participate in the oral tradition.

The sounds of Yucatec Mayan are regular in their articulation, and a great many of them are familiar to people who speak English or other European languages. Yucatec Mayan has five vowels, *a, e, i, o,* and *u,* pronounced with what linguists call European values, as in Spanish. Mayan vowels can also be elongated to change the meaning of words, and in some cases relative tone is important, although I have not noted tone in the transcriptions included in this book. An important distinction is made between glottalized and nonglottalized consonants, between those where the throat is constricted tightly during articulation and those where the throat is more relaxed. In the writing system I am using here, these two sets of consonants are expressed as follows:

Nonglottalized	Glottalized
c (always hard, even after vowels)	*k*
ch	*chh*
p	*pp*
t	*th*
tz	*dz*

In addition, Yucatec Mayan uses a *sh* sound which has conventionally been written as *x*.[2] Other consonants of Yucatec Mayan are *b, h, l, m, n, s, w,* and *y;* I have consistently used the symbol *y* where *u* is sometimes used in everyday writing in Yucatán. Yucatec Mayan contains many Spanish loanwords which use two additional Spanish consonants, *r* and *ñ*. The glottal stop, a constriction of the throat without other articulation, is an important part of the phonemic system as well; it is expressed here with an apostrophe. The glottal stop is sometimes used in English when a person says "u'uh" to mean "no" or when the *t*'s are left out of the word "bottle," rendering it "bo'le." In Yucatec Mayan glottal stops are often found between vowels, as in the word for "okay" or "good," *ma'alo*. All syllables are generally accented equally in Yucatec Mayan.[3]

The sounds of Yucatec Mayan take on significance in conversations between people. Alonzo Gonzales Mó, a storyteller and my own teacher of Mayan, suggested that I learn Mayan by learning a series of conversations. After the conversations were memorized, I would be able to talk with people in the situations that are common in Yucatán. The list of conversations Alonzo suggested included greeting people, talking about things in a house, taking a walk around town, making a milpa, taking a trip to do some work, and going to a fiesta. After I learned these conversational routines, Alonzo directed me to learn the words for the names of things, such as animals,

2. Yucatec Mayan has been written in the roman script since the mid sixteenth century, when Fray Diego de Landa attempted to give roman alphabet correspondences to hieroglyphic signs (Landa 1978). Alfred Tozzer, in his book *A Maya Grammar* (1921), lists the several alphabets used by colonial writers and linguists up to that time. I have adapted the practical orthography as it is used in Yucatán today for writing spoken Mayan in this book.

3. Complete treatments of the phonology and grammar of Yucatec Mayan have been carried out by Alfred Tozzer (1921), Manuel Andrade (1957), Alfredo Barrera Vásquez (1946), and Robert Blair and Refugio Vermont-Salas (1971). A readable summary of the Yucatec Mayan language has been written by David Bolles and Alejandra Kim de Bolles (1973). A more technical summary can be found in Norman McQuown's analysis (1979) of a Yucatec Mayan text.

birds, and plants. Then, he said, these words could be mixed together with the conversations so that I could begin to engage in folklore performances.

Mayan verbs carry a great deal of information in conversations. With prefixes, infixes, and suffixes, the verbs can indicate the subject of a sentence, whether the action is completed, still going on, or only hoped for, as well as the object of the action. Personal pronouns are bound to the beginnings of verbs. They are *-in-* (I), *-a-* (you, singular), *-u-* (he, she, or it), *-k-* (we), *-a . . . e'ex* (you, plural), and *-u . . . o'ob* (they). If one wanted to say "I am learning it" in Yucatec Mayan, the first person pronoun *in* would be put with the verb stem *can*, "learn," producing *tan-in-can-ic*. "They are learning it" would be *tan-u-can-ic-o'ob*.

The prefixes before the personal pronouns are important in changing the tense and aspect of verbs. The prefix used above, *tan-*, indicates continuing activity. Other significant verb prefixes include *dzo'oc-* for completed action, *ho'op-* for action which is starting to happen, *he'el-* for action that assuredly will take place, *bin-* for action that is intended to take place, *inca'ah-* for action which is planned, *tac-* for action which is desired, *cen-* for action which is expected to happen, *yan-* for action which is obligatory, and *kabet-* for action which is necessary. Often these prefixes are shortened in natural speech to their first sound, so that to say "I've finished learning it" one says *dz-in-can-ic*.

Nouns in Yucatec Mayan are always framed by a numerical classifier or a demonstrative. There are more than eighty different ways in which a noun can be specified with a numerical classifier, although the most common form is *ppeel*, which can be used for all inanimate things, as in *hun-ppeel-tunich*, "one inanimate rock." Some of the other important classifiers include *tul*, used with people and supernatural beings as in *hun-tul-maac*, "one living person," *xec* for plants and trees, *wol* for round balls such as tortilla dough, and *mal* for numbers of times, as in the name of the Mayan ruin Uxmal, "three times." There are demonstratives in Yucatec Mayan, one used to refer to things close at hand, the others to refer to things far away or not seen. *Le-tunich-a* means "this rock here," and *le-tunich-o* indicates "that rock there." *Le-tunich-e* indicates "that rock not seen."

Yucatec Mayan numbers are used for counting from one to four—*hun* is one, *ca'a* is two, *ox* is three, and *can* is four. The numbers after four are expressed in Spanish as *cinco*, *seis*, and so on. Although many people recall the Mayan forms for larger numbers, the Spanish forms are used in conversation.

Adjectives in Yucatec Mayan are few. Many adjectives are derived from verb forms. Common adjectives for size include *nohoch*, "large," and *chichan*, "small." Degree is signified by *hach*, "very," so that something very large would be *hach nohoch ba'alo*.

With these few notes about the pronunciation and grammar of Yucatec Mayan in mind, it is possible to follow Alonzo's path into the conversation he suggested should be learned first:

> *Bix a beel? Bix tamaansic ti acabah? Contento'ech wa?*
> How [is] your path? How did you pass the night? Are you happy?
>
> *Tech nuuctene than beyo, "Bix saasictech? Ma'alo?"*
> You answer the talk like that, "How did you wake up? Good?"
>
> *Cin wa'ic tun teche, "Ha'alibe, co'oxtun casic meyah.*
> I'll say then to you, "Well, let's start to work.
>
> *Ma'alo tun, co'oxtun casic meyaho ti'e kin behlay."*
> Good then, let's then start to work this day, today."
>
> *Canuucic tun tene, "Co'oxtun casic. Tancmeyah ti'a diaho."*
> You'll then answer me, "Let's then start. We are working this day."

There is much more to the art of speaking Yucatec Mayan than learning these few sounds and sentences. But, even in this first lesson, Alonzo has signaled an important feature of the Mayan conception of speech: he presents the language as a dialogue between two people, as a conversation.

Three of the narrative texts in this book are given in facing-page Mayan transcription with English translation. The rhythm and sound of the performances can be heard if the transcriptions are read aloud with the help of this short lesson on speaking Yucatec Mayan.

Yucatec Mayan Ethnopoetics

The oral literature of the Yucatec Maya can be best understood as a poetic form of speech in which performance is a dominant characteristic. As poetry, Yucatec Mayan oral literature does not rely on long, detailed descriptions of the context of events but, rather, assumes that the context can be understood by prosodic features such as voice quality, repetition of words and phrases, and gestures. Many of the narratives are short, lasting only a few minutes. This brevity is understandable if the forms are considered as poetic performances where well-chosen words and phrases are imaginative shortcuts to mythic concepts and actions.

The theoretical perspective that has guided this work combines a concern for the vocal quality of verbal art performance with a realization that a non-Western repertoire of oral literature can be understood only as it fits into a native system of the conception of speech. Understanding Yucatec Mayan oral literature includes the collection of stories, myths, and other examples in the repertoire as well as the discovery of the forms of speech that people recognize as significant and the place of oral literature within that system. This perspective draws on the work of Dennis Tedlock (1972), who brought a poetic approach to his translations of Zuñi verbal art, and on the work of Jerome Rothenberg (1972), who brought an interest in native American traditions to his own poetry. Together Tedlock and Rothenberg published the journal *Alcheringa/Ethnopoetics*, where for ten years poets and ethnographers found a common ground in the presentation of tribal traditions.

An interest in the social context of oral literature performance has recently come to the fore in folklore studies with the publication of Richard Bauman's book, *Verbal Art as Performance* (1977), although earlier interest in the acts and events of folklore performances includes Albert Lord's study of Yugoslav epic singers, *The Singer of Tales* (1960), and Melville Jacobs' dramatic analysis of Clackamas Chinook myths and tales, *The Content and Style of an Oral Literature* (1959). Jacobs suggested that "if folktales are interpreted in the light of native usage, manner of recital, audience behavior, content and design, they are often found to resemble the theater of Western civilization rather than its short story or novel" (1959: 211).

The place of stories and other kinds of verbal art in the conceptual world of native speakers has become an important theme in sociolinguistics. Richard Bauman and Joel Sherzer's book, *Explorations in the Ethnography of Speaking* (1974), provides many cases of how different kinds of talk are perceived and structured in languages other than our own, suggesting that, although *language* is a universal property of human beings, *kinds of speech* vary greatly from culture to culture. Dell Hymes' analytic schemes (1972) for understanding speech events and speech acts have stimulated much of the work on the ethnography of speaking. His own interest in the roles of storytellers and their interpreters has been a great influence on this work.

Few works have brought an ethnopoetic and performance perspective to Mayan materials. Collections of texts exist, such as Margaret Park Redfield's *The Folk Literature of a Yucatecan Town* (1935). This collection, although important for understanding Redfield's stated goal of discovering how oral literature dies out, was presented with no concern for performance. Some of the stories were told in Spanish and some in Mayan, but we are not told which these are. Daniel Brinton published a short article, "The Folklore of Yucatan" (1883), which contains one text and some "beliefs and superstitions." More recently several texts have been published in the International Journal of American Linguistics Native American Texts Series, including a translation of a humorous story by Norman Mc-Quown (1979) and a recollection of the Caste War translated by Victoria Bricker (1979). David Bolles and Alejandra Kim de Bolles (1973) have also published a set of texts from Ticul.

Munro Edmonson (1971) has brought a poetic vision to the translation of the most famous of the Mayan books written in Spanish script, the *Popol Vuh* or book of counsel, a highland Quiche Mayan book. Many similar books written in Spanish script by Yucatec Mayan people exist, such as the *Chilam Balam of Chumayel* (Roys 1933), the *Ritual of the Bacabs* (Roys 1965), and some sixteen other Chilam Balam books (Barrera Vásquez and Morley 1949). The available books of prophecy or Chilam Balam contain a rich treasury of Yucatec Mayan imagery and symbolism, but it is the imagery and symbolism of the Maya talking or, more correctly, writing among themselves. In contrast, the stories here present the Maya talking across cultural boundaries.

The one performance-oriented approach to Mayan oral traditions that has served as an important guidepost to this work is Gary Gossen's *Chamulas in the World of the Sun* (1974). Gossen's work with the highland Chamula Maya of Chiapas is a sensitive portrayal of the role of verbal art and other kinds of speech in the everyday world of the Chamula.

When Yucatec Mayan people tell stories, they separate the world of the imaginary from the world of day-to-day existence with words. Individual stories often have formulas or set routines which open and close a narrative. *Yan huntul maac, hach ich colile,* "there is a person, a real *milpero,*" is a common way in which stories are introduced. This formula is similar in function to "once upon a time" in our own tradition of children's literature or to "did you hear the one about . . ." in our tradition of joke telling. When a story is completed, a common way to end it is to claim personal knowledge of the last scene by saying something like *le cah manene, ti tubetku waho'ob,* "when I passed by there, she was making tortillas."

Other conventions in Yucatec Mayan storytelling are not found in our own tradition. Stories are told in sets by Yucatec Mayan people, and it is common for a narrative session to be separated from the rest of life by a story session formula or routine. An example of the ending formula for a story session illustrates this.

Imagine, for a moment, the following scene. On a hot April afternoon, a group of five or six *milperos* are finishing the cutting of the forest. The field is about nine miles from the village, and so they have built a small shelter where they can spend the night during the week of work. In the shelter, several small hammocks have been hung. Don Pas heard a dog barking while he and his sons were cutting down the forest that day, and so he tells a story about Box Peek, the Black Dog of the underworld. Since the story isn't very long, Don Pas follows it with several others. While he tells the story of Príncipe Moreno, the Dark Prince, his nephew Tino falls asleep. The other boys paint Tino's face with some ashes from the fire, a practical joke which will be recounted many times in the weeks to come. Everyone is tired, because cutting down trees to make a milpa is the most exhausting part of the milpa cycle. While Don Pas continues his story, several of the others sharpen their machetes with files imported from Belize. Young Daniel looks at the fine edge of his machete and remembers what his grandfather told him about the use of machetes in the bloody battles of the Caste War. Don Pas has been focusing his attention on Don Felipe while he tells his stories, and Don Felipe has listened attentively to every utterance. Sometimes Don Felipe would nod in agreement; at other times he would question Don Pas or even add a line to the story. The two voices of the men in dialogue have made most of the youngsters sleepy. A small fire was built to keep insects away and bring warmth to the shelter. Don Pas pauses at the end of a story, straightens up slightly in his hammock, and performs a story session epilogue with Don Felipe:

Don Pas: "Let's hunt."	*Co'ox dzon.*
Don Felipe: "My rifle's broken."	*Ca'ach in dzon.*
Don Pas: "Where are the parts?"	*Ce'enil u ca'achah?*
Don Felipe: "I burned them."	*Tin toocah.*
Don Pas: "Where are the ashes?"	*Ce'en u ta'anil?*
Don Felipe: "Eaten by a falcon."	*Ma'akil tumen cos.*
Don Pas: "Where's the falcon?"	*Ce'en u cosil?*
Don Felipe: "Went to the sky."	*Bin ca'an.*
Don Pas: "Where in the sky?"	*Ce'ex ca'anil?*
Don Felipe: "Fell."	*Huuti.*
Don Pas: "Then where did it fall?"	*Tu'ux tun huutil?*
Don Felipe: "Went in a well."	*Bin dzono'ot.*
Don Pas: "Where's the well?"	*Ce'ex u dzono'otil?*
Don Felipe: "Disappeared."	*Tzu'utzi.*
Don Pas: "Where'd it disappear?"	*Tu'ux tzu'utzil?*
Don Felipe: "Into your belly button."	*Yok a tuuch.*
Don Pas: "True."	*Ahah.*

Don Pas steps out of the hammock and stretches. Don Felipe lights a cigarette and comments on the Príncipe Moreno story. "It was beautiful," he says, "especially the part about the ring. Think of it, a magical ring." Don Pas looks out at the night. "I wonder if the federal government will build a road through here. Tomorrow you can tell some stories, Don Felipe."

This exchange, which ended the story session, does not seem to have an equivalent in Western European storytelling traditions, but similar exchanges are found in other oral traditions of the New World. A similar routine for "borrowing a flame" has been described by Brian Stross (1973) among highland Tzeltal Mayan people. Billie Jean Isbell and Freddy Roncalla Fernandez (1977) found that highland Quechua teenagers use a similar question-and-answer routine at the close of riddle-telling sessions.

This closing formula illustrates several aspects of the Yucatec Mayan tradition. The exchange is a dialogue. It is a formal conversation between a narrator and an interlocutor. The exchange exhibits several features of performance, including pauses which mark utterances, vocal qualities, and a penchant for brevity and understatement.

Dialogue

Yucatec Mayan myths, *uuchben tzicbal o'ob*, stories, *cuento'ob*, and other forms of narrative are conceived of as a type of conversation, *tzicbal*, in Yucatec Mayan. In the category system of the different kinds of speech that I found in Ticul and Señor, the term *tzicbal* or "conversation" included several ways of speaking, all characterized by dialogue.

Although Yucatec Mayan people themselves do not conceive of the different kinds of conversation as existing along a continuum, it is instructive to view them this way. The most common form of conversation, small talk, *chen tzicbal*, corresponds to our own use of the term "conversation." Small talk is found in the ordinary social encounters whose content reflects the everyday concerns and interests of life in Yucatán; it appears to be equivalent to the Chamula *lo'il kop* or "ordinary language" described by Gossen (1974: 50). A more formal kind of speech in Yucatec Mayan is the genre of story, *cuento*. Stories can be about tricksters, such as John Rabbit or Puma, as well as about princes and kings. Stories are told for entertainment and diversion while more formal and restricted speech genres, such as secret knowledge, *secreto*, are told to instruct. Secret knowledge stories describe the supernatural powers of deer and warn against arrogance in the hunt (see chapter 4). Even more formal in presentation than secret knowledge stories are ancient conversations or myths, *uuchben tzicbal o'ob.* Some myths are historical in nature and are referred to as *historias,* while others are accounts where historical chronology is not important and are referred to as counsels, *te'escunalo'ob.* In reciting these most formal narratives, performers sometimes speak out of a nonpersonal tradition. A narrator can take on the dramatic voice quality of a past historic figure or even become possessed by the Speaking Cross, the dominant symbol of the separatist Maya during the Caste War. One narrator concluded a counsel by dramatically reciting the following lines:

> I am Juan de la Cruz,
> I am the Noh Cah Santa Cruz Balam Nah.
> There isn't anyone else!

There are also several other kinds of speech, *thaan,* in Yucatec Mayan, *masewal thaan,* that are not conceived as dialogues. Monologues can be found in the genre of song, *kay,* whether they be sacred or secular. Likewise the mumbled speech of the shaman, *xwala thaan,* and playful speech, *baaxal thaan,* including riddles, are thought of as individualistic performances. The words of God, *thaan hahaldios,* include both monological prayers and archaic greetings and marriage petitions which are dialogues. Figures 1 and 2 illustrate the genres of conversation and speech as they were described to me.

In Yucatec Mayan, it is not possible to say "tell me a story." Instead, the only way to bring a story into verbal expression is to ask someone to "converse" a story with you. It is especially difficult for those of us who are used to listening to monologues in our mass media to recognize the importance of conversation and discourse in Yucatec Mayan oral literature. In the opening lines of the Quiche Mayan book of counsel, the *Popol Vuh,* the gods Tepeu and Gucumatz create the world by holding a conversation: "Tepeu and Gucumatz talked together. They talked then, discussing and deliberating; they agreed, they united their words and their thoughts" (Goetz and Morley 1950: 82). In contrast, in the Bible of Western European heritage the Word is singular, and it creates the world through a monologue, not a dialogue (Tedlock 1980b).

In ordinary conversations, Yucatec Mayan people, like their counterparts around the world, talk in groups of two, three, or more. The more formal kinds of conversed speech have more formal roles of participation. When stories are conversed, there are three roles that can be filled. The person who does the main telling of the story,

tzicbal "conversation"	*chen tzicbal* "small talk"	
	cuento "story"	
	secreto "secret knowledge"	
	uuchben tzicbal "ancient conversation"	*historia* "true narrative"
		te'escunah or *ehemplo* "counsel"

FIGURE 1. Categories of Conversation in Yucatec Mayan

thaan "speech"	*caslan thaan* "Spanish"	
	masewal thaan "Yucatec Mayan"	*kay* "song"
		xwala thaan "unintelligible speech"
		sawal thaan "prayer"
		thaan hahaldios "words of God" or "ritual greetings"
		baaxal thaan "playful speech"
		tzicbal "conversation"

FIGURE 2. Categories of Speech in Yucatec Mayan

the narrator or *lemaac uyohel lecuento'ob*, "the person who knows the stories," shares the central stage of story performance with a respondent, *lemaac uyohel nuucic lethaano'ob*, "the person who knows how to answer the speech." Together these two people perform stories with speech, gesture, and a judicial use of convenient sound effects in front of an audience, *tunyu'ubil lecuento tumen lemaaco'ob*, "the story is being listened to by those people."

The narrator, who is responsible for the performance of a coherent and meaningful narrative, does most of the talking in storytelling events. He or she supplies the opening and closing formulas as well as the episodes of the plot. Narrators have the widest range of vocal techniques and gestures at their command to insure that a story takes on a semblance of reality in the minds of the listeners. The conarrator (the respondent) must know the story as well. Respondents tend to be good storytellers in their own right, since the narrator and the respondent often alternate roles throughout the performance of four or five stories. In familial settings, the spouse commonly fills the role of respondent. In one performance of an ancient conversation, Alonzo began by telling about the epoch of miracles when firewood would follow a man home if he whistled, until a foolhardy boy carried the wood home and ruined life for the rest of mankind. Following this telling, Alonzo's wife, who had responded to this half of the myth, recounted the second half of the epoch of miracles. In this half the time is described when only one grain of corn was needed to make tortillas for a whole family, until some foolhardy girl soaked a whole bucketful of corn and made life forever difficult for womankind (see chapter 2).

The respondent's speech ranges from simple affirmatives to questions and comments on the speech of the narrator. The respondent and the narrator converse in front of an audience, people who are not expected to pay particularly close attention to every detail of the story but who may become interested in some exciting episodes. Sometimes, such as during late evening storytelling sessions, up to thirty-five people might fill a small Mayan house, listening at times, walking outside to smoke, and sometimes leaving to return near the end of an especially long story. Although it is common for stories to last less than fifteen or twenty minutes, some heroic tales take several hours to complete.

When more formal kinds of conversations are carried out, such as during the yearly reading of the Chilam Balam books at ceremonial centers like X-cacal near Señor, two "scribes," *ah dzibo'ob*, who are responsible for keeping the books, stand in front of audiences of five to six hundred people and take turns reading passages aloud, improvising on the lines or *thaan hahaldios* written in the books. In this case the two key roles are equal, while in the conversing of stories the narrator has greater responsibility than her or his interlocutor. The reading of the sacred manuscripts, as it was reported to me by one of the scribes in a small hamlet outside of Señor, could provide an ethnographic example of how hieroglyphic texts were read. Mayan archaeologists have found that the glyphs are usually written in pairs. Perhaps they were read in a style similar to that of the Chilam Balam reading done today, with two people reciting and elaborating on the visual expressions.

The manner in which I learned about the three positions of narrator, conarrator, and audience in story performances illustrates the importance of dialogue in the oral tradition in Yucatán. When I arrived in Señor after having learned to speak Mayan in Ticul, I began asking if there were any good storytellers whom I could record. A young man told me that there were such people, but I wouldn't be able to record their stories. I assumed that I was being told that it was inappropriate to tape-record performances or that the act of recording breached an ethic of language use in the area. This was not the case. Villagers soon heard that I had a recorder and began visiting our house so that they could record their voices and hear them played back. Several days later, I asked my friend why he had told me I couldn't record the stories. He said that I did not know the correct way to respond to them. If I sat in front of a narrator with a microphone in hand and kept perfectly still, I would be rude to the person telling the story. I asked how one answered the narrator. He said that I had to learn to say "*ahah*" and "*ahah, beyo*," "true" and "true, like that." This seemed logical and not too difficult, and so from that time on I began interjecting affirmatives into the pauses of storytelling.

It soon became apparent that there was more to responding than simply agreeing with the narrator. Good respondents also used questions, comments, and exclamations in ways that reflected the specific performance of particular stories. These more complex interjections into the stories were so performance-specific that my friend had not been able to tell me about them.

There are, quite naturally, skilled and unskilled respondents, just as there are skilled and unskilled narrators. Unskilled respondents rely on the stock affirmatives which can be applied across many genres of formal speech in Mayan, while more expert respondents utilize more complex utterances in storytelling sessions.

I have not included the responses to stories in this collection because this would lessen the impact of the narratives in translation.

Much of the respondent's speech takes place at the same time as that of the primary narrator, which makes it next to impossible to map the utterances onto paper with the main text without seriously disrupting the flow of the translations. A choppy, disjointed text results when the respondent's utterances are included. I have likewise not indicated the gestures or other similar contextual elements of performances in the translations. These decisions were made so that the texts themselves could be immediately appreciated and understood. Since the Yucatec Mayan oral tradition has imagery and verbal styles so different from those of European or North American traditions, the texts in this collection have been presented in their stark, direct form so that the impact of the Mayan tradition can be felt. The respondents or interlocutors in this collection are the readers who are listening to and understanding what the Mayan narrators are saying through these translations.

Oral Features of Performance in Translation

Except for a few of the short forms of verbal art, such as the riddles and Alonzo's definitions that he wrote in his notebook, which are presented in chapter 7, all the narratives in this collection were recorded with a tape recorder. The stories and other forms of verbal art were then transcribed with the help of the narrators and other Yucatec Mayan consultants. As a check on the accuracy of the transcription, many of the materials were then read back in Mayan. As I became more proficient in the tradition, I performed several narratives during storytelling sessions. My ability to participate in the sessions by being an audience member, a respondent, and at times a narrator clarified the importance of these roles and also sharpened my perceptions of features of performance that characterize the tradition.

Pauses and silences in the performance of Mayan stories are oral features which give rhythm and style to the material. The stories are translated so they can be read aloud. I have followed Dennis Tedlock's approach to translation (1972) by using the pauses in delivery as markers of each utterance. As with Tedlock's work with Zuñi oral traditions, I have used each regular pause in speaking to signal a new line of translation so that, by slightly pausing in between each line, readers can experience the speed of delivery and the rhythm of the original; an indented line is read as part of the preceding line. On the printed page this convention lends a poetic look to the material, and this suggests that the oral literature is more akin to

the sounds of spoken poetry than to the silent reading of short stories written in prose form.

The pauses which occur in the performance of Mayan oral literature are not necessarily hesitations or places where the storyteller
forgot what was supposed to happen next. Pauses "chunk" speech
into regular and expected utterances (Gumperz 1978), and longer
pauses or silences are used by narrators to bring semantic intensity
to particular passages. Linguists have found that silence in normal
speech is a very important feature which regulates the perception of
the speed of talk. Frieda Goldman-Eisler has pointed out that up to
one-half of speech is made up of silence and "pausing is as much a
part of the art of speaking as the vocal utterance of words itself"
(1964: 118).

Great clarity and accessibility to the literal meanings of original performances are possible by mapping the short pauses of speech
onto paper as part of the translation process. Compare, for example,
the following section, translated first without short pauses and next
with the pauses as line changes:

> *Example 1. without pauses*
> Well, later, he pulled the cigarettes from his pocket, he gave one
> to the important father of the girl. He gave one to him. Well, he
> lit it; he gave one to the mother too. The wife too. Well, they
> were lit. They were smoked. They were smoked.

> *Example 2. with pauses*
> Well, later,
> he pulled the cigarettes from his pocket, he gave one
> to the important father of the girl.
> He gave one to him.
> Well, he lit it; he gave one to the mother too.
> The wife too.
> Well, they were lit. They were smoked.
> They were smoked.

Confronted with the first rendering, it would be tempting for a translator to simplify and reword the text to improve readability. But,
when the short pauses are included in the translation, the section
becomes more readable and understandable without resorting to a
"free" translation. In addition, the style of the narrative performance
is maintained so that the important use of parallel constructions in
lines 2 to 4 and 7 to 8 is clearly visible.

Different narrators varied the length of their short pauses from
between half a second (this was a very fast talker) to a second and a
half. Pauses within stories are uniform, except when very long pauses

are brought into the narrative to emphasize utterances or to mark
the episodes. These longer pauses are indicated by dots between
lines, each dot representing a multiple of the length of the short
pause of the performance. The following passage illustrates the dramatic use of long pauses. In the story "The Man Who Was Such a
Hunter," a Nohoch Winic or supernatural guardian of the forest is
talking to the hunter who has been killing too many deer:

> He says to him, "Listen,
> •
> little
> •
> yellow-foot,"
> he says to him,
> "what have you come to do?"
> •
> "Me, father,
> I'm just passing through for a little hunting."
> •   •
> "Ahah.
> •   •   •   •
> The deer
> •   •   •   •
> you were chasing before, the one you say you shot,
> there it is, lying down.
> •   •   •   •   •   •   •   •
> You did it."

There are also times when a line is spoken with short pauses
within it, as in the case when the speech of someone confused is
quoted in a story. These pauses within lines are indicated with dots
between words, such as in the following case, when a vulture regis-
ters its surprise that a sparrow can sing:

> For my part—how . . . how does a little Sparrow . . . then how
>   do you know how to sing?

Sometimes the normal speed of speech in a line is increased so
that words and phrases run into each other. This quality is indicated
through dashes, as in the following speech of the hunter in "The
Man Who Was Such a Hunter":

> Here's that village, but there isn't a village—I know that there
>   isn't a village—but here's a village—

When vowels are lengthened to indicate emphasis or consonants are
held slightly longer than normal to also emphasize degree, dashes
within words are used. This occurs in a phrase stressing complete-

ness, such as "a—ll of them," or in phrases stressing a number, such as "fi—ve grains."

Storytellers control their voices during performances in order to intensify the dramatic effect of what they are saying in other ways as well. Loudness, which is signaled in the translations through the use of capital letters, is a common voice modification. In the example given above of the supernatural guardian of the forest and the hunter, loudness was used to further intensify the anger of the supernatural being:

> The DEER
> • • • • •
> you were chasing before, the one you say you shot,
> THERE IT IS, lying down.
> • • • • • • • •
> (*quietly*) You did it.

Lines spoken especially quietly, such as the last line of the above example, are indicated by noting the voice quality in parentheses in the text. Other voice qualities such as irony, disgust, or surprise are also indicated in this way. A common vocal quality in many narratives is a slow, quiet, but deliberate style which gives the impression of gravity. I have used italics to signal this feature:[4]

> What killed them?
> A . . . *sacred hunger killed them.*

The grammar of sentence construction and word choice differs in stories from that of everyday speech. One important difference is the use of constructions which put quotes around dialogue and description in stories. Such constructions consist of using the word *beya*, "like this," at the end of utterances, using the verb *cuyalah*, "it is said," at the beginning of utterances, and using the word *cah*, "that," which is normally used to introduce clauses, to introduce each line. These constructions give a nonpersonal knowledge base to the meaning of the speech. In this way the performers remind the audience that the narratives come out of the oral tradition and are not personal anecdotes. This effect is further emphasized in the narratives by the use of many passive constructions.

Verbs are often reduplicated in stories for dramatic effect. Distance can be exaggerated by saying "they went on, they went on, they went on." Combined with reduplication of other phrases, verb

---

4. In the texts which follow, any words italicized are spoken with gravity; other words of Spanish or Mayan derivation are not italicized.

reduplication can be used to call special attention to an action, as in the following case:

> Well, he got ready and left.
> He went, he went. Just to the mountains, just to the
>   mountains, just to the mountains.
> He saw that he'd gone over FIF—TY MILES.

Yucatec Mayan syntax is similar to Quiche Mayan, as described by Edmonson in his translation of the *Popol Vuh*, in that it also "leans forward" with the subject saved until the end of a sentence for a "final triumphant closure to a thought" (1971: xii). Although Edmonson kept a verb-subject word order in his translation of the *Popol Vuh*, I have found it necessary to transpose the order into subject-verb in most instances to conform to English usage and readability.

A common feature in Mayan oral literature is the use of parallel constructions. Sometimes a sentence or a phrase is repeated word for word in a line or in two lines. In such cases it is common for the narrator to modify her or his voice during the second half of a couplet. In the following line from "The Story of the Hunchbacks," Mr. Noey is told to build a boat:

> that he make a boat, (*quietly*) that he make a boat.

Although couplets of this type are common, as they are in the Quiche *Popol Vuh* (Edmonson 1971) and in Chamula tradition (Gossen 1974), in many cases the parallel constructions are extended into triplets, as Tedlock (1980a) has found:

> "I guess I'll shoot these deer."
> BAM! he shoots one there. POW! he shoots one there. BOW! he
>   shoots one.

Some grammatical features cannot be directly translated without seriously disrupting the meaning and voice of the stories. Numerical classifiers, for example, are explicit features of the language which are left untranslated. *Hun tul maac* could be translated as "one animate, human or supernatural person," but I find the simple "one person" to be a translation which keeps the original meaning and also preserves the syllable count of the original.

Narratives use several kinds of formula or stock words and phrases which are not found in normal conversation. The phrases which begin and end a story or *cuento*, "there was a person . . ." and "when I passed by . . . ," are common although not mandatory in performances. *Uuchben tzicbalo'ob*, ancient conversations, tend not to have such formulas, as they arise more directly out of a regular conversation and end only with a final statement of the narrative. Sometimes they are signaled with a title given in a declaration by the narrator, such as "Mr. Allan Burns, I am here to tell you an example, the example of the Hunchbacks."

Another stock phrase in narratives is a rest phrase, *ha'alibe, tuno,* "well then." This formulaic phrase is used to suggest that a change in scene or a change in episode is about to occur.

Very few people are named in stories. Most narratives are about unnamed corn farmers, so that the overall effect is one of a generalized character. A few trickster stories have named protagonists, such as the boy trickster Ahau or the rabbit trickster Juan Thul or John Rabbit. Place-names are also not common in stories. In most cases action occurs in "town" or in "the milpas." Some of the ancient conversations use extant cities or ruins as the locus of activity, such as Ti-Ho (Mérida), Uxmal, and Tulum.

Sound effects are used in narratives. Most sound effects are onomatopoetic words and noises made vocally, although in some cases a narrator might use the physical props of his or her surroundings to make a noise. Bird songs are very often onomatopoetic and are interpreted as having meaning. One dove song is quoted as *tah sapatan,* an utterance which does not at first glance have meaning. Later in the story the narrator interprets the bird song as saying *taaseh, ppaatah tan* or "bring it, a house is left." Other animal sounds are often included in stories, but they are not semantically loaded as are the bird songs. Cows say *me'e'eh* and an eagle calls *hi—n pi—iu,* both of which are not meaningful words. Exaggerated action by humans is also dramatized through onomatopoetic words, as in the following case where a narrator describes someone hurrying off:

> (*quickly*) He jumped up running—gone!
> HA—ALAH he went.

Sometimes sounds that are more hypothetical than real are expressed through onomatopoetic forms. In a story about the underworld, a woman's flesh and blood magically leave her as she emerges above ground. The narrator used the words *benach benach benach* to indicate the sound made by her flesh and bones as they fell to the ground.

Taken together, these features of narrative performance give Mayan oral literature a recognizable style that is translatable into English through a set of conventions. The silences, voice modifications, and grammatical features of the narratives all create rhythm and meaning in the oral tradition.

Yucatec Mayan Oral Literature

The selections in this book have been chosen from many of the genres of speech in Yucatec Mayan in order to present a description of contemporary Mayan life-styles and culture as the people themselves talk about their lives; these myths, stories, and plays on words represent the Yucatec Mayan oral tradition. Their arrangement in this book follows the logic of the different genres of speech in Mayan, beginning with the highly stylized *uuchben tzicbalo'ob*, ancient conversations, and ending with the less formal wordplay of stories and short forms of verbal art. The presentation of the oral literature also follows a chronological order, beginning with those narratives which explain the origins of things and ending with a narrative which suggests future earthquakes in the Mayan world.

Chapter 2 is made up of examples of ancient conversations concerned with origins. Although Yucatec Mayan people today do not have myths which retell the several creations of the world, as found among highland Mayan people, they do believe that we are now in the fourth creation. Before our creation lived the hunchbacks (*ppuuso'ob*), who died in a flood, an event which is now syncretized with the biblical account of Noah. Other narratives in the second chapter include conversations about the origin of corn and the milpa as well as a story about the travels of Jesus Christ. The appearance of biblical characters and other features of the European world is expected in the Yucatec Mayan tradition, since the Yucatán Peninsula has been under Spanish and Mexican control for over four hundred years. As a result, even these highly formal ancient conversations give recognition to the fact that the Mayan world exists alongside of other cultural worlds.

The third chapter contains other ancient conversations, which deal with events more recent than those of the second chapter. The narratives in this chapter are from the genres of *ehemplo'ob*, examples, *historias*, true narratives, and *te'escunalo'ob*, counsels. The dominant theme in the narratives of the chapter is the conflict between Spanish and Mayan cultures. Several narratives which recollect events of the Caste War are included in the chapter.

Chapter 4 contains narratives from the genre known as *secreto*, secret knowledge. These narratives are not thought of as secret in the usual sense of the word: they are not made up of knowledge which is guarded. Instead, the narratives deal with esoteric phenomena of the nonordinary world of the Maya, the world seen in dreams or during visitations by supernatural beings. In everyday parlance, Mayan people often refer to the events of the "nighttime" world as the converse of those found in the "daytime" world. The nighttime world is inhabited by beings in the form of children, *aluxo'ob*, who play practical jokes on people who venture out in the dark. The nighttime world is also the realm of deer and other animals which are hunted and the world of poisonous snakes which can kill the unwary.

Stories or *cuento'ob* which are told for entertainment, diversion, and fun are included in the fifth chapter. Some of the stories are filled with slapstick actions by protagonists, while others are filled with fantasy. The *cuento* repertoire contains many narratives with European and African features, such as the story of Aladdin and his lamp or the story of the rabbit trickster. "The Seven Towers of Marble" is one such story which has many European themes and characters in it. The story is included because it illustrates how well the Mayan oral tradition incorporates ideas and themes from European folklore.

The sixth chapter contains a narrative which I asked the narrator to perform. It is an elaborate description of how a person makes a milpa, from setting out to find good land to harvesting the crops. The narrator referred to the performance as a *cuento*; this indicates how the logic of narration can be applied to ordering and communicating information. I elicited the narrative by simply asking Alonzo to talk about how a milpa is made. He might have chosen to provide a life history by talking about his own milpa but decided instead to use a traditional speech form to present a cultural rather than an individual description of this important activity.

Chapter 7 contains many short forms of Mayan oral literature: types of *baaxal thaan*, playful speech, such as riddles and jokes; a song, *kay*; and several short definitions for common phenomena of the Mayan world. These definitions were written by Alonzo in a notebook which he kept. They represent the first time he had attempted to put some of the wordplay and narrative vignettes into writing, as I had taught him to write in Mayan.

Chapter 8 presents a story of the Feathered Serpent, an important supernatural figure for both the Aztecs and the Maya in Mexico. In the Aztec world the Feathered Serpent is known as Quetzalcoatl, the Shining Serpent, while in the Yucatec Mayan world it is known as Cuculcan or Nohoch Can. In Quiche Mayan the Feathered Serpent is Huruacan, a word which has come into English as the designation of the powerful hurricane.[5] In the Feathered Serpent story,

---

5. I am indebted to Dennis Tedlock, who first brought this case of Mayan to English word borrowing to my attention.

a small child is born who is half person and half serpent. The boy is called Colas, a shortened form of Nicolás. It soon outgrows all places of nurturance and is put into a cave. One day it flies up to the sky and causes the earth to shake. Every year on the anniversary of its birth, it flies again, causing another earthquake. This story, which was the last one collected for this book, was told by Alonzo Gonzales Mó. It was, in his words, a story that he had been wanting to perform for several years, a story which is especially beautiful and good to tell people beyond the Mayan world.

The final chapter of the book summarizes how Yucatec Mayan people use narrative to order and explain their world. The logic of narration, intimately tied to the talk of everyday conversations, is a cognitive process that is not disappearing. Rather it is changing as the times change, providing Mayan people with intellectual skills useful to the issues of today as well as those of the past.

2. ANCIENT CONVERSATIONS

In the time before the Spanish conquest, the Yucatec Maya along with their highland relatives used an elaborate calendrical system for plotting agricultural cycles, divining the future, keeping genealogical records, and tracking the different heavenly bodies. One feature of the preconquest sense of time which the Maya held was that time was cyclical (Coe 1966: 149). Every fifty-two years, the ritual and solar calendars would coincide with the same dates to begin another cycle or "generation" of thought and action.

This cyclical sense of time is still important for Yucatec Mayan people today, even though they do not retain the pre-Columbian calendar names or dates like the highland Maya do. Yucatec Mayan people rely on the European calendar today, although a few month names and day names from the pre-Columbian system remain in the oral tradition.

Even though the calendar itself is not in use, Yucatec Mayan people continue to pay close attention to the count of days, whether for divination, curing, or agricultural advice. In the less rainy areas of the northern part of Yucatán, in towns like Ticul and Oxkutzcab along the Puuc Hills, farmers and artisans alike do the *xoc kin* or "count of days" during the month of January. The *xoc kin* is a divination system which uses the weather of the month of January to predict the weather for the coming year. Although both Robert Redfield (1941: 99) and Arthur Rubel (1965) have noted that this particular divinatory system is probably of European origin, it has been grafted on to an earlier Mayan system such as that found in the Dresden Codex (Thompson 1972).

The present system works as follows. During the first twelve days of January, the weather experienced each day will correspond to that of the twelve months of the year. From January 13 through 24, each day again corresponds to a month, only this time the months are in reverse order: January 13 corresponds to December, January 14 to November, and so forth. During the six days from January 25 through 30, the months are again predicted, only this time each day is divided between the morning and the afternoon, so that the morning of January 25 corresponds to the month of January, the afternoon of the same day to February, the morning of January 26 to March, and so on. Finally, on January 31, each hour from 6:00 A.M. until 6:00 P.M. corresponds to each month of the year from January to December. The repeated cycles of the *xoc kin* are similar in form and function to ancient Mayan calendrical uses and are, in a collapsed form, a continuation of a world view based on repeated cycles of life.

Much of present-day Yucatec Mayan thinking about the creation of the universe has been influenced by the over four hundred years of Christian missionizing in the peninsula. Yucatec Mayan narrators do not have a specific origin myth which tells about their beginnings, nor do they continue the traditional knowledge of the four creations as described for highland Mayan groups like the Chamula (Gossen 1974: 22). Instead people know that we are the latest in a series of "generations" of people and that the most recent generation before our own was made up of the hunchbacks or *ppuuso'ob* (see "The Story of the Hunchbacks"). Our own generation has been predicted to end just like those before us, only, unlike the flood that drowned the hunchbacks, our own generation is expected to die through drought. The last prophecies of Yucatán before the conquest, the Chilam Balam of the town of Mani, are the focus of the knowledge about the end of the present generation: as the Chilam Balam narrative in this chapter points out, the "old lady" at the cave in Mani will demand a small boy for every cup of water. When she has taken all the boys, no more water will be available.

When our own generation comes to an end, when, as I was repeatedly told, "the days of Chilam Balam come about," the earth will be transformed again and a new generation of people will come to inhabit this world. The next cycle will begin again, and perhaps some of its origin myths will be stories of the destruction of the world through drought.

Origin Stories in the Form of Lessons

The first narratives about the origins of things that I learned were dictated by Alonzo to me. I wrote them directly onto paper without recording them on a tape recorder because they were part of the long hours of Mayan lessons that Alonzo was creating and not performances per se. Alonzo was fifty years old at the time and had lived a varied life as a *milpero*, as a foreman on a henequen plantation, and, most recently, as an assistant at his brother-in-law's market stand. He could no longer engage in hard physical labor because of what he called "nerves." Alonzo spent hours and hours teaching me Yucatec Mayan, and only after a month or so did I realize that he was a first-rate performer.

The lines of the following narrative "conversations" are based on the points where Alonzo paused long enough for me to write down his phrases, a kind of silent "responding" to his speech. The titles in this section were supplied by Alonzo before he began each piece. All other titles in this book were supplied by the narrators before the performances.

CONVERSATIONS IN MAYAN

I'm going to bring you something,
I want to talk in Mayan like this.
When I'm done, I'll translate into Spanish
and English.
To do all of this, you have to write each line on the paper,
just as I'm telling you right now.
There are things I'm going to talk with you about that are
    large.
There are things I'm going to talk with you about that are
    small.
There are things strange;
there are things regular.
Maybe a small story can be put onto paper like this,
that's good.
Or if a small story can't be pulled out, then that's fine too.
That's how it will be.
Perhaps you'll have to write twenty pages for just one thing;
you'll have to do it.
Just the same, if you have to write one page about something,
that's what I'll bring you too.
I want to bring you a lot of things in Mayan.
I want to see how the words come out,

I want to learn how the words go.
I want to understand how they are sent around the world.

CONVERSATIONS AMONG PEOPLE

If you want a couple of stories, I'll want to tell them to you.
Likewise, if you want conversations about how stories are
        heard in the fields or in the huts or in a house,
likewise, if you want more examples or counsels, they'll be
        told to you.
Or jokes, "The Counsel of the Rope," "How They Made
        Churches in Mérida, Ticul, and Uxmal."
"The Man Who Wanted to Make the Devil His Compadre."
Or any of the other conversations.

BIG THINGS

The Chilam Balam,
"The Old Lady of Mani,"
how the well will go dry, how this generation will end there,
        how the last generation ended, how the generation began.
"The Epoch of the Miracles," long ago.
How men got firewood long ago, how the corn grew long ago.
How the corn was harvested long ago, and all the other things
        that happened in "The Epoch of the Miracles."
"Frightening things." How many there are, what their forms
        are, how they live, how they grow,
how they kill, how they are driven out.

HOW JUST ONE POOR MAN LIVES

How he found his life long ago,
how he finds his life today,
how he'll find his life tomorrow.
How a person is born,
how he grows among everything,
how a boy learns to work,
how a girl learns to work too.
How the boy finds a sweetheart,
how they "close their paths."
How they die too.
How a funeral is made for them,
for the dead.

THINGS THAT HAPPEN TO YOU

What Mérida looked like the first time you were there.
And all those things like that.
How things are made in a house;
how a kitchen is made to cook with too.
The house: how a house is built,
what a house is for too.
Corn: how it grows, what it is for.
The town: what it is for, what people do in it.
How it grows.
How a person goes hunting in the forest.
How a communal hunt is created to find deer in the woods.
How you catch gophers in the fields,
how you bake the meat.
How a "canteen" is made by people in the fields.
How things are made with honey and with bees.
How corn drinks are made; how a woman makes a meal.
Whatever you want to talk with me about.

Not far from Ticul, where Alonzo has spent most of his life, is the town of Mani. Mani today is a quiet town, about eighteen miles off the main highway between Muna and Felipe Carrillo Puerto. In addition to the fame Mani has as being the home of the prophet who predicted the coming of the Spaniards to the New World, it was the location where Fray Diego de Landa, in an act of faith, burned a large pile of Yucatec Mayan picture manuscripts soon after the conquest. This next narrative was untitled, although the story was referred to at other times as "The Old Lady of Mani." This version was written down by Alonzo in a notebook he kept after we had worked together for a year.

THE OLD LADY OF MANI

Well, there in the town of Mani there is a deep well.
There's a huge box there;
there's a huge rope there, rolled up in the box.
It's a thick rope.
The thing is, the rope lives—it has blood.
There in the middle of the town of Mani it is rolled up.
Half of the rope.
When it is cut, blood runs out.
When you try to roll it up again, it won't go.
Long ago it was cut like that,
it was put in two huge boxes.

That's the only way it can be rolled up, because one box can't
    carry it.
There at the deep well there in the middle of the center of
    Mani,
there is water,
because the well is enchanted.
It was made that way by the ancient Makers.[1]
It was spoiled in the old times.
At midday strange things are heard.
Roosters sing and turkeys shout.
People talk, dogs bark.
Burros shout, pigs, goats, cows, horses—it's enchanted like
    that.
There is a big path inside the Deep Well that runs to the town
    of Ho.
There underneath the cathedral the big path comes out.
That road keeps going, it doesn't have an end.
It just keeps going, it doesn't have an end.
Because the path that runs there goes all the way to Jerusalem
    too.
That rope that goes from Mani to Ho,
there is where the "poor people's horse" is going to run—the
    squirrel.
There is where the "rich people's horse" is going to run too—a
    real Spanish horse.
There they will be sent to get some hot tortillas from Ho and
    bring them to Mani.
When the horse gets on, it falls because its feet slip like that.
Because it can't go like that.
That "horse of the poor people"—the squirrel—has feet too.
When it grabs the rope—the "horse of the poor people"—with
    its claws, then it can't fall like that.
"Tha'—tha'—tha'" it goes like that.
It comes right away running with the hot tortillas to Mani too.
There is the Old Witch Who Sells Water too.
There is the Feathered Serpent.
There water will be sold:
you'll be given a little nutshell of water;
you'll give one boy child for it like that.
These things are coming to pass.
The day is growing closer too.

---

1. The word used here was *hmen,* which is often translated as "shaman." The
word is derived from *meentic,* "to make" or "to create," so I have translated *hmen* as
"maker" here.

Stories about the Ancient Times

The next two narratives were tape-recorded in a village in Quintana Roo from an old, respected narrator, Paulino Yamá. Paulino, close to one hundred years old when I met him, had founded the town in which he lived. He was an effective political leader in the towns surrounding the shrine center of the separatist Maya of X-cacal (Villa Rojas 1945). During his life, Paulino had traveled to Belize, had met with people from the United States at the ruins of Chichén Itzá, and had remained faithful to the separatist movement of the Speaking Cross which formed the motivation for the Mayan uprisings of 1848 through at least 1900 (see Reed 1964).

The narratives concern the birth of corn, the most sacred aspect of Yucatec Mayan life today. Indigenous corn in Yucatán is the staff of life and is most commonly referred to as "sacred grace," *santo gracia.* Corn symbolism is a strong part of Mayan thinking today. Young children are referred to as corn kernels and, just as some kernels are short, or turn out bad, so is it with children. Eating corn in the form of tortillas is done with particular relish, so that every meal becomes a reaffirmation of a very sacred attitude toward this food.

Two versions of the origin of corn are included here to show how a theme, such as the origin of different activities and the form of different birds, can be elaborated. The first version was recorded in January, the second in March. While the story is about the origin of corn, it is also about the origin of the milpa and the kinds of animals that are associated with corn farming.

WHERE THE SACRED CORN SEED WAS TAKEN, I

The town, sacred town of Xuuch,
the town where people die because of . . . because of sacred
　　HUNGER.
A—ll of the people, important people—angels—important
　　people, all *kneeling* by a *tree trunk.*
Kneeling; just as you look, already *dead.*
Well, it passes over them lying there already dead—killed.
What killed them?
A . . . *sacred hunger killed them.*
Well, then, the sacred *field mouse*[2] came;
it came.

---

2. *Xpukiicho,* the word used here to refer to the mouse, was not in any of the dictionaries I consulted. I was told it was a field mouse.

It stole *sacred corn*.[3]
Fi—ve kernels of corn it stole.
Stole.
It took them to the town of Xuuch with *fi—ve* beans, *fi—ve*
    red beans, *fi—ve* squash seeds.
It *took*
fi—ve lima beans.
Well, they were brought to the house of a *saint*;
they were brought to the house of a *sa—int*.
The . . . the important woman, the important person . . .
    important person awoke.
The husband said,
(*higher*) "Is it possible, my True Master, my True Woman?
How was the Sacred Corn brought to the house of the
    sa—int?" he said.
The wife answered, "Ahah."
The woman awoke.
What did the woman do? She took the sacred corn—*five*
    kernels,
She ground them on a metate.
Then she cooked it, then ate it with the . . . with the important
    person.
Well, the sacred field mouse watched,
the field mouse just watched.
That evening, it went again to rob the sacred corn.
They were given.
The sacred corn they drank
was for *planting*,
not for eating, not for drinking.
It robbed them, it robbed others, two more. There where the
    round part of the house is,[4]
the little field mouse went there to rob, to see
what they would do.
Well, he saw. He saw at daybreak.
(*higher*) "Is it possible, my True Master, my True Woman, look
    at the sacred kernels, the Sacred Corn.
Fi—ve kernels."
    •   •

Well, just the sacred kernels—the . . . the other foods weren't
    eaten.

---

3. I have left "sacred corn" in lowercase letters when the Mayan word *nal* or
ixi'im, "corn" or "grain," is used. When *santo gracia* is used to refer to corn ready to
be eaten, I translate it as "Sacred Grace."
4. The lengthwise rafters in Mayan houses are called *beh chho'ob* or "roads of
the mice" because the small mice that live in the thatched roofs often run back and
forth on the rafters at night.

Well, he said,
(*aside*) three times the Sacred Corn, "Let's plant it.
Let's plant the Sacred Corn; it's for planting." The five kernels
    of sacred corn
began to be watered.
Five times it took it. As it was taken like that, it was planted
    there.
It is said,
thre—e months
there they saw the beautiful Sacred Corn become yellow.[5]
It began to break through, (*higher*) row by break, row by—no—
    row by row, row by row, row by row.
"Is it possible that the sacred corn
is for planting?"
said the Old One of the town where people died because of
    sacred hunger.
Well, af . . . afterward,
•

then the sacred corn was seen to have been robbed.
A . . . a thing came to pass:
the *fire.*
The flames of the fire went up over the tops of the trees.
Who entered to steal it?
Nobody entered; it was sealed off,
that sacred corn.
Well, then, a—ll of the classes of birds began to be searched
    out,
WELL dressed, WELL clothed,
to sing a song to see
what they . . . how it could be given to the fire.
Well, the master wasn't found,
the *master* wasn't found.
Well, afterward then,
then the little Sparrow[6]
wasn't given a chance.
They didn't think if it had . . . if it would lower the fire.
The Sparrow came . . . the Sparrow
sang its song to see.
It said—(*aside*) it made three songs;
the fire was left . . . it was lowered, just CHARCOAL SPREAD
    OUT.

5. The color yellow here refers to the tassels on corn plants.
6. The sparrow here is most likely *Arremonops rufivirgatus,* the Olive Sparrow.
I have used Raymond Paynter's work (1955) on the ornithology of Yucatán for bird
identifications, Ralph Roys' work (1931) on ethnobotany for floral identifications, and
Santiago Cruz's work (1958) on the fauna of Yucatán for animal identifications.

The little Sparrow said:
(*sung*) "Pocchin-chin samamamah."

•

Well, the fire is *going down.*
(*sung*) "Pocchin-chin samamamah."

•

Well, it *went down further.*
The third time: (*sung*) "Pocchin-chin samamamah."
The fire was *out.* Just spread-out charcoal like that.
Then the peccaries
entered, wild pigs entered, tzubs entered, halebs[7] entered; then
     A—LL of them entered.
to be given the seed of the *Sacred Corn.*

•

So many people
went
to take, to grab the seeds of the Sacred Corn.
The *Motmot* said, "I sleep SO GOOD, I sleep SO SOUND.[8]
(*higher*) I guess I'll go to the road edge.
I'll feel who ever comes by wake me,"
said the Motmot.
Then the Motmot went and stretched out on the road.
What? It slept SO SOUND.
The sacred corn was robbed; all of the sacred seeds, ALL were
     taken by all of the people.
A lot of crowds of people went there;
they each took a sack.
IT WOKE UP.
Well, the Motmot SCREAMED so loud,
(*higher and sung*) "Wucpic wucpic wucpic," *it went.*[9]
What seed did the sacred Motmot take then?
It just took the only one, just the *tomato* seeds.
Well, that's how it is.

•

*That's what happened to the Sacred Corn seeds, that's what
     happened to the people*
at the town of Sacred Xuuch where the people died because of
     HUNGER.

---

7. The wild pig is *Tayassu* species; the *tzub* is a spotted agouti; the *haleb* is a
tepescuintle, most likely *Geologenys paca.*
8. The motmot is a colorful bird which has two long tail feathers that are bare
for an inch or so part of the way down.
9. *Wucpic* is an adjective used to describe crowds of people.

WHERE THE SACRED CORN SEED WAS TAKEN, II

(*quietly*) Shall I begin to tell it?
•   •

Where the seed of the Sacred Corn was taken.
•

Where the seed of the Sacred Corn was taken.
Sa—cred To—wn of *Xuuch*
is where the seed of the Sacred Corn was taken.
Also, people were dying there of HUNGER.
If you have grabbed a tree trunk, you've grabbed it.
You just die, just kneeling there.
You HOLD on to a tree trunk,
kneeling there, you just *die.*
But it was given . . . was given. Sacred town of Xuuch
was the town where the Corn was.
The thing is, people also died there because of *hunger.*
•

Well, then, the little field mouse, as it is so small,
•

it stole,
it stole the sacred corn.
(*higher*) FI—VE GRAINS of the sacred corn it stole from the
      town of Xuuch,
and FI—VE SQUASH SEEDS
and FI—VE beans, FI—VE lima beans,
FI—VE red beans, (*normal voice*) all of them.
•

Well, they were brought . . . they were brought to the house,
      . . . to the table where the Most Holy *Cross* was,
where an important person was
with his wife like that.
(*higher*) An im—important person.
•

Well, (*higher*) they didn't even sleep because of hunger.
Well,
they went to sleep for only a minute—then awoke.
When they awoke, the sacred candle, (*aside*) truly the house of
      the saint, didn't go out.
The important man awoke,
(*higher*) "Is it possible, my companion?
•

(*higher*) Look at the Sacred Corn here—where did the seeds of
      this Sacred Corn come from? Here, *fi—ve grains of sacred
      corn,*
•

fi—ve sacred beans,
fi—ve red beans,
fi—ve squash seeds,
fi—ve sacred lima beans."
•   •

Well, (*higher*) "Is it possible, my True Master, my True Woman,
from where did they come—did they come from heaven?"
•

He spoke like that, the important man said,
(*higher*) "Truly they came from heaven, where else could they
    come from?"
he said when he spoke.
The other person grabbed the corn then,
she put it on the metate,
she ground it up fine.
When it was finely ground, she put it into a bowl of WATER.
It was drunk.
Well, if you are going to think that the sacred corn, the *five
    grains of corn*, had a LOT of SUBSTANCE . . .
it didn't . . . it didn't even whiten the sacred water; but it was
    all drunk.
(*quietly*) They drank it.
Well, afterward,
then the little rat, the little field mouse,
was there in the round part of the house.
He saw *what they were doing.*
Then when the sun set again, the small field mouse got up and
    went again
to the sacred town of *Xuuch*
to rob some more corn.
But that corn that was . . . was eaten, was drunk,
HE GOT SOME OTHER.
Those other foods weren't touched by the people; he didn't get
    more of them.
•

Well, (*higher*) when the . . . the important person awoke again
    another day, (*normal voice*) some other sacred corn was
    there.
•

Well, that other was drunk; then the little *field mouse* brought
    some more.
(*higher*) "Ahah,
(*higher*) that's good, my dear. (*normal voice*) No, we are not
    going to drink it. What we will do,
we will PLANT IT."
•

THEY PLANTED IT.
They planted the SACRED CORN.
(*higher*) Ev—ery grain of the sacred corn
came up as sacred corn.
It is said that *the tassels were yellow*
when it came up in three weeks. Two by two, two by two, two
    by two the tassels of corn appeared.
But, A LOT OF CORN.
Well, the *Old One* of the town,
where people died of hunger,

•

said,
(*aside*) it is said that they didn't die,

•

(*higher*) "Then what will I do with the Sacred Corn? Now we
    already have seeds today."
Then it began to give.
Then the Sacred Corn grew
(*higher*) row by row, row by row, row by row, row by row.
It was for PLANTING.
They say that within thre—e weeks of planting the Sacred
    Corn it was watered.
God, the Sacred Corn was yellow!
It was already given . . . already given

•

by . . . to the poor people who were dying of hunger. It
was given to them by our Master True God.

•

Well, (*aside*) sacred town of Xuuch, where the seed of the
    Sacred Corn was like that, was a large town.
Well, Beautiful True God saw then—(*higher*) "How's that?
(*normal voice*) That one has to continue stealing."
Then Beautiful True God,
our Master True God,
our Master Jesus lit a fire.
The FIRE BURNED up to the *tops of the trees*,
all around the town,
the town of *Xuuch*.
A—ll of the kinds of animals came together,
GOOD ANIMALS, IMPORTANT SE—EDS OF ANIMALS,
like WILD PIGS, like DEER, like whatever class of ANIMAL
    that would come to pass over the earth.
THEY CAME TOGETHER
along with all of the SPECIES of birds; their plumage was
    BE—AUTIFUL: IMPORTANT SE—EDS.

Well,
(*higher*) the little Sparrow went there. (*normal voice*) Because it
    was so small,
(*higher*) it wasn't noticed whether it had any thoughts or
    whether it had understanding.

•

The larger ones pushed it behind them.
They sang songs. How could they lower the fire? How could
    the fire be brought down? What day could this Sacred Fire
    be put out?

•

The Corn was there in the *middle*; fire was ALL around. This
    fire really burned to the tops of the trees.

•

Well, (*higher*) then all of the animals sang. Whatever kind of
    animal there was sang its song.
Instead of the fire lowering, IT WENT UP even higher.
Well,

•

the little Sparrow said,
(*higher*) "I'm figuring . . . I'm figuring
that there is a way that this fire could be lowered.

•

(*higher*) I, I say . . . as I understand the songs that you are
    making,
(*higher*) well, don't you see that with
EVERY song you make,

•

the fire RISES UP; it goes higher.
IT DOESN'T GO DOWN," it said.
(*higher*) "Well, don't you see that the songs you make . . .
the songs you make don't sound good to me,
those songs you make.
For my part—how . . . how does a little Sparrow . . . then how
    do you know how to sing?"

•

"If I don't know it, you can hit me. I'll sing a song for you to
    hear.
I was just figuring, I'll make one, I'll say it.
My . . .
my song that I'll make will *lower* this fire.

• •

That's what I'm saying to you. I guess I'll just sing then for you
    to hear:
(*sung in a higher voice*) Pocchin-chin-chin
    samamamah . . . "

Well, instead of going higher,
THE FIRE WENT DOWN.
"How does it look to you?"
(*quickly*) "Well, sing again!" (*sung*) "Pocchin-chin
    samamamah . . . "
The Sacred Fire was finished;
it had lowered.
CHARCOAL WAS SPREAD OUT.
Then WILD PIGS entered, then PECCARIES entered,
then HALEBS entered, then TZUBS entered, then DEER.
ALL of the classes of birds entered.
They entered and knew to eat the Sacred Corn.

  •

Entered to take the seeds.
Well, then, that Motmot . . . that Motmot
slept so well.

  •

It said, "I sleep so VERY well. Who knows why I sleep so VERY
    well?
I guess I'll go to the road there and stretch my tail across it.
When all of the crowds of people just pass by,
let them say that I'm stupid if I don't *wake up.* I'll awake."
Well, he went and put his tail across the road.
What happened, Beautiful True God?
A large crowd of people came there,
pa—ssed over him
there.

  •   •   •

They said, "Wake up!"
The rest of the people . . . all of the people went.

  •

THEY FINISHED TAKING the seeds, all of them.
That one didn't wake up.
So many people passed over his tail that it was left hairless,
    hairless.
(*quickly*) He jumped up running—gone!
HA—ALAH he went.
(*sung higher and quickly*) "Wucpic wucpic wucpic," he came
    to where the seeds were taken.
He took only tomatoes.
That Motmot took the seeds of *tomato.*
(*quietly*) That Motmot
took the seeds of tomato, mister,
at the town, the sacred town of Xuuch.
That's where those things happened.

  •

That,
I am THINKING, is
HISTORY.
That is ANCIENT CONVERSATION. Very ANCIENT
    CONVERSATION, mister. That is the reason.

•

That is how
it happened that the seeds of *Sacred Corn* were taken.

A very common story throughout indigenous America tells how things were easier in the epoch of miracles. In some myths of the coyote trickster from California, for example, it is Coyote himself who ruins things for the rest of humanity by carrying firewood rather than having it walk along behind him (see de Angulo 1973: 23). In the Yucatán Peninsula, this short counsel about the epoch of miracles is often told by both a man and a woman. Once when I was in Alonzo's house, he told the first part about the boy and his wife told the second part about the girl. The version presented here was told by Paulino Yamá, the narrator of the above two stories.[10]

THE EPOCH OF MIRACLES

Well,
there was

•

the SON-IN-LAW.
That son said
(*quietly*) to his father,
(*hurried*) "Father," he said, "do you know," he said,
"there is a girl I saw there,
SO PRETTY.
If it isn't an insult,[11] could you go and ask for her,

•

ask for her for me,
so I could marry her?" he said.

•   •

(*with doubt*) "Do you really mean what you say, then, son?"
(*hurried*) "Who knows how, father, but I wouldn't be saying it
    if I didn't mean it. She's so good to my eyes, so pretty.

10. See Margaret Park Redfield (1935: 330) for a version of this narrative which combines elements from the hunchbacks story.
11. "If it isn't an insult," that is, if his family and that of the girl are on good terms.

If it isn't an insult, will you go
and

•

ask for her for me so I can marry her?"
This is what the boy said.
Well, the old man got up and went with the "Name of
    Wonderful True God" and a number of cigarettes and all.
    He went.[12]
He arrived and said,

•   •

(*with ritual dignity*) "AMARIA OLD ONE."[13]
(*same voice as above*) "CONSERBIDA OLD ONE, ENTER.
Here's my chair, Old One;
sit down."

•

"Ahah, Old One."

•

The father of the girl got up.
He sat down.
Well, lat—er,
he pulled the cigarettes from his pocket, he ga—ve one
to the . . . important father of the girl.
He gave one to him.
Well, he lit it; he gave . . . one to the mother too.
The wife too.
Well, they were lit. They were smoked.
They were smoked. The one who is asking for the daughter, he
    smokes too.
Two, three cigarettes are smoked.
They get up, the "words" are said,
the words that are said then.

•

(*higher*) The asking for the bride goes on.

•

(*with slight surprise*) "My daughter?[14]
How . . . what are you saying to us about my daughter?
Are you agreed
to lend us my daughter,
agreed to loan my daughter?[15]

---

12. This refers to a ritual exchange called "sweet words."
13. This ritual greeting phrase is now used only on ceremonial occasions. Assistants stated that it was the common greeting pattern in the past.
14. The surprise of this line is one of etiquette, as the previous actions have signaled to the father of the girl what is taking place.
15. A circumlocutory way to refer to the bride service traditionally required of the husband by the wife's family.

(*higher*) Then I will complete it with your son."
"Fine then. That is why I've sought your wishes concerning
      your
daughter."
(*with obvious contentment*) "Father!" said the son-in-law.
Well, then the . . . boy was married to the . . . daughter of the
      rich man.

•

The boy said,
(*with arrogance*) "How will she see if I'm a MAN? Yeah," he
      said.
The boy grabbed his ax and went to CUT FIREWOOD.

•

Well, after all, in the town where he went to be given a woman,
the elders, when they went to cut firewood, they would cut up
      to te—n, twen—ty loads of wood.
Then they'd just WHISTLE,
then the WOOD would just come.
The boy said,
after he had gone to do his bride service, (*with arrogance*)
      "How will she see that I'm a MAN?
Well, after all, isn't that why I've begun this bride service?"

•

He pulled out his ax. He grabbed his ax and he went.

•

Well, after he found the firewood, after finishing,

•

he CARRIED IT when he came.
That's how it was with the wife too.
(*with arrogance*) "How will he see if I'm a WOMAN too?" she
      said.
Well, she made corn dough with five pounds of corn.

•

After all, when dough was made, it was made with ONE-half a
      kernel.
Just one kernel of the sacred corn was taken up and cut in half.
Well, then, it made dough.
Well, enough for a dinner for six or eight people.

•

Well, that one, she made dough with FIVE POUNDS—five
      pounds of corn were used.

•

IT SPLIT OPEN A STONE HOUSE.

•   •

That's what happened.
That's also how the . . . son-in-law
ruined the town like that.

•

Well, that's how it is.

•

Today, (*higher*) isn't it bad for us then today?
When you go to get firewood,
YOU CARRY IT!
But before, just by whistling, before.
(*quietly*) So good, before. Just whistled.
But he, because he was so smart,
so valiant, he carried a load of firewood.
He CARRIED IT, the split wood, the hard wood.
Well, the daughter-in-law too, she made dough from five
     pounds too.
The dough she made,
it split a stone house open too.

•

Well, that,
that's not good like that.

The next narrative combines the biblical story of the flood with the explanation for the end of the hunchbacks.[16] One of the ubiquitous artifacts found in lowland ruins is a trough carved out of stone. Whenever these were spotted on trips to the ruins, someone would invariably say that they were the boats of the hunchbacks, thus lending physical credence to the story of their demise. While such logic appears strained at first glance, it is, in fact, the same logical process Western evolutionary biologists use when they point to fossils in stone to verify their own stories of floods and other ecological catastrophes. This story was also recorded from Paulino Yamá.

16. For comparative texts, see Robert Redfield and Alfonso Villa Rojas (1934: 153) as well as Margaret Park Redfield (1935: 24).

THE STORY OF THE HUNCHBACKS

STORY OF THE HUNCHBACKS.
   •   •
The EXAMPLE of the Hunchbacks.
Ahh . . . what I will tell,
the example of the Hunchbacks.
How the Hunchbacks happened to *end*;
what the Hunchbacks did—their days ended.
   •   •   •   •
Huh? Ahh.
Who . . . who will I send it to? To . . . to you, Allan Burns?
Mr. Allan Burns, I am here to tell you an example, the example
    of the Hunchbacks.
   •
The Hunchbacks that were; their days ended.
He said . . . it was said to Yum[17] Saint Noey
by Yum . . . Yum Jesus Christ in the time when the world was
    new before, they say
(*quietly*) a new world before.
It was said then to the Saint Noey
   •   •
that he make a boat, (*quietly*) that he make a boat.
Well, that Yum Saint Noey had good thoughts. Not bad
    thoughts.
All of the Old Ones of the town, the People of the town,
he said to them: "Well, all of you, it was just said to me that I
    make a boat.
But I'm telling you,
   •
you have to help me as it's such a BIG job I have to do, a large
    boat I will make
so that ALL of the various animals can enter."
   •   •
The . . . the Hunchbacks answered, (*with confidence*) "You're
    just jacking off.
What day?
What's a boat for?
For how many days it hasn't . . . it hasn't rained water here.
The land is constantly moi . . . moist.
The land, the land gets water all of the time."
   •

---

17. *Yum* can be translated as "mister" or "master," although it is closest to the meaning of the Spanish term *señor*. I have decided to leave it untranslated in this context, as "mister" or "master" seems stilted in English. These terms also depart unduly from the metric structure of the lines.

LE CUENTO PPUUSO'OB

CUENTO'I PPUUS.

. .

U EHEMPLO'I Ppuus.
Haah . . . le cinwa'alal,
u ehemplo'i Ppuus.
Bix uuchul *chheehi* Ppuuso'ob;
ba'ax tumeetah Ppuuso'ob—cah xuul ukiino'ob.

. . . .

Huh? Haah.
Maax . . . maax cintuuxtic? Ti . . . ti tech, Don Allan Burns?
Señor Don Allan Burns, naca'anen intzicbaltech humppel
    ehemplo, u ehemplo le Ppuuso'ob.

.

Le Ppuuso'obo' cah yanlaho'ob; xuul u kiino'obe.
Cah tuyalah . . . cah a'alal ti Yum San Noene
tumen Yum . . . Yum Jesucristo'e ti u tiempo tumben yani
    yokocab ca'achi ci
(*quietly*) tumben yani yokocab ca'achi.
Cah tun a'alal teh le San Noeno

. .

cah tun umeetcu barco, (*quietly*) cumeetic u barco.
Ha'alibe, Yum San Noeno tune, utz u tuucul. Ma kaas u
    tuuculi.
Tu laacal u Yuumil le caaho, u hente la caaho,
cah yalah ti'e: "Ha'alibe, yun xtropa'e'ex, be'orita dzuyalahtene
    cah inpool le barco.
Pero cinwaicte'exe,

.

yanawaantkene'exe tumen hach tah NOHOCH meyah
    ceninmeetice, nohoch barco ceninmeetice
ti uyoocol tu LAACA u layasi alako'ob."

. .

Cah tunuucah le . . . he Ppuuso'obo, (*with confidence*) "Chen
    tuuscep cameetici.
Ba'ax kiin?
Ba'ax uti'al barco?
Buca'ah kiine mina'an . . . mina'an le cukaaxal ha weye.
Le lu'umo, constante humede . . . humedecernaha'an.
Le lu'umo, tadz ora ukum ha le lu'umo."

.

Well, then,
for one hundred . . . one hundred years
that Yum Saint Noey made that boat.
It was finished. He wasn't helped one bit by the Old Ones of
    the town, the Hunchbacks.
Then the Hunchbacks saw so QUICKLY that truly the clouds
    were rising up.
To the east, a—ll, all was covered by the clouds.
"Ahh . . ." the Hunchbacks said then,
(*with confidence*) "ahh, that . . . boat that Noey is making will
    quickly rot. He won't get off with it.
Wood.
    •

Not like ours, . . . let's make our boat then,
    •

limestone." [18]
    •

After they carved the boat out of limestone,
they drilled a drain hole so that the water wouldn't fill it up.
When the water would fill the little boat, it would drain out.
Ahah, like that.
Well,
the rain began to fall. *Forty days and forty nights.*
Eighty days [19] the sacred water fell.
The sacred water rose up quickly, went right up above.
It went up TWENTY-FIVE FEET until it touched the horizon. [20]
The sacred water finished falling.
    •

Well, how much, then . . . everything ENDED then.
    •

Well, he saw then, . . . then he saw the . . .
animals, all of them there in the forest.
All of the animals came together then.
The day came when the boat was finished.
It is said at TWELVE midnight.
Hm—mm, how many came? All of the animals.
    •

18. The word used in the Mayan at this point was *pilatuunich*, a combination
of *pila* (Spanish), "baptismal font" or "trough," and *tuunich* (Mayan), "rock." The assistant who aided in the translation of this narrative into Spanish said that it referred
to limestone. The fact that a hole was drilled in one end might imply that bathtubs
are known in this part of Yucatán, but the narrator was not aware of this.
    19. The "eighty days" include forty day "days" and forty night "days." This
double count of days and nights also finds expression in the following riddle from
Ticul:
    [What is] a tree with twenty-four fruits: twelve black and twelve white?
    A year [of twenty-four months: twelve of them light and twelve of them dark].
    20. The horizon in Yucatán is seldom higher than twenty-five feet, as there are
few hills higher than this.

Pues, ha'alibe,
ti sientos . . . sien años
cumeetic u barco le Yum San Noeno.
Cah dzo'oci. Ma yaanta'ah hunpuli tene le Yuumil le caaho,
le Ppuuso'obo.
Cah tun tuyilah le Ppuuso'ob hach TAATONI to haahil
tunliikil tun munyal.
Ti'u actan laakin tu la—acal tu lah cubrirtico le munyalo'ob.
"Ahh . . . " cah tuyalah tun le Ppuuso'obo,
(*with confidence*) "ahh, le ti . . . le barco cumeetic Noeno, *seb
cunla'abal. Yete mun liikil.*
Che.
•

Ma seto'ono, . . . co'one'ex polic tun le barcoto'ono,
•
pilatunich."
•

Cu dzo'ocupolce pilatuncho,
cah tuhoolol bey u yiit yo'la mu buuthul ha'i.
Chen oohce ha teh chan xpilatuncho, pitman.
Ahah, beyo.
Cah tun,
Cah ho'oppu kaaxa ha. *Cuarenta dias yete cuarenta noches.*
Ochenta dias cukaaxa santo ha.
Cah liik le santo ha cooxol, bin tumeetah ca'ana.
SIETE METROS ubin utaakal ti na ca'ane.
Cah xulu kaaxa santo ha'o.
•

Ha'alibe, buca'ah tun tulaaca ba'alo . . . tun CHHEEHI.
•

Ha'alibe, cah tun tuyilah tune le he . . . cah tun tuyilah tune le
he . . .
le alako'o, tu laacal yan teh kaaxo.
Cah juntarnaho'o tu laacal le alako'obo tuno.
Cah liik le kiin dzo'oce barco tuno.
Cah tuya'alah LAS DOCE akabo.
Ci—il, buca'ah tah? Tu laacal le alako'obe.
•

Came to enter the *boat*.
•

Well, Yum Saint Noey got up, too. He looked, (*with
        surprise*) "What's coming? What's that noise?"
The animals were coming, coming like so many horses.
They all went into the boat.
•   •

Well, just when Saint Noey looked, (*with bewilderment*)
        "What next?"
He didn't know what the boat was for. He didn't know—
        wasn't told what the boat was for, the one he made.
He was just told to build the boat with a LO—T of rooms.
•

Well,
they,
•

all of the animals were stuffed in, all in pairs.
Two by two. Two of ev—erything, like two peccaries, two . . .
        two deer, two wild pigs, two yucs, two tzubs, two halebs,
two of all of the . . . the species, even the birds.
All in pairs, all went there
into the boat.
Well, then, later
came a small baby girl. Her eyes were just YEL—LOW-
        GREEN. A little WOMAN.
(*quietly*) A little woman.
She said, "Mr. Noey,
please take me into the end of your boat.
I'm so poor. I'll . . . I'll have to die here too;
I'll also have to DIE here."
•

That's what the woman said.
That woman, what was she?
When it was done, that woman wasn't a person—*an evil thing*,
        (*with disgust*) *a snake*.
The snake, it just had *yellow-green* eyes.
It went, asked for a place.
Well, if it wasn't received then, today there wouldn't be any
        seeds of that *snake*.
Well, then, the sacred water
•

went up TWENTY-FIVE FEET. It touched the horizon.
The rain just fell. *Eighty days it fell,*
forty nights and forty days it fell.
•   •

Uti'al oohc ichile *barco.*

•

Ha'alibe, cah liik yum San Noeno. Cah tuyilahi, (*with
 surprise*) "Ba'ax cutal yambalo'obo?"
Tun tal le alako'obo. Ciil buca'ah le cutal ya'acach tzimno'obe.
Puro iche barco ti cubino'obi.

•   •

Ha'alibe, chen tuyilic San Noene, (*with bewilderment*) "Ba'ax
 tun mas?"
Le ti ma yohel ba'ax ubil le barco. Ma yohe—ma yalah ti ba'ax
 ubil le barco cumeetco.
Chen tuya'alal ti'e cumeeteh barco, YA—'AB u bodegasil.

•

Ha'alibe,
cah tun,

•

cah tun lah buuth tulaacal le alako'obo, puro u parese'i.
Ca'aca tuuli. Ca'atul tula—acal bey citamo'obo, ca'atul . . .
 ca'atul ceh, ca'atul kaaxi ke'eken, ca'atul yuc, ca'atul
 tzub, ca'atul haleb,
ca'atul tu laacal le . . . u layasi tac chhiichho'obe.
Lah u paresi, lah bin teh
ichil le barco.
Ha'alibe, despues, tune
cah tal tun huntul chan niña'i, chen YA—'AXCALE'EN u
 yiich. Chan XUUNAM.
(*quietly*) Chan xuunam.
Cah tuyalahi, "Señor No'i,
meet favor akaancen tu punta abarco.
Tene, otzilen. Tene, yanin . . . yaninciimil xan ten weye;
yaninCIIMIL ten xan weye."

•

Citac tun le xuunamo.
Le xuunamo, ba'ax u bin?
Cudzo'oce, le xuunamo, ma wa wiinci—*kaasiba'al,* (*with
 disgust*) *le ti caano.*
Le ti *caano,* le ti chen *ya'axcale'en* yiich.
Cah bin cah kaanil.
Ha'alibe, wa ma uuchul kaanil, behlac mina'an u semilla le
 caan ca'achi.
Ha'alibe, le santo ha tuno

•

SIETE METROS u bin. Cah takac na ca'an.
Cah chen ukaaxa le ha'o. *Ochenta dias ukaaxa,*
cuarenta noches yete cuarenta kiin ukaaxa.

•   •

Well, the *vulture* was sent then. To see then.

•   •   •

Forty days
and forty nights,

•

the rain just came down.
The . . . the vulture was SENT
to see if the earth had dried up.

•   •

Well, the vulture came down to the earth here.
What did it carry off then as a sign? As a sign then,
it carried off something. What did the . . . vulture carry off?
It carried off (*with disgust*) WORMS, the WORMS OF DEAD
       THINGS,
of all of the dead people, that's what it carried off.
It came to the presence of True God. It threw up what . . .
       what it carried.
It just threw up WORMS,
that VULTURE.
True God said, "No, not very good.
Bad.
It will be: what you will see . . ." The vulture was cursed:
"Anything spoiled that you will see,
you will just have to eat it. That is how you will live," it was
       told.
It was sent then, the . . .
then it was sent,

•   •

the cuckoo.[21]
The cuckoo
just ate seeds.
The dove[22] was sent
to see how the world was.
The dove arrived on earth here.
What did the sacred dove swallow? Just sacred corn.
It carried it off.
Well, because of this, that sacred . . . sacred

•   •

dove, that one
wasn't killed. It can just dive into sacred water and doesn't die.
They say that it's nourishing.

•

Well, those . . . well, then, a—ll of those millions of
       an—imals,

21. Cuckoo: *Crotophaga sulcirostris*, the Groove-billed Ani.
22. Dove: the word *paloma* was used here, referring to many kinds of doves.

Cah tun tuuchita'a tune le *chhom* tuno. Uyih tune.

• • •

Cuarenta dias
yete cuarenta nochese,

•

chen cukaaxa ha'i.
Cah TUUXTA'ABI le . . . le chhomo
uyih tuni wa dzusa'appal le yokocab.

• •

Ha'alibe, cah eeme chhomo, yo le lu'uma.
Ba'an tubisa'a u señal tuno? U señale
yan ba'ax tubisa'a. Ma ba'ax tubisa'a le . . . le chhomo?
(*with disgust*) XNOOKOL tu bisa'a, u XNO'LI
    ANIMASO'OBO,
le dzulah ciimno'o, le ti tubisa'a.
Cukuuchul tun ti icnal Hahaldiose. Cah tuxeehe le . . . le ba'ax
    tubisa'aho.
Puro XNOOKOL tuxe'ah,
le CHHOMO.
Cah tuyalah Hahaldiose, "Ma, ma ma'alobi.
Kaas.
Cah tun ppaat tune: he ba'ax binawileh . . ." Cah
    maldicionarta'a le chhomo:
"He ba'ax binawileh tu'e,
chen le ti cenahaanteh. Le ti cenacuuxtale," cuya'alah.
Cah tun tuuxta'a tune le he'ela . . .
cah tun tuuxta'a tune le,

• •

xchhicbulo.
Le xchhicbulo
chen xi'im tulukah.
Cah tuuxta'a tune le paloma
cah yilah bix yanil yokocab.
Cah kuuchul paloma wey yokocabe.
Ba'ax tulukah santo paloma? Chen santo xi'im.
Tubisa'a.
Ha'alibe, le ti meetice, le santo . . . le santo

• •

paloma, le ti'o
ma'nciinsic. Teh ich ha cubuulce, mu cuciimil.
Hach alimento ya'alal.

•

Ha'alibe, le he tune . . . le tun tu la—acal buca'ah millonese
    a—lak,

LARGE seeds, LARGE animals,
all were killed, all were ended.
Well, why did the poor Hunchbacks end? Why? *So bad a*
people.
(*formally, almost sung*) They went and slept . . . at the side
of their mother.
They went and slept . . . at the side of their daughter—even
the father.
They did not respect . . . if it was a daughter.
They had no respect . . . if it was a mother.
They had no respect . . . if it was a sister.
They had no respect . . . if it was a brother.
They went and slept at the side of the brother;
they went and slept at the side of the sister.
•

Well, Wonderful True God saw all of this,
"Their seeds be ended."
The Hunchbacks, that's how the Hunchbacks ended.
So EVIL.
•

The . . . the other people that we have here now,
those who are here now then,
there is respect for people.
You understand that you have a family;
you have a mother, you have a sister, you have an older
brother, you have a younger brother, all of them.
Well, that's how we are now. The Hunchbacks *ended.*
Ended because it was seen that they were *evil seeds,*
not very good seeds, those Hunchbacks.

NUUCUCH semilla, NUUCUCH alako'obo,
lah ciimo'o, lah chheho'o.
Ha'alibe, ba'anten chheehe otzil Ppuuso'obo? Ba'anten? *Hach*
    kaas u raza'o.
(formally, almost sung) Tac tu xaax u maama'i . . . ti
    cubin weene.
Tac tu xaax u hija'i . . . ti cubin weene—cex tatatzil.
Mix turespetartah . . . wa u hija.
Mu respetartice . . . wa u mama.
Mu respetartice . . . wa u ciic.
Mu respetartice . . . wa u yi'itzin.
Tu xaax yi'itzin, ti cubin weene;
tu xaax u ciic, ti cubin weene.

   •

Ha'alibe, cah tuyilah tun ci'ichcelem Hahaldiose,
"Cah cuchheeho'o semilla'ilo'o."
Le Ppuuso'obo bey uuuchul chheeh le Ppuuso'obo.
Hach KAAS.

   •

He . . . le u la tun generacion yanico'on tune,
le ti'a yanico'ona tune behla'a tuna,
yan u respeto tun maac.
Tana'atic yan a laak;
yan a mama, yan a ciic, yan a sucu'un, yan a wi'itzin, tu
    laacale.
Pues he'elo le ti tun yanico'on behla'ah tune. Le Ppuuso'obo
    chheeho'o.
Chheeho'o pero tumen dzuyilah *kaas u semilla'ilo'o,* ma
    ma'alo semilla'ilo'obi, le Ppuuso'obo.

The next story, about Santo Muerte or Saint Death, the angel of death, was also recorded from Paulino Yamá. After it was told one of the audience members present, a grandson of Paulino's in his mid twenties, said, "That story wasn't any good, he told it backward." Since I had understood the story as it was being told, I did not know how to take this comment. The words were certainly coherent; no Mayan equivalent of pig latin was being used. After questioning my friend about his aesthetic commentary, I found that the story was backward in that it ended with the birth of Jesus Christ and started with death. The chronology was reversed from the expected way of telling this particular origin story.

SANTO MUERTE

Good day, Mr. Burns,
Now I'm going to tell you where we are today.
I'm going to present a counsel.

•

Santo Muerte was ordered by Rey de Dios Padre to go,
to go and get the Sacred Spirit.
Well, that saint, Santo Muerte, asked Wonderful Old Dios
     Padre,
"How can I go and get the Sacred Spirit? It goes like the wind."
Wonderful True God answered, "It's possible.
If you go like the wind, most of the spirits will escape you."
"What?"
"You should travel the way *thoughts* do, that's how *you should*
     go."
"Ahah, okay, then. Since you order, I'll do it. What else can I
     do?"
Well, Santo Muerte went on.
He caught the Sacred Spirit just like he was told and came
     back.
He was told,
(*aside*) *Santo Muerte,*
"The spirit you caught is BAD.
It has a bad mind."
This, Santo Muerte doesn't forget. He doesn't forget funerals.
The Sacred Spirit escapes, but other spirits are caught.
They are brought—the spirits are brought—to the presence of
     Wonderful True God.
He's told,
"No, not that one. I didn't send you to get that one.
You'll have to get another one. That's an order.
Go and bring another."
Santo Muerte goes back where he came from. He doesn't
     return the bundle;[23] he puts it in a tree.
Well, then the Sacred Wind comes.
The spirit is grabbed and begins to scream.
It screams like that.
It happens just like that, just like that.
Well, then he goes to get another.
If Santo Muerte loves the sacred spirit,
it is just taken and brought through a sweet path;
doesn't go over many thorns.
But if he doesn't return it, Santo Muerte just throws the spirit
     out into the thorns. It goes through torment.

23. That is, the spirit.

How much does it suffer? How much pain?
Santo Muerte does it.
He ought to be honored.
The funeral rites ought to be watched over, ought to be
   honored
so the spirits will be taken care of, so they will be taken in by
   Wonderful True God.
He does it, mister.
All of the counsels told by the old ones are taken into account
   by True God.
They should be listened to, they should be heard.
Nothing happens without the order of Wonderful Father there
   in heaven.
That's how a piece of gold is,
that's how a piece of silver is:
true!
That's how it ought to be watched,
because, who told it?
Not, who told it, *Wonderful True God* the Rey of heaven
and the Rey of the sacred earth.
He invented the earth, he invented the heavens. He put in all
   of the stars, all of the sun,
the morning where we go and find our lives,
all creatures, all day,
he made everything.
He put all of the people in the towns.
He put them in the towns like that.
Gave them thoughts.
Well, there aren't any thoughts that belong to True God;
   whatever he looks at, like a lake, like the sun, like stars,
   like anything at all, is his.
Wonderful True God who remembered the world, who made
   the sacred heavens, who made the sacred earth.
He isn't remembered.
Well, Wonderful True God said, "I'll make the earth, I'll give
   myself to you, I'll sacrifice myself, I'll spill my blood for
   you.
You won't have to say you love me,
but if you are going to throw me aside like that, well, I'm going
   to throw you aside too.
You can go where you wish, wherever you want, GO AHEAD
   living the way you do. If the town sinks, then stay in your
   stone house.
Live there in your town, live until you get to limbo!"
Well, then, the sacred earth sank again. Then the earth rose
   again, the earth of the town.

Well, that, mister, is why I'm explaining the reason why people
     live over the earth.
The advice really ought to be followed.
The sacred words shouldn't be passed over. SACRED WORDS.
     Sacred words are not toys.
The words of our father,
the one who sacrificed for us,
the one who sent his Wonderful Son to give himself here on the
     earth.
That one died for us, the Wonderful Son of the Father Rey de
     Dios Padre.
Beautiful Mother Venerable Mary, she was the mother. The
     father was Mr. San José.
He was also the stepfather.
The twelve apostles said,
(*higher voice*) "X-Mary,
The Angel that is coming has to be born."
"MINE?"
"Ahah. Since it's yours, tomorrow you will have to be married.
     Tomorrow.
The sacred staff has seven colors.
If a flower opens on the sacred staff, the wedding mass will
     begin. That will be a true sign that the child is growing
     inside Venerable Mary."
Well, she kneeled to be wed. The sacred mass was to begin
     with the woman Mary.
They looked at the staff—no flowers appeared.
"Well, what do you say? It is just because you *like* the Beautiful
     Woman Mary. You say she's pretty. Is she your wife? NO!
Well, tomorrow, another will come to be married." It went on
     just like that, just like that, just like that. The twelve
     apostles tried to get married to that woman Mary.
That sacred staff never had a flower.
Mr. San José
put his boat on the shore.
They came to get Mr. San José so he would come.
"An order is out for you to come. I've been told to come and get
     you. It's urgent that you come with me."
"Eh? Why? I'm listening, but I haven't finished working. I have
     a lot of work to do. I'm all by myself
here at the edge of the sea."
"Ahah.
That's fine, but I was told to come and get you."
"But I'm poor;
you can see all of my sores. My body is covered with sores. My
     clothes are dirty, my clothes are torn. I'm covered with
     dirt. Why me?

The rest of the people are well dressed. They're important
people. They all have beautiful clothing.

•

Go ahead and tell me it isn't so."
"It's true." "Then why me? My body is covered with sores. I'm
dripping with pus. So let's not go."
Well, he brought him against his will. The father, Mr. San José,
arrived. The twelve apostles said,
"Ave María Santísima, look at that horrible thing coming! Look
at the sores, they're all swarming with flies! That is what
is going to be wed to X-Mary?"
The mass began. They entered into the marriage part with that
Woman Mary. The Gloria was said. The sacred staff grew a
flower. They said, "Finish the mass, because the sacred
staff has grown a flower!"
The sacred staff WAS COVERED with flowers. The twelve
apostles were frightened!
"How was X-Mary touched like that? How was she touched?"
(aside) She had no sins.

•

The Sacred Angel that grew inside her was given to that
Woman Mary.
The Sacred Book[24] came to her, was given to her.
It is said that that Woman Mary was visited by an angel.
"Es posible, Sacred Angel? My hands are dirty. I'm sweeping
my house."
The Beautiful Woman folded up her dress.
"Even my clothes are ragged."
The Sacred Book fell into the fold in her clothes.
Well, then, afterward, she gathered the broom together, then
washed her hands.
Then the book was put where she would forget it.
When she remembered, she said, "Es posible, my True Master!
The Sacred Book!"
When she looked down, it had entered her flesh, all except a
small part.
Ahah.
She started to cry, she began to cry.
Started to cry, began to cry.
Father in heaven, the one who sent the book, saw all of this.
He sent word to her: "Go and tell X-Mary not to cry. Tell her
not to think about it."
(high voice) Piclic-Piclic the Sacred Angel went to tell her.
"Well, X-Mary, Our Father sent me to tell you that you

24. The impregnation of Mary by a book is an indication of the high value
placed on literacy in Yucatán.

shouldn't think about the Sacred Book. So don't think
about it."
The Woman Mary began to cry again. She said, "The *Sacred*
Book has already entered my skin."
"Well, that isn't a sin.
That is just a blessing of Wonderful True God Rey de Dios
Padre."

•

That is how the Savior Jesucristo was given to us by Wonderful
Father
to save the sacred earth.
All of the evil people who killed True God in the world were
separated. That is how the world came to be saved.
They were separated up until today. Even today they are in
another place, a town of gold.
Well, that is a history, a good one.
That isn't any bad talk, it's a history, a history of Wonderful
Rey de Dios Padre. A history of wonderful Father Mr.
Jesucristo.
A history of Beautiful Mother Venerable Mary. Mr. San José,
the stepfather, he did it.
There!

Yucatec Mayan people consider themselves Christians, as most sub-
scribe to Catholicism. Recent missionary activities by evangelist
and Mormon groups in this part of Mexico have had some degree of
success. Mayan religious thought today is a combination of indigenous ideas as well as Judeo-Christian ideas, as the last several narratives have shown. This next narrative was recorded from Alonzo
Gonzales Mó in Ticul. The story has an obvious moral to it—one
should not lie—but it is of greater interest because of the way birds
are central to the action of the chase between the Jews and Jesus
Christ. This is a similar use of birds to that found in the birth of corn
and the hunchbacks stories. This narrative was transcribed directly
onto paper without the use of a tape recorder, so, like the narratives
which begin this chapter, no indications of vocal qualities other
than line length are present in the translation.

JESUS CHRIST

There is a person coming to catch Christ.
Christ comes to a milpa and asks the milpero,
"What are you doing, old man?"
He says to him, "I'm planting." "What are you planting?"
"I'm planting palm trees."

"Okay, if God wills it, I hope the palm trees you're planting
grow large."
Then he goes on, Christ goes.
He comes to another milpa and goes into it.
"What are you doing, old man?"
"I'm planting." "What are you planting?"
"Coconuts."
"Okay, if God wills it, I hope the coconuts you're planting grow
large."
Then Christ goes on. He continues to go, he goes.
He comes to another milpa where a man is planting. He asks
the man who's planting,
Christ says, "What are you doing, old man?"
"I am planting." "What are you planting?"
"Stones."
"Uhuh, okay, if God wills it, I hope the stones you're planting
grow large."
Christ goes on. He goes.
He comes to another milpa.
He begins to ask, "What are you doing, old man?"
"I am planting."
"What then are you planting?"
"I am planting a bit of 'grace,' a bit of pepper, mix all mixed
up[25] in my milpa."
"Okay, if God wills it, I hope that you have a large harvest in
the milpa."
Then
Christ goes on, he goes.
Then, while the Jews are going along looking to catch him,
they come to a road there where Christ first passed by.
The man says, "Did a man come through this milpa?"
"He has. When he passed by here I was planting palm trees."
The Jews say, "Wow!" The Jews say, "It's been a long time since
he's been here.
You can already hear the bats in the palm leaves."
The Jews say, "It sure has been a long time since he passed by
here, look how large these palm trees are."
"Well, I guess I'll go."
They come to another milpa.
Those Jews find the owner of the milpa and ask,
"Did a man come through here a little while ago?"
"Yes, a man came through here a bit ago; I was still planting
coconuts."

25. This refers to multiple cropping, the usual growing strategy of Yucatec
Mayan *milperos*.

"Wow!" says that Jew, "it's been a long time since he was here,
    look how big these coconut trees are!"
The Jews go on. They go on.
They come to another milpa.
They come into the milpa with great difficulty because there
    are many large stones there.
They see the owner of the milpa and those Jews ask him,
they say, "Did you see a man come through here a while ago?"
"Yes, he just came through here a bit ago; I was planting
    stones."
"Wow, it's been a long time, look at these stones: they're
    already falling apart."
"Well, I guess I'll go on."
Well, the Jews go on.
They come to another milpa.
The man is harvesting.
"Hello, old man," they say to him,
"by chance did you see a man come by here?"
"He's already gone. I was planting 'grace' when he came
    through."
"Wow, it's been a long time since he came through. The corn is
    already old;
it's already drying."
The Jews go on.
They go on searching for him like that.
Well, as they are going down a road, Christ goes onto a road.
The little sutzuy[26] says,
"Suutzuy beh."[27]
The Jews hear that.
"Wow, we won't be able to go down this road because it's
    closed."
While Christ is going then, a quail flies up in front of him,
    HOOM!
That quail frightens Christ like that,
so Christ says, "From now on you have to sleep in dirt. That's
    how you will live."
They were cursed like that.
Then Christ went on.
Then the Jews came to find Christ.
The Jews came and the sacpacal[28] said,
"Chumuc pocche, chumuc pocche, uhuh."[29]
The Jews said, "Well, he's in the middle of the low forest.

---

26. The *sutzuy* is a Caribbean Dove, *Leptotila jamaicensis gaumeri.*
27. "The road's closed."
28. The *sacpacal* is a White-winged Dove, *Zenaida asiatica asiatica.*
29. "In the middle of the low forest, in the middle of the low forest."

Let's get him. Let's go in there to find him."
When that bird sang again, "In the middle of the low forest,"
    they were close to catching him.
When they came to where Christ was, they found him sitting
    on a stone.
That's where he was.
They tied him and carried him off.
The man where he first passed by said,
"That wasn't a man that came by here. It was beautiful God. I
    didn't know it.
Now I have to keep planting. I didn't know it was Jesus Christ
    who passed by here.
I didn't tell the truth.
If I would have said the right thing before, that I was planting
    corn,
perhaps today I would have a good harvest.
I told him I was planting palm trees. Now I am planting them.
He gave me plenty of palm trees; that's all I have now."
Another one says, "Me too.
I told him I was just planting coconuts. I told him, 'Coconuts.'
If I would have said, 'I'm planting corn,' today I would have a
    good corn harvest.
That man who passed by here wasn't just a man, it was Jesus
    Christ.
Oh well, what more is there; I've spoken."
The other one joins in. "That happened to me too when he
    passed by here.
I said, 'I'm planting stones.'
Then I was left with lots of stones at harvesttime."
Well, they left.
That other one says, "When he passed by me,
He asked me what I was planting.
I said to him that I was planting a little 'grace' and pepper.
I gained too; he gave me a lot because I didn't lie to him."
There it ends.

3. COUNSELS

Narratives which have historical referents and historical significance are subsumed under a Yucatec Mayan category of verbal art known as a counsel, *te'escunah*, or a true narrative, *historia*. They are ancient conversations, *uuchben tzicbalo'ob*, and so have an archaic sound to them, an obscurity which demands that one pay close attention to the events, places, and people mentioned in them. These ethnohistorical stories can serve as admonitions as well as points of argument. As admonitions, they can be invoked, for example, if younger men in a village do not want to take the time to perform their regular guard service at the shrine center where one of the many sacred crosses is held.

After the Mayan uprisings of 1848, the Caste War, many separatist Maya fled to the sparsely inhabited areas of east central Quintana Roo. There they continued to fight a guerrilla war against the Mexicans under the symbolic icon of a Speaking Cross. The Cross spoke, wrote letters, and planned strategy throughout the latter part of the nineteenth century. In 1900 a Mexican general, Ignacio Bravo, captured the center of the rebel Mayan forces, a town they had come to call Noh Cah Santa Cruz Balam

Nah or Santa Cruz—present-day Felipe Carrillo Puerto. The separatist Maya then split into a number of small groups and set up small village clusters, each with its own Speaking Cross.

Today these clusters of villages remain as effective political and social units, centered on a shrine village where all younger men are expected to perform a guard service for the Patron or Cross of the region. Of course, with the availability of wage labor and motorized transportation and with the end of the guerrilla warfare between the Maya and the Mexicans, many younger men prefer not to perform this community service. The counsels often have sections admonishing people not to forsake their traditional service to the Patron or Cross. Counsels are often performed at agricultural ceremonies, when eight or ten people might be gathered to eat some of the produce of a milpa. The ritual occasion serves to lend authority to the message of the counsel, making it something that the younger men might listen to with greater attention than they might if it were performed under less ritually charged circumstances.

Counsels of a historical nature can also serve as part of the rhetoric of argument. Once, during a harvest ceremony in the fall, a young man asked me to tell the elders what I had told him about the origin of rain clouds. I said that rain clouds were the result of the evaporation of water, especially the water from the sea. Paulino Yamá, an elder statesman of the village, then began an argument with me, saying that rain came from Chac, the rain deity who turned his water gourd upside down when he wanted to send rain down to the earth. To prove his point, he asked me how the evaporated water "knew" it was time to start falling. I could only reply weakly that the water "got heavy" and fell. "There," he said, "that is when Chac turns the water gourd over." Paulino went on to perform a counsel that included a reference to a time during the Caste War when the water from the sea joined with the water from the sky to destroy many enemy troops. Later I recorded a version of this counsel from him which is included in this chapter.

The ethnohistorical narratives in this chapter are among the most obscure and difficult to translate examples of Yucatec Mayan oral literature that I collected. Sparse in delivery, they can be understood only as highly stylized encapsulations of Mayan thought. Some are no more than outlines of historical events, names, and places mentioned briefly either to be elaborated by another narrator or to pique the interest of younger listeners. In this sense they closely resemble the performance of the sacred books which some villages still retain as a community function. In a small village near Señor, I met one of the two community secretaries or scribes who kept the sacred books and copied them over for future generations. These books of prayers, incantations, and historic anecdotes, the books of Chilam Balam, are still read from, or rather performed, every year or two in some villages. I did not see their performance, but the scribe of the village told me that he and his counterpart from another village stand before the temple where the Cross is kept and take turns reading from the books. I asked him to illustrate how they are read. He used the notebook as a mnemonic for his performance. Each line of the notebook contained some of the words of his counsel, but he did not read each line verbatim. Instead he elaborated what was written down, and so his verbal example was much longer than the words contained on the written pages.

This method of literary performance is remarkably similar to the way hieroglyphic texts may have been read in pre-Columbian times. J. E. S. Thompson, in his review of the Dresden Codex (1972: 7), relates how Bishop Landa described glyphs as being read and then expanded into discourse. Thompson argues that hieroglyphic texts were directly succeeded by the books of Chilam Balam. This suggests that the economy of expression in the glyphic codices, in the Chilam Balam books, and in the performance of counsels and other types of ancient conversations is a feature which allowed for elaboration, improvisation, and interpretation. The ethnopoetic format that I have adopted here for translation best reflects this special characteristic of Mayan verbal art.

The counsels and true narratives that refer to historical events and times are not invariant records. They are creative reworkings of history intermingled with prayer, made new each time they are told. They often arise out of conversation in answer to a question or to provoke a discussion. One narrative about a historic figure of the Caste War, Venancio Puc, began when my next-door neighbor, Paulino Yamá, asked me who the president of the United States was at that time. I answered that Nixon was the president. Paulino picked up the microphone of the tape recorder and began to send the president a message about Mayan life. "Mr. President Nixon," he began, "you are the United States." After telling me the counsel, Paulino admonished me to take it back to the United States and translate it, and in that way his voice would be heard beyond the confines of his village. It is not as if Paulino wanted the personal fame of an individual performer when he asked me to bring his words to a wider audience. Paulino and others who told counsels spoke out of a cultural tradition, not out of an individual one. The words, the narratives themselves, took on life when they were spoken.

When some of the counsels and prayers were played back to people in the village, I was often asked to play sections over again where Paulino took on the voice of *Hahaldios,* "True God." Those sections, commented on by people as being especially beautiful, were listened to for their poetry and power as much as for their meaning. When I later researched the relationship of these stories to the Caste War (Burns 1977), I found that those sections bore a striking resemblance to speech attributed to the Speaking Cross during the nineteenth century. It appears that some narrators can be so possessed by or entranced with the cultural symbol of the Speaking Cross that the Cross begins speaking through them. This explains one of the difficulties scholars have had in understanding the proliferation of crosses during the Caste War and the varied ways in which God was reported to speak to the Maya through the crosses. If the Speaking Cross is interpreted as a cultural idea, not as a material object, it can take the form of many things: people, pieces of wood, paper with writing on it, and so on.

Narratives about Mayan Political History

"The History of Don Francisco Xiu" is a very common narrative throughout the Yucatán Peninsula. Descendants of the Xiu dynasty, which ruled the area around Uxmal at the time of the conquest, are still living in towns along the Puuc Hills. This version of the story was told by Paulino Yamá in the X-cacal area of east central Quintana Roo. Paulino's story is especially obscure in that the audience is expected to know the plot well. Because of this, the narrator chooses to leave out certain elements, and this makes the story difficult to follow if it is heard only once. Very early in the narrative, a group of wizards or magicians known as the Itza Maac—called "they" in line 3 of the story—are referred to as the people who can disappear and change form. A Mayan audience would be clued into the identity of these people by the emphasis on the word "disappeared" that Paulino provides. The Itza Maac, according to him, were the original inhabitants of Chichén Itzá who quite literally went underground when the Spaniards arrived. The Spaniards are here referred to as fishermen. The narrator used the Spanish word *pescadores* here but later switched to Yucatec Mayan to refer to them as the ones who caught fish, *chuc cay.*

Like many historical narratives, this one provides a rationale for the continuing conflict between the separatist Maya and the Spaniards or Mexicans. In this case the Spaniards are unable to see milpas, carry hot tortillas, or put a mysterious rope back in its box and so are not favored by True God as the English and North Americans are. Alonzo Gonzales Mó's story of the old lady of Mani in the second chapter includes the same theme found in this narrative.

THE HISTORY OF DON FRANCISCO XIU

When the fishermen
had come over the sea,
they DISAPPEARED into their milpa.
They made their milpa disappear.
When they appeared about
A HALF A LEAGUE AWAY, THEY SAW THE MILPAS
of the Disappearing Ones.
Well, the FISHERMEN came;
they came down.

•

The fishermen CAME DOWN, they came down then.
Well,

•

when they got there
EVERYTHING WAS GONE. They just looked at the milpas
    over the sea,
but the milpas, just as they got there, at the edge there, WERE
    GONE.
Pure THORNS, SACBAC thorn trees, BE'EB trees, SIDZMUC
    trees, CHHOM, XDZEREBAYO trees.[1]
There wasn't anywhere for a person to walk there.
Well, it looked bad to the people like that.
Well, they went on.
They continued fishing.
They went to catch fish.
Well, (*higher*) afterward, afterward,
afterward,
on ANOTHER DAY they went there again.
EVERY DAY they came back to look, EVERY DAY they saw
    the milpas.
Well, Don Francisco Xiu GOT FED UP WITH THIS.
He said,
"Well, let's wait and see what they are going to do."
There were daughters, THREE OF THEM,
of Don Juan Titul Xiu.

---

1. *Sacbac* is a creeping cactus, *Cereus donkelaarii; be'eb* is *Pisonia acleata,* a bramble; *sidzmuc* is *Celtis* species, a hackberry; I was unable to identify *chhom,* literally "vulture," or *Xdzerebayo.* The narrator said that these were all thorn trees.

There were daughters, three of them. PRETTY ONES,
    WOMEN.[2]
The FISHERMEN were told to go.
Well, mister, it was a WHITE ROAD, in truth, a big FINE road.
It didn't stop them, it didn't stop the SPANIARDS.
The SPANIARDS made it.
Don Juan Titul Xiu said, he said then,
"This thing isn't going to end well.
It isn't going to end with love.
It has to go bad."
That's what Juan Titul Xiu said.
They went back.
EVERY DAY they began to come. Every day, every day from the
    east
they came together. Then there at UXMAL,
there at MANI town,
there at CHICHEN ITZA,
then there at
YAL COBA.
At all of these places they disappeared.
Then there at COBA they made the tortillas.
There they made the *tortillas.*
There at the town of Siiho[3]
they made the food,
the "relleno."
That was where the table was too where the DINNER was to
    be held.
That is where the spoon was, that is where the PLATE was, all
    of the settings of the dinner were ALL THERE.

•

Well, the tortillas were coming out and were piling up.
The tortillas came out and were piling up. The tortillas came
    out and were piled up.

•

Because there was a
little kitchen.
Well,
the tortillas were all wrapped up.
The KING said then,
the KING of the nobles,
"Well, go and bring the tortillas,
GO AND GET THE TORTILLAS WHILE THEY'RE HOT,

2. In another version of the same narrative, the three daughters become married to the Spaniards.

3. In other versions of this narrative, Siiho becomes known as Ho or present-day Mérida.

so they can arrive at Siiho for dinner."
THEY WERE PUT on a horse.
How will the horse of the Spaniards
get there?[4]
IT HAS LARGE HOOVES.
It can't get on.
(*higher*) It got fed up trying to do it.
Well, then, it was said to the KING of the Mayan people,
"Well, you go and bring the tortillas."
"Okay."
That one put the SADDLE on his horse,
the King of the Maya.
The horse was the little squirrel, the Kam'ex squirrel.
They just put the tortillas on his back.
Cooxol (*quickly*) tatatatata it ran.
It went right through the ring there,[5]
HEEEM it went right through the ring
there at the CASTILLO at Chichén. It went through and went
    on.
It had gone.
Why? Because THEY DISAPPEARED.
Well, it brought the very hot tortillas.
Well, the KING of the nobles said,
"By God, look how fast the tortillas got here.
THEY'RE DRY!
Dry and moldy!
They can't be eaten. I can't accept them."
Why?
Because it was
because they broke the old rope.
What happened was the ROPE was cut.
Everything was lost when that happened.
THE FATHER of the heaven,
the Rey de Dios Padre, and his wonderful Son *clearly saw,*
they knew what had happened. They knew what had been
    done.
Well, then,

•

what happened then, they were told,
"The ROPE you cut,
you have to replace.
You have to put it back. This will decide.

---

4. The narrator has not yet mentioned that the "road" between the two towns
is really a rope, but most audiences would have already known this. The rope becomes the focus of the next episode as well.
    5. This refers to the ball court ring still in place at Chichén Itzá.

If you can't replace it, you will lose."
(*higher*) "How will it be replaced?
(*higher*) It can't be put back the right way.
Well, there's only ONE WAY to replace it,
tie it in KNOTS."
"No, no, it shouldn't be done like that.
This old rope
has to be put together again.
It has to be PUT BACK again
because it had been PULLED APART."
"But how can it be made good; there isn't any way to make it
     good."
(*higher*) The leader of the Disappearing Ones changed into
     termites, XTULULI termites.
They all changed.
The rope that had been cut
was measured to fit an old trunk.
It was eaten by the leader of the town, he ate it.
But they saw the xtululi termites,
the leader of the Spaniards said,
"This trunk is being eaten.
MAKE ANOTHER ONE."
He said to the carpenter,
"How many days will it take to finish?"
"*Three days.*" "Ahah."
After he made that trunk in three days
he *brought it over.*
Well, they put it on one side of the old trunk that *was eaten.*
They rolled up the rope, rolled it up.
It wasn't even unraveled.
How did they roll it up? They did it.
He said, "Only half fits in the old trunk, the one that was
     eaten.
The new trunk
IS FILLED WITH HALF!"
"Caramba," he said,
"how could it be? They were both made the same height, the
     same width, the same depth.
How can it be?"
Well, he didn't want to CUT IT.
He had a pocketknife in his pocket.
"PUT THE ROPE OUT AGAIN.
I'll have to do it. Since it's eaten, it was all eaten, what more
     can I do?
It has to be finished.
I put it in the new trunk but it didn't all fit."
Well, they ROLLED IT OUT OF the new trunk.

It was put into the old trunk again.
(*higher*) Only half fit in the new trunk;
the old trunk was filled. ALREADY FILLED AGAIN.
"*Ave María Santísima.*
What happened here?
Well, what can I do?
There are TWO TRUNKS,
one trunk is filled and the other is half-filled."
Well, the King of the Spaniards said,
"I guess I'll have to finally cut it." He pulled out his
    pocketknife and he began to cut it.
The rope pulled the knife to it.
WE'EH when it was cut everything within three feet was
    covered with blood!
"*Ave María Santísima.*"
They began to scratch their heads.

•

"It wasn't just a rope, by God!
It was ALIVE, BY GOD! THERE IS BLOOD IN IT, BY GOD!"
They WERE ALL FRIGHTENED, all of them.
Well, they lost because of this,
the Spaniards lost.
Not one of them won.
The ones marked by Wonderful True God in truth were the
    English and the Americans.[6]
Those ones, in truth, can read the Night Writings.[7] They will
    win.
That's what Wonderful Jesus Christ said
when he went there to heaven,
to the presence of our Wonderful Father Rey de Dios Padre.
That one created it, that one created all of this.

This next narrative describes a visit between Paulino Yamá and a famous North American archaeologist, Sylvanus Morley, renowned for his excavations of the ruins of Chichén Itzá. The meeting referred to in this counsel has also been reported on, from the side of Morley, in the book *Sylvanus G. Morley and the World of the Ancient Mayas* by Robert Brunhouse (1971: 260–269). The Morley side of the event is of great interest because of the importance he and his colleagues placed on the political leader of the time, Concepción Cituk. In this

    6. The narrator is using the story to explain why the Maya today look to the English and the North Americans as allies in the continuing conflict with the Mexicans.
    7. The glyphs at the ruins are often referred to as night writings. The narrator noted that the Itza Maac still appear at night and that they were the inhabitants of Chichén Itzá.

counsel, Cituk's leadership is questioned. Political leadership among the Maya of the X-cacal region is not absolute today and most likely was not absolute at the time of the meetings, in 1934 and 1935. Morley and his colleagues, accustomed to a Western model of unitary leadership based on contractual legitimacy, saw the meetings as taking place between "chiefs." This counsel, narrated by a member of the expedition that visited Morley in 1934, indicates that that view was not correct. In Brunhouse's description of the meeting, much is made of the tour of the ruins and the showing of some Charlie Chaplin movies, which supposedly impressed the rebel leaders. These aspects of the meetings are not mentioned in the counsel. Instead, the narrator complains that Sylvanus Morley did not seem to understand the requests of the Maya and put them off with polite greetings when they wanted to talk about arms and assistance with the continuing struggle.

This particular counsel resulted from a conversation between myself and Paulino, in which he asked if I knew Sylvanus Morley. I did not know Morley but did say that I knew who he was. In the narrative the Patrons or crosses are referred to as belonging to the Maya. This theme, common in counsels of this type, was used as a stylistic marker to signal the reference point of all separatist Mayan life, the Speaking Cross.

THE FIRST THING I SAID TO DR. MORLEY

"HELLO, DR. SYLVANUS MORLEY,
we came to talk to you in person here
at 'Chhe'en Kuha'[8]
so you can give us some ADVICE, some SATISFACTION.
We've already talked with you, MISTER, with satisfaction.
You've been asking us, 'WHAT HAPPENED TO US?
What has been done to us?'
WE'RE SO POOR, MISTER, so INNOCENT, so CLOSED.
We don't know what to say.
That important Captain Cituk
that spoke to you
doesn't have any BRAINS.
He doesn't have any UNDERSTANDING.
He just talked even though people told him what he should
    have said.
What I'm saying IS TRUE.

---

8. This is an alternate name for Chichén Itzá. A literal translation would be "Well of the Nest."

Uhuh. Well, you shouldn't do that, you ought not to do it that
    way.
You ought to say what happened to you,
your head isn't just for your hat.
It isn't just for your hat, it's for carrying thoughts up high
and IN FRONT of you.
That's why I'm going to talk to you, I'm going to give some
    advice.
You came to talk to me here,
here in 'Chhe'en Ku.'
Well, now, . . . now,
after you've come, well, WHAT do you have to say to me?
All of the people act like they don't have MOUTHS,
they're like mutes.
That can't talk at all.
Ahah, well, I'm going to say this,
Señor Jefe, the time has passed.
Every time we come, every time we come, every time we come
    here,
well, you don't say anything to us.
We don't say anything either.
Well, NOW then, Señor,
I'm taking account, Señor.
The land, our nation, what is
the reason it is called 'Mexico'?
It is SO FAR AWAY.
They say it's the same land
but I don't believe it's TRUE:
because this land
is separate.
This land of the Territory is separate:
Nohoch Cah Santa Cruz Balam Nah Kampocolche nation.
The FIVE PATRONS are all here in this land, the Territory.
THE OWNERS of the Territory are the MAYAN INDIANS.
    They serve the five Patrons here.
The SAINTS are certainly ordered . . . ordered to stay with the
    Maya.
They weren't ordered to stay with the nobles,
not with the ENGLISH,
not with the FRENCH,
not with the TURKS,
not with the SPANIARDS,
not with the MEXICANS,
not with the GERMANS,
THEY HAVE TO REMAIN HERE.
ALL FIVE SAINTS, PATRONS, should remain here at
NOH CAH SANTA CRUZ BALAM NAH.

They should remain in the land of the Territory.
There they are served by the POOR PEOPLE.
It is said that they are among us.
THE SAINTS SHOULDN'T STAY WITH THEM.
Well, now, that's how the Saints are.
I've given you some advice.
I've said it to you when you came here.
Well, Señor, I believe the time has passed.
That big captain didn't say anything to you.
That Captain Cituk.
Well, I've told you now.
That Noh Cah Santa Cruz Balam Nah is for me
and for you.
My town and your town."
In truth, it is good.
That's how I spoke long ago;
it's been a long time now.
That's how I sought aid long ago.
Now I'm SO HAPPY.

The next narrative or, more correctly, oration is an admonition to
continue serving the Speaking Cross. Paulino recorded this short oration. In this case he spoke in the voice of the Cross. This particular
example of his narration was very well received by people in his village—they often came to the house in which I was staying and re-
quested that I replay this oration. They listened with great contentment; one woman referred to the admonition as a prayer, although
most people referred to it as a counsel from an old and respected
leader.

THE PATRON, I

That Patron,
the Patron remains with us.
Isn't ordered to remain with the ENGLISH,
isn't ordered to remain with the FRENCH,
isn't ordered to remain with the TURKS,
isn't ordered to remain with the SPANIARDS,
isn't ordered to remain with the MEXICANS.
ORDERED, ORDERED by True God to remain with The
    People. Ahah.
Then who will win? No one will win. True God will win,
along with The People.
Well, now,
the thing is, the Sacred Cross is confused, I tell you. Listen
    now while I explain it to you:

you don't serve a Patron like this.
It was ordered to REMAIN WITH YOU.
Really ordered to remain by . . . by *Yum Jesucristo,*
really ordered by *Rey de Dios Padre*
that it would remain with you.
THAT IS WHY, if you let it go, if you suspend service, if you
    abandon it,
it will abandon you too.
If you lose it, it will lose you too.
That is why you should listen to the counsel I'm giving you.
Believe what I am saying to you. This isn't just play,
I am not just breathing air;
I am not just breathing for you.
You won't be left behind,
nor will you be ground into the dirt.

This counsel was performed by Paulino Yamá so that I might carry a message about the Maya of the X-cacal shrine center back to the United States. In keeping with the Mayan penchant for phrasing political oratory through the vehicle of a narrative, the performance continues, after a short introduction, with several episodes from the Caste War of the last century. Like the narrative about the meeting of Sylvanus Morley and the Maya in 1934, this narrative shows some of the conflict and factionalism of Mayan political history—Venancio Puc led the Maya in the 1850s at the time when the Speaking Cross came into being. As with all counsels, this one relies on understatement and brevity to examine present-day interpretations of the Caste War.

THE STORY OF VENANCIO PUC

WHAT, what is the name of the president of the United States?
    (*answer: Nixon*)
Nixon, ahah.
MR. PRESIDENT NIXON, you are the United States.
You have the power within you.
Your town was marked by Beautiful True God.
Not in time will you come apart;
not in time will you lose.[9]
The first time Wonderful True God was given,
it went to Wonderful Heaven.
Yum Jesucristo and Beautiful Woman
Honored María went to the Sacred Town of Jerusalem,

9. This concludes a greeting.

to heaven . . . they left us again.[10]
Truly no man is going to put the tower on the church.[11]
The one there in *Noh Cah Santa Cruz Balam Nah.*
The building there is a huge ancient work of the people . . .
    NO:
it is the building of the Spirits.
   •

That's who did some of the building of the church.
That one there;
the one without a tower.
   •

Venancio Puc,
he did a lot of killing.
He did a lot of killing, he did.
He always looked for ways of being a traitor, besides. [A traitor]
    to the governor . . .
to the governor, the commander, to the captain, to all of the
    officials.
They met every day for nine days.
There was a meeting held every day at sunset.
Well, every month Venancio Puc,
every month, each month didn't end before
he brought together six hundred people.[12]
Then he picked the ones to be killed at random.
That's what scared the governors.
The generals thought in their hearts,
"How can we put Venancio Puc to the side?
He's gone too far killing people;
he's become a traitor."
Then the next day they held another meeting.
A mule with a saddle and bridle [was prepared].
Well, after nine days, Venancio Puc said,
"Well, Wonderful God, I guess my time has come. What
    more?"
They came out and tied a rope around his head,
they then tied a flag around his neck.
They brought him to where the governors wanted.
Well, then he bowed down and asked for mercy from the
    honorable governor.

    10. These five lines are more of an interlude before the first episode of the nar-
ration begins.
    11. The church still stands in Felipe Carrillo Puerto. It was built by the separat-
ist Maya during the 1860s and 1870s. Venancio Puc was perhaps responsible for its
construction.
    12. Nelson Reed (1964: 170) found that Puc took some 550 captives at Bacalar
and killed many of them. This counsel is, in effect, commemorating this particularly
violent episode of the Caste War.

When he asked for mercy from the governor,
CHAH! The people grabbed him.
They beat and kicked him.
He ran to find the mule with the bridle;
he jumped on it and got his foot tangled in the ropes, that
    Venancio Puc.
The mule was hit. It began to run.
The mule ran about seventy feet and dragged him there.
His leg was pulled out.
That's how Venancio Puc was killed.[13] Then Venancio Puc was
    dead all right.
Well, they let the people go, then, to make a little milpa.
The first milpa the people made was 120 feet by 120 feet.
The people made the milpa.
That's how the people found their lives in time past.[14]

•

It was told to Wonderful True God;
he was told what happened.
Don Felipe Yama was governor.[15]
He said to his generals, "If you are killed, then it is not your
    fault if you don't have eyes.
Well, I'm going to have real justice. Who will be afraid?
Now I'm going to ask whose fault it is. I'll ask he who bled, he
    who sanctified himself."
He then asked. Lightning flashed in his eyes! Whose?
The official. The one who was killed was General Felipe Yama.
He was dead.
He was down.
He lay there on the ground for three days.[16]
He got up and rubbed his eyes.
He began to say his name.
Lightning flashed in his eyes.
LEEM! He was down;
he fell.
Well, then, mister,
True God said, "My name is the General Felipe Yama.
There is my temple.

13. Grant Jones (1974: 675) notes that Puc was executed along with two assistants. This counsel indicates that the execution was less direct than a simple murder.
14. These four lines also serve as an interlude between the episodes of the counsel.
15. Felipe Yama was a political leader during the 1890s (Reed 1964: 227). At that time, the separatist Maya suffered great population loss through epidemics and continuing skirmishes with Mexican forces.
16. In this episode, Felipe Yama is about to be possessed. Lying dead for three days is an idea taken from the Christian Bible.

No one is going to put up that tower
except those that are called English
and those that are called Americans, red-red men.
They will put up the tower on my temple.
That is the only truth.

    •

I've made it true until the sun ends.
There you will get whatever the things you need, there with
        those who are called English,
with those who are called Americans, red-red men.
They are my servants;
they are my sacred people.
I am Juan de la Cruz,[17]
I am the Noh Cah Santa Cruz Balam Nah.
There isn't anyone else!"

This ethnohistorical narrative by Paulino again explains why the
Maya continue to think of themselves as separate from Mexican
society. Instead of referring back to the Caste War, however, this
counsel brings in the events of the Cuban Revolution as part of the
argument. Although Americans from the United States and the English are seen as natural allies of the Maya, this counsel expresses
some doubt about the willingness of such allies to join in the struggle. In the early 1970s, I found that the separatist Maya were very
aware of the U.S. involvement in the war in Vietnam. Some separat-
ists suggested to me that the U.S. army might be better off support-
ing the Maya than the government of South Vietnam.

THE PATRON, II

The . . . the . . . the PATRON,
the Patron of my town,
Noh Cah Santa Cruz, the real town,
the real town of Xoken, Chindzonot town.
There it appeared; there it came out of a cave.[18]
My town is Noh Cah Santa Cruz Balam Nah Kampocolche
        town.
Now,
THE LAND HERE HAS BEEN DIVIDED by the Mexican
        masters.
Well, now, I'm thinking . . . I'm thinking that

---

17. Juan de la Cruz may have been the founder of the Speaking Cross icon in
the 1850s (Bricker 1977).
18. The Speaking Cross was from a small well near Santa Cruz or Felipe Carrillo Puerto.

it isn't very legal. It isn't legal because they don't care about
   us.
They don't like us; they don't give us any respect. They don't
   AID US like they should.
Well, whatever . . . all the conversations that are heard now
are understood. A long time ago, long ago, we were all VERY
   IGNORANT. ALL IGNORANT.
Our eyes were closed, as they ought to be. Now, in the time we
   are living,
WE ARE ALL "campesinos of the Mayan zone." All of our eyes
   are open. All of them.

•

Well, now,
we're thinking about all the things that have happened, all that
   has been told to us.
Like what happened in Havana, Cuba.
Havana, Cuba, in the time of . . . what, what what was his
   name? (*answer: Batista*)
Batista was overthrown, overthrown by Fidel Castro. Beaten by
   Fidel Castro.
Well, all of the . . . all of the THINGS that were put on those
   streets by the Americans were left there.
They were all taken by Fidel Castro.
Since the Americans didn't want anything, didn't want to
   fight.
All of the goods were left. Left there,
left for Fidel Castro.

•

We are POOR now. Well, now we are thinking that the SAINT,
the Noh Cah Santa Cruz, ought to be served.
It ought to be respected. It ought not . . . not be left to become
   old and useless. We ought not sleep through the dusk. It
   ought to be respected.
Even before sunset it ought to be lit up with lights. How good
   that would be! How beautiful that would be!
All of the Sacred Candles
ought to be given to . . . to . . . to the SAINT. And all of the
   Sacred Incense ought to serve the SAINT as it should.
If it is served as it should be,
even Old One Rey de Dios Padre would SEE. The Wonderful
   Father, Yum Jesucristo, WOULD SEE. Beautiful Woman
   Venerable María WOULD SEE, if it were rightfully
   respected.
Respected as it ought to be.

•

We are in poverty.
Well, now, we, The People,

are poor. That is how the Most Sacred Patron is also, poor.
A leader hasn't arisen to HELP US AS HE SHOULD.
Well, as we are now,
the Mexicans HAVE ENTERED Noh Cah Santa Cruz Xbalam
    Nah. They have TAKEN EVERYTHING. Everything has
    been grabbed by them, everything has been eaten.
Who owns the land? Who? The People, the "campesinos of the
    Mayan zone."
They get nothing. They aren't paid a good wage.
They are in real poverty. All poor. Well, we are taking all of
    this into account.
When will we be given respect? When will we be helped?
We are serving the Patron who was left to us here on earth.
We have no STRENGTH,
we are POOR: in POVERTY. We don't have BOWLS, we don't
    have CALDRONS, we don't have anything.
Well, now,
we are thinking to ask
aid from Mr. President . . . Mr. Governor, because they have
    the Territory.
They hold everything in the Territory.
Where else can we ask for help?
We cannot ask any other nation. We cannot ask the English, we
    cannot ask the Americans, not them.
They are not the ones who are holding the Territory.
The president and the governor, they are the ones holding the
    Territory. They have robbed us of everything. They ought
    to give us ALL the implements, everything.
Things like the
ORCHESTRA that is needed for the Sacred Ceremonies.
Everything like TRUMPETS. Everything.
They ought to give us everything, so we can serve the Patrons
    of our town.
   •   •
That is it.

Divination and Signs

Signs foretelling events, signs of the weather, and signs of people's
thoughts are critical features of Mayan conceptions of the world.
The *xoc kin* described in the second chapter is a way to use the
month of January as a metonymic sign for the entire year. Events,
activities, and relationships between people are calculated and commented on like so many days of the *xoc kin*. When I asked Alonzo
why he wasn't surprised when I paid him a visit one year, he replied

calmly that he knew I was coming, even though I hadn't written, because the cooking fire had made a noise like my Volkswagen bus that morning. "Allan is coming," he had said to his wife. Sure enough, my family and I arrived later that day. On another occasion, I was out in the fields during the cutting phase of the milpa cycle. Don Benito, my next-door neighbor, and I were about to leave the fields, as we had finished our work for the day. Don Benito placed a small leaf in the path. I asked what he was doing. He said that his brother-in-law and the others who were working in a nearby field would notice the leaf and know that we had left. The leaf was a sign, something out of place, a pattern disturbed which could be comprehended by other Mayan people expert at pattern recognition.

Mayan dreams are signs as well. In villages that lack telephones, it is common to rely on a kind of extrasensory perception through one's dreams. The following illustration shows the structure of dream signs. One day a well-known musician from the shrine village of X-cacal came to my house. I had not met him before, although I knew who he was and had been discussing his abilities with his brother the day before. I was planning to go to the shrine village soon with my tape recorder to record some of the ceremonial music that still existed there. Don Marcelino came into the house and began a protracted ritual greeting. He sat in one of our hammocks while his wife and children examined some of our possessions in the house. Finally, when I ran out of things to say, I asked why he had come to our village that day. Don Marcelino replied with some surprise that he thought I wanted to see him. I said that I did but asked how he knew that. He answered that I had been in his dream the night before and we had been talking. He was there to see what we were supposed to be talking about. I then made arrangements to record him and his musical colleagues.

When I asked others if such events were unusual, I was told that they were quite regular and expected signs. Mayan people are more surprised when the dream-calling system does not work than when it does. One young man even compared dreaming about talking with people to using a telephone. "How else can we get in contact with people?" he asked.

The following two narratives by Paulino are reports of signs during the time of the Caste War. The first describes a comet, most likely Halley's Comet, which appeared in 1910, ten years after Ignacio Bravo entered Santa Cruz. When Bravo entered the town, he found it deserted: the Maya had escaped into the surrounding jungle. The second narrative reports on a gorilla-like monster that was found around the same time; it also describes a flood which is interpreted as a sign that the Maya were correct in their uprising against the Spaniards.

SIGNS, I

In the TIME of Ignacio Bravo,
there were a lot of SIGNS that were given to us by Sacred Yum
    Jesucristo and Beautiful Father Rey de Dios PADRE and
    Beautiful Virgin María.
Why were so many given to us? The miracles were given by
    Beautiful True God because of True God's great love for us.
He helped us as it ought to be, just like it can be.
We ought to kneel next to the trunk of a tree, just as at the end
    of your hammock you ought to kneel.
Also, you shouldn't lie to True God ONE BIT, you shouldn't
    forget Wonderful True God one bit.
Well, then,
a thing came to pass—there came a Xbuudz Ek, the thing that
    is called a comet.
It was REALLY big. It was really big when it came long ago.
It was about three . . .
about three when it appeared.
That Xbuudz Ek had a tail
that was about TWELVE FEET long.
That Xbuudz Ek
moved. It moved.
Before it came there was a big noise.
That Don Bernardino Cen said, "It will kill us."
Well, it went back. It went back because Yum Jesus made the
    noise all the way to Jerusalem.
One day, about TWO THOUSAND cannons came.
One day so many WERE FIRING, like rifle shots.
The guns fired, but it was a pure mystery how they fired.
They say that it wasn't just one cannon, there were ONE
    HUNDRED shots of a rifle that sounded.
Well, when the sound was made there wasn't even an echo.
They say that that cannon
MADE THE SUN SET.
It made it dark.
When the sun was out there at the town
it made the sun set. They say that cannon and the sound
    darkened the sky.
That wasn't a big sign.
Another miracle was given, another BIG SIGN was given to the
    Mexicans.
It happened over there at Santa Cruz, the Noh Cah Santa Cruz.
They didn't win.

It was just a horse. They just won horses like that.[19]
Ignacio Bravo killed all of them because of Ariero there at
      Yo'Co'opo.
Ariero said, "If Wonderful True God wants me killed,
I'll go behind the trail of them on my horse."
FOR THREE DAYS the poor man came along.
He got to the town of Carrillo,
the town of Noh Cah Santa Cruz Xbalamnah.
There was a Siperes tree
at the entrance of the temple.
There is where the horse was caught.
After he caught the horse he went.
Well, he came into the house of Ignacio Bravo there at Co'opo.
He said, "I found this horse at an abandoned town.
There's a huge temple there of cane and a Siperes tree, a big
      Siperes tree.
There's a palace to the north, a palace to the south, a palace to
      the east, a palace.[20]
Well, I couldn't tell where but it showed where people passed
      there in the dust.
It showed where people passed.
The town ISN'T there,
but it showed where people passed.
No one saw me; neither did I see anyone."

SIGNS, II

I want to tell you something.
There was a thing I saw, *I saw*
during the TIME . . . the time of Ignacio Bravo.
There was an animal
that GAVE a real fright
to all of the Maya.
That animal gave fright to ALL OF THEM.
It was at Chaccho'obe where that animal began to make a
      growl.
Then all of the people were frightened.
From afar the growl was heard, even as far as
about forty leagues.
Ahah. Well, True God gave that thing, that big sign.
It was ordered to be.
Well, there were some people there making their guard service.
They all went into the church

19. This refers to the desertion of the town by the Maya prior to the coming of
the first scout.
20. In the shrine center of X-cacal today, houses for the rotating guard com-
panies surround the main temple.

where the Important Patron was.
They put out three guards.
It was the time when "mama moon" barely, barely came out.
It was the time of the Yaxkin,
the month of *May.*
Well, they saw the animal.
They shot it. They shot it.
Its tail was three hands wide . . . the tail.
It even had hair.
It had hair of ALL KINDS of animals.
There was hair of RODENT,
there was hair of BROCKET DEER,
there was hair of DEER,
there was hair of AGOUTI,
there was hair of WILD PIG,
there was hair of BOAR,
hair of jaguar, hair of ocelot.
It had hair of all of the animals,
it had EVERY KIND OF HAIR.
That animal had all kinds of hair.
Its claws were like the claws of a cat; that's what the claws
    were like.
But the growl couldn't be understood.
If it growled, no one would know what it was.
Well, all of the people, A THOUSAND PEOPLE, were
    frightened.
Wonderful Leader said it was ordered to come.
He ordered a big sign for all of the people who could hear it.
All of the people heard it.
No one person did it,
True God Santo Gloria, he's the one who did it,
that's the one who gave the signal
so all the people would come together and pray.
Because prayer is needed. It's needed by the Maya and all the
    people.
Why, then?
Because Wonderful True God ordered all things to happen.
He doesn't want us to let loose.
A bad thing has come to pass because of the Mexicans,
because of the Mexicans.
That's how we are.
A monster came to the Maya during the time of Ignacio Bravo.
It was a frightening thing.
But because the POOR Maya had guns
no one could kill them.
That Ignacio Bravo rose up against the Maya,
but Wonderful True God gave him a big sign too.
The sea ROSE UP to the sky

like it had done before.
It went to be with the sky.
The . . .
federation of Mexicans was there at Noh Beh;
they were going to come into *Noh Cah Santa Cruz Balam
    Nah.*
When they got there THE RAIN FILLED THE ROAD.
The water was up to the tops of the trees.
It broke down and piled up wood.
It was up to the tops of the trees.
(*higher*) All the trees were flattened down by the water that
    came over the land.
How did this happen? God did it.
The water wasn't too wide, just about thirty feet.
The water was from the little sea.
The water from the little sea is a
woman.
The water from the large sea is a *man.*
When they come together they are the "rain" water and the
    sea.
The two waters rose up,
went as HIGH as the SKY UP THERE.
That's what True God said.
That's how True God gave the sign
to the Maya;
he gave a signal that the enemies and Ignacio Bravo's people
    would hear,
so that they would see that they weren't correct. They
    wouldn't win.
"What I think is what is going to happen.
I don't have any guns; what I have is just a CUP and a GLASS
    OF WINE."
All of the people of Ignacio Bravo will end with that.
JUST with that, the hail came. Just with those grains, HE
    GAVE IT TO THEM.
That's how their days were ended.
Ignacio Bravo's people's lives were ended.
"I'm the only true one. I am speaking the truth to you all.
I love all of the Maya; I TAKE CARE OF THEM,
I watch with loving eyes so they continue to pray,
so they wash their knees, so they take care of me.
That's why I tell you.
Why? Because I, I spilled my blood for them.
I love them.
That's why
I am sad for errors that are made
even when they're without fault."

4. SECRETS

Secret knowledge about the more esoteric or mystical aspects of Mayan life makes up a genre of oral literature in itself. The term for narratives of this form, *secreto'ob*, does not refer to the distribution of this knowledge; it refers to the mysterious content of the stories. Anyone can hear secrets; there are no limitations on who can tell stories from this genre. On the other hand, such stories are not told merely for pleasure, as they are likely to be able to influence the natural or social world in a way that other stories cannot.

One of the secret stories in this chapter concerns a man who travels to the clouds in order to understand where the rain comes from and why it does not fall equally on all plots of land. The story itself was told in early June, when the first rains of the season should have arrived. There was a drought that year, though, and the story was told in part because many *milperos* had the drought on their minds. A few days after the first telling of the story, it rained. The narrator did not make any connection between the story and the rain, except to call attention to the story when we heard the thunder and in this way lend more credence to the events of the narrative. When the story was tape-recorded a week later, it began to thunder and lightning in the middle of the narrative. Mayan narrators would not go so far as to say that such stories can cause rain to fall. Rain ceremonies are reserved for that function. But there is often a close synchronization between secret stories of this type and actual events, a point that narrators enjoyed emphasizing whenever such stories were performed.

Many secrets concern different kinds of deer and their activities. Yucatec Mayan people consider the deer to be special alters or guardians themselves; deer are beings who live in the forest and jungles in counterpart to people who live in cities and towns. Deer are watched over in a corral deep in the jungle so that harm does not befall them. If unusual harm comes to a deer who is a person's alter, that person will become sick and perhaps die. In such cases a traditional curer who knows the guardians of the forest is called in to correct the relationship between a person and her or his alter.

Deer are also hunted regularly. Milpas attract them with the abundance of corn, and hunting deer at night in a milpa is an enjoyable and profitable enterprise. But too much hunting can result in an upset in the balance between deer and people, as the first narrative points out. The second narrative is also about deer hunting. It concentrates on one of the secrets of the deer: the existence of a small stone that can be found in one of its stomachs. The deer stone must not be used to undue advantage, as the narrative explains.

Secrets are the most esoteric genre of Yucatec Mayan oral literature. In secrets one can meet up with the big deer with a bee's nest in its antlers, be carried off to the sky, or travel through the levels of the underground. Secrets are supernatural in character. They are told with the full expectation that they will be believed, even though they may contain comic actors or episodes.

Two Deer Stories

The first two secret stories, "The Man Who Was Such a Hunter" and "The Deer Secret," were told together as a set of narratives about deer hunting. The narrator, Alonzo Gonzales Mó, had been out hunting several times with me, although we never were able to shoot a deer. At the time of the telling, a farewell dinner was being planned, as my family and I were leaving after a two-year stay in Yucatán. Alonzo, who knew that we enjoyed the pit-oven cooking that is done on ritual occasions such as this, took great delight during the two stories in describing the process of cooking the deer in a pit oven.

THE MAN WHO WAS SUCH A HUNTER

Well,
•   •
it will be completed, there is a
person. Such a *great hunter.*
But such a great hunter.
•   •

Every time he goes
to *hunt*
in the *jungle,*
the sun doesn't
go down without a deer.
Every day he goes, each day he has to hunt.
•

Well,
one of those
DAYS like that then,
•

he goes to a *road* like that.
Just as he's going,
•

he sees a LARGE DEER.
•

(*higher*) But it's a big thing!
•   •   •   •

He says,
(*quickly*) "I'll shoot this deer right away."
As the deer is standing there,
he
•

LOSES it there in the forest.
•   •

Then the man, such a hunter, enters; he entered
to see WHERE
the deer passed, where it WENT.
•   •

Well, he *enters* the *forest,*
a little *dark trail,* like that.
He starts to go to find
where the deer went.
As he is SEARCHING, he SEARCHES; he goes walking where
     he ought
to find it, where the deer went.
•

There, at the edge of a
vil—lage,
(*higher*) a small town like that,
•   •   •

then he sees
•   •

the deer fenced in a
corral. But SO MANY deer, not just one,
SO MANY deer, all of the kinds of deer are there.
However it is wished, there they were!
•   •   •

Well, he says, "GOD!" he says.
•

"Look *how many* deer there are over there!"
•   •   •

Well, as he is just going on like that,
he turns;
he goes on.
Then he GOES UP to the gate like that.
•

Then just stopped, he thinks.
•

He thinks with the deer in his sight like that.
•

An *Important Person*
just appears.
His *beard* is pure white;
his *hair*, white;
his beard, *white.*
A LARGE beard.
•   •

He says to him, (*lower*) "Listen,
•

little
•

yellow-foot,"
(*quietly*) he says to him,
"WHAT . . . have you come to do?"
•

(*higher*) "Me, father,
I'm just passing through for a little *hunting.*"
•   •

(*quietly*) "Ahah.
•   •   •   •   •

The DEER
•   •   •   •   •

you were chasing before, the one you say you shot,
THERE IT IS, lying down.
• • • • • • • •

(*quietly*) You did it, . . . my animals,
•

it's that you do evil to my animals.
Every . . . every time I look, I'VE LOST ONE.
• •

You, by God, do evil to it—you KILL IT!
•

Well," he says like that,
"little yellow-foot,
• • •

here are the deer,
•

(*quietly*) my herd.
CHOOSE
which one looks good to you.
CHOOSE
the largest; shoot it!
• • •

Carry it!
•

But it will be finished like that,"
(*quietly*) he explained like that.
•

(*quietly*) "Okay, then, father."
•

He shoots the deer.
He shoots it like that, he . . .
"Well, there it is—
but LEAVE!"
he says to him like that.
• • •

The man ties up the deer.
He enters into that corral,
•

he LEAVES.
• •

(*quietly*) "Well," he says, "Christ!" he just says.
• • • •

(*quietly, to himself*) "Where will I find the trail?
• • •

I'm lost here
in this forest.

Here's that village, but there isn't a village—I know that there
   isn't a village—but here's a village—could I go to the edge
   of the trail? I don't know . . .

   •   •   •

(*normal voice*) I guess I'll go with the deer on my back.
I'll see where I end up. I'll find the trail where the road enters."

   •

Well, he shoulders the deer, he begins to go.

   •   •   •

Well, not VERY much farther, about . . .
not far from the road where
he came in,
about FORTY FEET from there
from the trail where he saw the village like that,

   •

well,

   •

he began to go,

   •

he began to go to his town,
his town like that.

   •   •

Well,

   •

he ends up, by God,

   •   •

there on the road, by God.
He
CUTS A MARK in a tree like that,
a MARK to show where he came out.
Where he can enter again where he came out—he marked it
   like that.

   •   •

Well, he went on.

   •   •

He came to his town.

   •   •

He said to his wife,

   •   •   •   •

(*higher*) "Here's a deer;
I shot a deer."
(*normal voice*) "Christ! Look, by God, at the big thing you
   shot,

   •

mister!"
she said like that.

"I shot a large, large deer."

•　　•　　•　　•

Well, he

•　　•

threw it down!
He said that she ought to prepare the
CONDIMENTS,[1]
the FIRE PIT ought to be dug out,
because the deer will soon be skinned.

•

Well, the CONDIMENTS were prepared like that, the PIT
　　WAS DUG.
The beec[2] WOOD was found,

•

to make the fire pit.
The FIREWOOD,

•

the ROCKS.

•　　•

Then he began skinning the deer.

•　　•

When he had skinned the deer like that,

•　　•　　•

well,
the MEAT was taken off.

•

After it was A—LL skinned, A—LL of the meat taken off like
　　that,
then,
well,
the pit was LIT,
the pit was LIT.

•　　•　　•　　•　　•

He LIT the PIT like that.
Rocks were put over
the pit.
The rocks were piled up OVER EACH OTHER.

•

Then after
the pit was lit like that,
about,
about . . .

•　　•　　•

　　1. The condiments include the spices and onions that are cooked along with
the venison.
　　2. *Beec* is a species of oak, *Ehretia tinifolia*.

ONE HOUR after the pit had burned,
(*aside*) or less than one hour after the pit had burned like that,

•

after it had burned, WATER WAS SPRINKLED.
Water was sprinkled over it like that.
After sprinkling the water like that,
the rocks were all spre—ad out even.
RED-HOT, ALL OF THEM.
About TWENTY were taken off, all of them RED-HOT,

•

because this is when the venison is brought and SPREAD
        OVER the pit.
Then, when it was evenly spread over the pit,
it is all RED-HOT like that.
Then rocks are placed over the deer . . . the deer meat,
so that it cooks FAST like that.

•

After it is SPREAD OUT like that then,
the . . .

•

that beec wood goes over it,
those beec branches go over the meat.
It is all evenly spread out.
After it is all well SPREAD OUT like that,
REAL THICK like that,
the dirt has to go;
the dirt is spread over it.
After the dirt is SPREAD OVER IT like that,
then when the dirt is well SPREAD,
no place is seen where air can enter—if the air enters like that,
well, a little more dirt is just put on.
Because where air enters like that, smoke comes out.
Well, dirt is put on it then,
over where air enters like that so that it is covered up where
        AIR CAN ENTER like that;
the head doesn't escape.
The deer COOKS well.

•

Then, after it is buried like that, it stays,

•

say . . .
TWO HOURS, I guess.

•

It is just

•   •

thought like that.
Then the meat is pulled out like that.

When the meat is pulled out, even the AROMA—when it is
    pulled out, even the AROMA OF THE VENISON IS
    COOKED.
COOKED, WELL COOKED.
Then it is carried to the house like that.
Then it is divided.
The meat is CARRIED to town

•   •   •

(*quietly*) to be sold.

•   •

Well,
after all of this like that,
then he says to
a friend,

•   •

(*higher*) "I have to go back there;
I saw a corral there—so many deer were there.
I have to go and see WHE—RE it is,
how it is there, at the edge of the road.
I have to go and see,
I have to get another *deer*."

•

(*normal voice, but concerned*) "But man, where are you going?
You tell me that there is a corral of deer that you saw . . .
WATCH OUT that evil doesn't happen to you!
The one you say you saw was a *Master of the Deer*, an
    Important Person," he answered like that.

•

"I have to go and see."
Then the man went to see.

•   •

He CAME to where the tree was slashed,
he TURNS;
when he TURNS, he ends up who knows
HOW FAR AWAY.
He looks through the forest for a block square—NOWHERE,
    NOWHERE is the cow . . .
(*laughing*) the DEER CORRAL found.[3]
HE NEVER FINDS THE DEER CORRAL.

•   •

"Well," he says, "well,

•

well, I guess I've LOST SIGHT OF IT;

---

3. The narrator laughs at his own mistake here. He began to refer to the corral
as a cow corral rather than a deer corral. The use of the term "corral" indicates that
the deer are domesticated by the deer guardian in the story.

but I can't have lost sight of it.
Here I can see for forty yards along the side of the road;
there WAS a corral,
there WAS a village.
I'll find it."
He goes in,
he returns to his town.
The man returned.
Within TWO DA—YS after he came back to his house,
there . . .
        •

there
came a FEVER for him.
But a FEVER was given to him;
        •

a FEVER was given *to the man*.
(*higher*) But a real fever.
    •   •

Well,
    •   •   •

it KILLED THE MAN,
it KILLED HIM.
WHEN I PASSED BY, HIS FUNERAL WAS IN PROGRESS.

THE DEER SECRET

The other one?
    •   •   •   •   •   •   •

Well, it would be completed, a person;
    •   •   •

one of the fields.
This one of the fields
        •

has to hunt
    •   •

each time he goes to the fields.
    •   •   •   •

Whenever he goes to look,
he is sure to hunt.
    •   •   •

The field where he is
is a very LARGE FIELD.
Well, every time like that,
that he goes, he *hunts*.

Well, one of those
DAYS like that,

•

he finished off a
DEER like that, a large deer.

•   •

Well,

•   •

as he begins to skin the deer
that he shot,

•   •   •   •

as he begins to remove
the deer shit there from the belly,

•

when he squeezes it,

•

when it falls,

•

there is a *little stone.*

•

He says like this, (*higher*) "Jesus," he just says.

•   •

"A little thing fell here;

•

I guess I'll take it."
He grabs the little stone, he sees that there is an
image of a small deer there *on the stone.*
Not large.

•   •

Well, he grabbed it.
He didn't tell anyone like that.
(*quietly*) "Well, what's it for?"

•

Well,

•

(*quietly*) it is left like that. He . . . well, he
makes an earth oven.

•

He digs out the oven.
He finds the WOOD, he finds the *stones*—hard stones. He
   buries it BY HIMSELF, because nobody came with him like
   that.

•

Well,

•

after the deer is cooked like that,
well, he returns to his town.
(*quietly*) He goes like that.

•

Well, he arrives at his house like that,
he . . . about . . . about DUSK.

•

He arrives at his house.
His wife says to him,
"You've returned, 'big man'?"—(*higher*) "I've returned.

•

I shot a deer."
"WHAT DID YOU SAY TO ME?"—(*higher*) "It's true, (*quietly*)
    there it is in the basket."

•

Those baskets are for carrying deer.
"It's there in that basket.

•

The thing is, let's prepare to eat a little STEW.

•

(*quietly*) We'll eat a little stew like this," like that.
Well,

•

since he had
that little deer stone like that, well, when he went,
(*higher*) he was sure to hunt.
As soon as he's on the road he hunts like that, because he has
    the stone like that.
When he goes into his fields,

•   •

EVEN IF HE DOESN'T GO TO LOOK, JUST GOES TO A
    ROAD, JUST TO GO INTO HIS FIELD,

•

a *deer* appears.

•

He doesn't go to look for it,
he just goes into his field
to see how his field is, how . . . where the corn is,
a deer just appears.

•   •

BAM! he shoots a deer.
What did it?—the deer stone did it.

•   •

Well, because that person
was such a hunter, which means to say

•

such a person so . . .

•   •   •   •   •

a person . . . so . . . *addicted*
•   •

to DEER,
•

he didn't stop
with ONE,
•

he hunts *every week*.
As it's seen that he has balls,
whenever one appears, he SHOOTS IT.
Well, constant . . . every day, every day of the week, (*higher*)
    how many deer will he shoot?
A lot of deer.
Well, he *really abused* the . . .
that . . . that . . . that which was given, the
•

st . . . deer stone. OVERUSED.
Hmmm. Overused what he should have.
•

He didn't MEASURE it.
Well, then,
•   •   •

he's . . . he hunts deer during the DAY,
•

not satisfied.
He goes looking in the *night*.
•   •   •   •

Well,
•   •   •

one of those days then like that, he says,
•

(*quietly*) "I've already shot a deer, there is a deer,
•

but I want to shoot another!"
Because the deer . . . if you sell deer every day, HOW MUCH
    WILL A DEER GET YOU?
One deer will get you about eight dollars.
Every day.
Well, how much does he get? A lot.
Besides, he has his fields.
Well, then, he goes to LOOK, he shoots another deer.
Then,
•   •   •

he is approached by
that important one of the deer, an Important PERSON then.
•   •

Well, the
Important Person like that says that he quit it.
•   •

Well, he GOES AGAIN.
He ties a place to look from in a tree there
•   •   •   •

(*quietly*) in the field like that.
•   •

(*higher*) Well, he climbs to the thing, around
•

seven at night. He climbs up the tree to LOOK.
(*quietly*) Well, he stays there
to look.
•   •   •   •

Well, he was
WARNED
•

by the Important People.
•   •   •

WARNED, I'm telling you,
because at every CORNER of the field,
•   •

they WHISTLED.
At every corner the Important People WHISTLED. It's that
      they WHISTLED,
•

the Important People, so he'd LEAVE,
because the *Evil*
•

was coming behind;
because the thing . . . because the deer . . .
because the *Animals*.
•

It's that he was STUB—BORN;
•   •

he didn't go. "You, what . . ." He finds and kills another DEER.
•   •

A little later, the Important People whistled, a little later, they
      whistled.
•

WARNED by the Important PEOPLE that he LEAVE
because Frightening Things
were coming behind.
•

(*higher*) But he didn't go!
Well, the Important People got tired like that. He was given . . .
      he was told to leave like that.

They even hit trees there, BAM! BAM! BAM! they hit the trees
   there in the FOREST. They went to the CORNERS of the
   field there in the forest and hit the

•

trees there, so that he'd go, but he DIDN'T GO.

•

He was STUB—BORN, he didn't go.

•

Well, then, he just hears that the deer are coming.
Then they come: "Heeyin . . . HEEYIN . . . (*louder*) HEEYIN!"
   come the deer. They come there, they come over there,
   they come there . . . well,

•

they are

•

coming all around.
Well, he begins to say,

•   •

(*higher*) "I guess I'll shoot these deer."

•

BAM! he shoots one there. POW! he shoots one there. BOW! he
   shoots one.

•

BUT NOT ONE OF THEM DIES. HE REALLY SHOOTS, but
   not one DIES.
He finishes off his bullets; well, he stays there then.
He finds a tree there, a STOUT tree,

•

like that.
He zooms up it like that.
Then high up there he TIES his little hammock then;
(*quietly*) he looks there.

•   •   •

Well, he's finished off

•

his bullets on the deer. He's certainly shot them.
He sees that NOT ONE IS DEAD.
Not one of the deer is dead. Not ONE.

•

He sees that the deer have gathered around the tree trunk.
   There they are DIGGING WITH THEIR FEET.
They're DIGGING, they "bah, BAH, BAH." They . . .
well, they're digging like that.

•

Then, there at the tree trunk, they BUTT the tree trunk, they
   BUTT IT.

Look how they BUTT the tree trunk. The man up there is
    SWINGING.
•
The deer begin to EAT, to MUNCH on the tree trunk. They
    MUNCH on it.
Well, the MAN says,
•
he's SHIVERING there high in the tree,
•
LOOK how many deer! Not . . . not fifty, not even twenty-
    five, ONE HUNDRED AND TWELVE. A LOT.
•   •   •
So many . . .
he says, (*quietly*) "My True God, I'll be eaten,
what will I do?
•
Hmmm. What will I do? The tree is being eaten! The trunk is
    getting narrow. When the tree is felled,
I'll be eaten by the Animals.
•
What will I do?"
•
Well,
•
this
•
was said to him:
•
"GIVE UP THE . . .
•
THE STONE,
you'll be *free.*"
•
But he wasn't able to say
if the deer
SPOKE. He just heard
the WORDS, just heard the WORDS
"Give me
•
the stone, or give the stone to
the deer.
•
YOU'LL BE
•   •
Free."
•

Well, he heard the words.

•

He had FORGOTTEN
that he had the deer stone,
FORGOTTEN.
Then he remembered what he was told:

•

(*quietly*) "Sacred Mary!"
the man says like that, "I guess I'll take the stone with the
     image from the tote sack." He grabbed it, he THREW IT to
     the deer.
When he THREW IT, he saw that it was PICKED UP like that.
The deer WENT AWAY.
The deer WENT AWAY.
(*quickly*) Well, the poor man came down from the tree, from
     the lookout. Around midnight or ONE A.M. he CAME
     DOWN.
THE MAN WAS HALF-DEAD.

•

He was trembling, he was SHIVERING as he came down.
He looked at the tree trunk, but it,

•

the tree had ALMOST FALLEN.
"Ahah, THEN LET'S GO, BODY."
Ahh, the man really went to his . . .
to his FIELD.
To the HUT.

•

He stayed there.

•

A friend came there to the hut then. He told him what had
     happened like that.

•   •

(*quietly*) Well, when dawn came like that,

•   •   •

(*quietly*) they went.
(*quietly*) He didn't even stay in the field.

•

Then, it came to that, the Important Man never went back to
     shoot DEER.

•

Never.
There it is finished.

A Secret about Rainfall

This narrative by Alonzo explains why rainfall is not regular. In Yucatán, especially in the northern part along the Puuc Hills where this narrative was told, rainfall is not predictable. The area around Ticul receives about thirty inches of rain a year, and so it is ecologically in a transition zone between the plantation areas of the northern tip of the peninsula, where henequen is grown, and the corn-producing south. In the area around Ticul the *chachac* or rain ceremony is still commonly held, while in the southern villages of the peninsula farmers reported that they knew what the ceremony was, but they seldom had to resort to it as rainfall was generally sufficient.

THE OWNERS OF RAIN

There is a man
of the milpa.
He plants the milpa like that.
•
But,
as for the corn of the milpa . . .
when the rain RISES UP,
it doesn't fall on the milpa. The water FALLS TO ONE SIDE.
It's that the corn
is almost half-dead like that.
•
The poor milpero says like this,
•
(*quietly*) "My Most Beautiful God,
why then?
The water doesn't
fall here on my milpa.
WHY are the neighbors' milpas
well watered?
(*quietly*) Because every storm that rises,
there it falls.
For my part,
when a storm rises,
IT GOES to the side.
I say, for me, it never rains."
•   •
Well,
there is a narrow-mouthed cave in the middle of the milpa.
There, a THING does EVIL.
An evil thing like that.
•

LE YUMILE CHAACO'OB

Yan huntul maace
ich u coole.
Cupakal u cool beyo.

•

Pero,
le u nal le coolo . . .
le can LI'ICE chaaco,
ma tu kaaxa ich u cool. TANXE TU'UX cu kaaxah le ha'o.
Es que le u nale
casi tu medio ciinlahlo'o beyo.

•

Ci'a'ic beya le otzil yumile cool beya,

•

(*quietly*) "In Hahaldios cichcelen,
ba'ax ten tun?
Ma tu kaaxa
le ha waye ich in coola.
BA'AX ten le u chucano'obo
cu buula ha ich u cool?
(*quietly*) Tumen tu lah li'ce ha'o,
ti cu kaxli'i.
Tene
le can li'ce ha'o
BIN cu beetic tanxe tu'ux.
In tya'ah tene, ma tu hoya'tic."

•   •

Como,
yan humppe xomoh sahca bey ich u chumuc u coolo.
Ti yane BA'AH cumeyah KAASO'O.
Tentasion beyo.

•

Then the important man, the milpero like that,
says this,
(*higher*) "My True God,
why doesn't the water fall here in my milpa?
What's the reason?"
He begins to pray.
While he is making his prayer like that,
an Important Man appears. He talks.
(*aside*) A long MUSTACHE, long hair. White, the hair on his
    head—on his face.
He says to him like this,
"Son,
what happened to you?"

•   •

(*higher*) "Ay, Important Man,
here's what happened to me:
I'm THINKING . . .
because here in my milpa,
the RAIN never falls.
When a big RAINSTORM rises up like that,

•   •

it rains to ONE SIDE.
(*higher*) My milpa's JUMPED OVER.
It doesn't rain here in my milpa."

•

(*quietly*) "Ahah . . ."

•

"If I could see
where the Owners of Rain
get the water,
I would go too, to get water to bring here to my milpa.
I would water the corn of my milpa."
"Ay, son,

•   •

you would really COME?"
(*higher*) "I would come, Important Man, Important Father.
(*quietly*) I would come.
What I would look for is water for my milpa. I could then see
my corn grow a little in my milpa.
If not, it will die like that.
No water.
(*higher*) Here only dust rises up,
(*higher*) even you see that."
"Fine then, son.
Are you brave enough to know, to go where the rain is found by
    the Owners of Rain?"
"I'm brave enough, I'd go."

Ha'alibe le nohoch maac tun, yumile cool beya,
ciya'ic beya,
(*higher*) "In Hahaldios,
ba'ax ten ma tu kaaxah ha waye ich in coole?
Ba'ax o'olah?"
Cah ho'opu rezar.
Mientras cabeetic u oracione beyo,
cah tiip tunu huntul Nohoch Wiinic. Tzicnale.
(*aside*) Nuucta cu ME'EX, nuuc u pol. Sactuce'entaco'o tu
    pol—u me'ex.
Cah alah ti'e beya,
"Hijo,
ba'ax ciuchutech?"
•   •

(*higher*) "Ay, Nohoch Dzuul,
ma ba'ax ciyuchutenene:
tin TUCLIC . . .
tumen wey ich in coole,
ma ti kaax le HA'A.
Le can li'ceh NOHOCH CHAACO beya,
•   •

TANXE TU'UX cu kaaxlahlo'o.
(*higher*) Es que in coole CUPPITIC.
Ma ti kaaxa waye ich in coole."
•

(*quietly*) "Ahah . . ."
•

"Wa cinwila'ah
tu'ux cubin chhaabil le ha
tumen le Yun Hoya'abo,
he'in bin xan in chha'i, cah in taas waye ich in coole.
Ca in hoya'te nal le in coola."
"Ay, hijo,
•   •

haah TAALEH?"
(*higher*) "He in talleh, Nohoch Dzuul, Nohoch Taat.
(*quietly*) He in taaleh.
Ba'ax in caaxceh tin hoya't ich in coola. Cah paatic inwilic
in logurartic humppiit u nal le in coola.
Wa ma beya tuciinla'a.
Mina'an ha.
(*higher*) Waye polvo culi'cil,
(*higher*) tac tech ilic."
"Ma'alo tun, hijo.
Kucha'an wa tun a wooli catalcech tu'ux cuchha' le ha'o
    tumen yum Hoya'bo'obo?"
"Kucha'an inwooleh, he'in tale."

"Good. You'd truly go?"—"I'd go."
"Well, FRIDAY I'll come here to get you. I'll come by to get
    you,

•

if you'll truly come."—"I'll come,

•

Important Man."
"Well, fine. Friday, wait for me here. I'll come by to get you. We
    will go.
I will bring you there."
"Fine then."
"Well, I guess I'll go.
Friday, I'll await you here;
I'll come by to get you." (*quietly*) "Fine then."
Well, the Important Man, the Important Person left.
The milpero was left there.
That man thought,
"Just . . . stories, what he was saying."
He's thinking,

•

"What he said wasn't real, like that."
Well,
Friday,
the man came
into his milpa, just like a milpero would.
He
went to his little hut like that.
Then, just a LIT—TLE after he arrived,
the Important . . . Man, the Important Person, appears.

•

He says to him,
"Well, let's go, son, if you'll truly come. Well, let's go.
I came to get you, that's why I came."
"Well, let's go then,
mister . . . Let's go."
Then the milpero
was taken away.
(*higher*) In a moment they are going. As they are going, they go
    down a path; he sees it disappearing.
He's carried away.
Who knows where he is carried to?
He is carried on a journey.
He arrives, carried along to where he is going.
He is among many Important People like that, OWNERS OF
    RAIN like that.
(*higher*) Well, the man isn't thinking anything.

"Bueno. Haah tah?"—"He'in tale."

"He'elo, VIERNES he intale chha'ech waye. He inman
    inchha'eche,

·

wa tumen hah tale."—"He intale,

·

Nohoch Dzuul."

"He'elo, ma'alo. Viernes, apaa'cen waye. Inchha'ech. Cah
    xiico'on.

Cinbisech."

"Ma'alo tun."

"Hali paa'tic inbin.

Viernes in paa'cech waye;

he'in maneh chha'ech." (*quietly*) "He'elo, ma'alo tun."

Ca'ah binah Nohoch Wiinic beyo, Nohoch Dzuul beyo.

Le maace, cah ppaate.

Le tuclic le ti'e maaca,

"Chen . . . boladas ti a'alah, beyo."

Tu tuclic,

·

"Ma hach ba'ax ti a'alah, beyo."

Ha'alibe,

Viernese,

cah taale le maaco

tech ich u coolo yumele cool beyo.

Cah

bin yan u parsel beyo.

Ha'alibe SA—AN kuchce'e,

cah tiip le Nohoch . . . Dzuul, Nohoch Wiinic.

·

Cah alah ti'e beya,

"Pues co'ox waye, hijo, wa tumen hah taale. Pues co'ox.

Tal inchha'ech, le tal inbeet beya."

"Pues co'ox tuni,

taat . . . Co'ox."

Ha'alibe cah bisa'abi

yumeli coolo.

(*higher*) Chen ichi tu bino'obi. Sigue cah cahe, tubino'o ti
    humppeh beeho; cah tzile dzusa'atah.

Bisa'abi.

Tu'ux bisa'abi?

Le ti'e tubisa'a tu beetah.

Hali, cah bisa'abi, cukuchu bin tu'ux bin bisa'abo.

Ichi ya'aba Nuucuch Wiinco'o beyo, Nuucuch HOYA'ABO
    beyo.

(*higher*) Ha'alibe, le ti'e mix ba'ah tu tuclic.

When the sun sets,
he is given supper to eat. There are all kinds of things to eat.
He's given just PIIB food, CORN DRINK.
Things are given him like that. A fine dinner.
Well,
then the . . . Important Man says like that,
the RAINMAKER says like that,
"Listen,

•

let's go and water.
Choose one of those horses there.
Which one looks good to you?"
the Important Person says.
"That one, the FAT one can carry me."

•

"No—," he says like that.
"It won't do. That horse can't carry you, it's SO fat.
If that fat horse carries you, you'll be LEFT BEHIND.
You won't get there,
(*quietly*) you'll be left behind.
There's a horse there, very skinny.
That rib . . .
the one with its ribs sticking out.
(*quietly*) That skinny one, that's the one you get."
"Fine, then,
Important Man."
"Prepare it."
He prepares that horse, prepares it well.
He puts the . . . saddle on.
Well,

•

"Let's go, man.
Fill your water gourds."
He fills his water gourd like that.
"YOU,

•

son,
when you get right over your milpa,
you know where it is, your milpa,
turn your water gourd upside down.
Your milpa will be watered."
"Fine then,
mister."
(*quietly*) Well, then they went.
When he saw . . . when he saw like that, when he saw that he
      was (*higher*) over the earth,

Le cah ococ kiine,
tutzeenta'a tu haanal. Yan tu laacal ba'al tuhaanten.
Puro PIIB cutzah le ti, SA'CA.
Ba'alo cutza le ti beyo. Ma'alo'obo haanal.
Ha'alibe,
cah alah ti'e tumen le . . . Nohoch Wiinic beya,
le YUM HOOYA beya, ti a'alah tie beya,
"Uye,

•

pues co'ox tun hooya.
Walo teh ta tziimno'o.
Le macamac utztawicho'obe?"
cah ti alah Nohoch Maac beya.
"Le ti'e tu hach POLOC ceninbiseh."

•

"Ma—," ti alah ti beya.
"Ma tu pahtah bisceh nohoch tziimin, hach TAH poloco.
Tumen cah bisceh tziimin hach tah poloco, CAPPAATAH
    PAACHIL.
Ma ta tah,
(*quietly*) cappaatah paachil.
He u tu tziimin yan hach dzoya'ano.
Le ti'e che . . .
chehecbal u baacilo.
(*quietly*) Le dzoya'ano, le canachha'i."
"Ma'alo tun,
Nohoch Dzuul."
"Prepararti."
Cah tu prepararte, prepararte fino.
Cah tu tza u . . . u halma.
Ha'alibe,

•

"Pues cone'ex tun wale.
Chuupa chuuhe'exo."
Cah tu chuup u chuuh beyo.
"TECHE,

•

hijo,
le cah maancech tu tohi a coole
awoohe tu'uxan a coolo,
cah chinchincuuntic a chuuho.
Cah ppaatac u hoya'ata ich u coolo."
"Ma'alo tun,
taat."
(*quietly*) Hali, cah bino'o.
Cah tyilah . . . cah tyilah beyo u ca'ah tzile (*higher*) yo' lu'um,

(*higher*) as he was looking, it DISAPPEARED. As he went it
    DISAPPEARED. He couldn't even
see one TREE.
They went into the clouds, who knows how many layers of
    clouds were there?
Well, they went on together,
whipping the horses like that.
(*quietly*) Well, they went on.
Well, then he says,
(*higher*) "My Most Beautiful God!
The Important Person, the Important Man said that to me.
WHERE I am going . . . is to my milpa.
THERE I will turn my water gourd upside down.
(*higher*) But where . . . where is it?
Will I see it?
But how will I see it?
How will I know where it is?
(*higher*) Well, I guess I'll just have to do it."
•

Well, they went on like that.
He then said to him,
"Well, turn your water gourd upside down here!"
•

"Fine then, Important Man." The man opened up his water
    gourd.
He turned his water gourd upside down like that.
(*quietly*) Then it rained like that.
(*quietly*) Well,
•

for NINE DAYS, he was brought to water the milpa like that.
When they returned one time
where . . . where they were,
(*quietly*) "Well," he said to him, "well, rest, horse;
rest you too.
Tomorrow I'll bring you back.
FRIDAY.
Be ready."
"Fine,
•

Important Man."
•

Well, Friday morning . . .
"MAN, I guess we'll go.
I guess we'll go where I took you from."
(*quietly*) "Fine then, Important Man, Important Mister."
He returned.

(*higher*) chen ca'ah tzile, u SA'ATAH. Tu bin u SA'ATAH.
    Chen cah tu ppaatah ma tzilic
mix humppe KAAX.
Ich muyalo' yani, pero quien sa' hayppe yaala muyalo yaani?
Ha'alibe, ket bin tunu,
le u chicote'obo beyo.
(*quietly*) Ha'alibe, cubino'o.
Ha'alibe, ciya'ic tune,
(*higher*) "In Hahaldios cichcelen!
Tiya'ah tene Nohoch Wiinic beya, le Nohoch Dzuula.
TU'UX bin . . . yan in coolo.
TI bin cinin chinchinpool in chuuho.
(*higher*) Pero tu'un in . . . tu'un in?
Cin inwileh?
Bix in wiceh?
Bix in wey tu'uxane?
(*higher*) Ha'alibe, yan in beetic wale."

•

Hali, tubino'o tun beyo.
Ciya'alah ti'e,
"Pues chinchinpoolcinta chuuh waye!"

•

"Ma'alo tun, Nohoch Dzuul." Cah tu heehu maac u chuuho.
Cah tu chinchinpoolcintu chuuho beyo.
(*quietly*) Ha'alibe hoya'to'o beyo.
(*quietly*) Ha'alibe,

•

NUEVE DIAS bisa'an cu hoya'tic u cool beyo.
Cah suuna'o tu ca'atene
tu'ux . . . tu'uxano'obo,
(*quietly*) "Ha'alibe," ciyalah ti'e, "ha'alibe, he'elsa tziimno;
he'elsabah tac tech.
Saamal in biscech.
VIERNES.
Preparartabah."
"Ma'alo,

•

Nohoch Dzuul."

•

Ha'alibe, saastah viernese . .
"A co'ox wale XI.
Co'ox wale tu'ux in chha'ech."
(*quietly*) "Ma'alo tun, Nohoch Dzuul, Nohoch Taat."
Cah su'uti.

He returned there to the milpa where he was taken from. He
    was left there. "Well, son,
I'm taking you where I got you from.
Here I'll leave you.
I guess I'll go back to where I live too."
"Fine then, Important Man."
He sees the milpa then. WATERED, but WONDERFUL corn,
    BEAUTIFUL corn.
ALIVE, all of them.
When he GOES to where the cave is, the narrow-mouthed
    cave,
broken rocks there.
BROKEN even under the ground, that CAVE. BROKEN
    ROCKS.
Something reeked at the mouth of the cave.
The thing reeked.
SMELLED
where it was hit by LIGHTNING.

  •

Where it had died,
the EVIL THING, the bad thing, the thing that did evil to the
    OWNERS OF RAIN,
to the RAINMAKERS.
Hmmm.
"Well," says the man, "thank you so much.
You killed it for me;
there's water in my milpa too."
When I passed by, the man was happy:
a BEAUTIFUL milpa, BEAUTIFUL corn in the milpa,
a well-watered milpa.

Cu su'utile teh ich u coolo tu'ux chha'abah. Ti ca'ah ppa'ati.
    "Ha'alibe, hijo,
Tin chahech wey in chhaheche.
Wey cinin ca'ah ppaateche.
Es que paa'tic in bin tu ca'aten tu'uxanen caha'anen xano."
"Ma'alo tun, Nohoch Dzuul."
Tzilic ichu coolo. BUULUH, pero CIICHCELEN nalo,
    HATZUTZ le nalo'obo.
CUXA'ANTACO'O.
Le cah TU BIN tun teh tu'uxane le sahca, x'omo sahcabe,
ti'i xi'ixicabo'o tuuncho.
BU'LA'A tac iche lu'umo, le ti'e SAHCABO. XI'IXICE
    TUUNCHABO'O.
Es que tu ba'ale tu holubooc.
Tu boocancil le ba'alo.
TU
tu'ux hatzah tumen RAAYO.

•

Tu'ux ciinsa'abi,
le ti'e TENTASION, le u kaasile ba'alo, le tu meya kaso'o'bo ti
    YUN CHAACO'OBO,
le YUNTZILO'OBO.
Hmmm.
"Hali," cay tiyalah maac, "hach ya'aba Dios bo'oyti'o.
Tu ciinsuten;
ti hoya't in cool xan."
Cah maanene, le maac u ciimacyool:
HATZUTZ cool, HATZUTZ nale u cool,
hoya'tan u cool.

An Orpheus Story

The next narrative by Alonzo describes a journey to the three levels
of the underworld by a corn farmer in search of his wife, who was
seduced and dragged down into the earth by a Feathered Serpent—
who appeared in the guise of a handsome man. In this story the pro-
tagonist has as a hero a small boa, referred to as Xtziciluulme. Yucatec Mayan farmers generally will kill any snake that appears in the
milpas, although I was told that this snake, like the small mice referred to in chapter 2, is a friend, a pet of the milpa. The story contains some comic relief in the form of a priest who is brought into
the underworld by the *milpero.* The priest becomes more and more
frightened the deeper they go into the earth, so frightened that he
cannot pray and in that way fend off the evil things. When I inquired

about this story being a secret, the narrator said that the use of a
Xtziciluulme snake as a friend was a secret, as was the use of a
skunk to enter the underworld. Caves in Yucatán are damp and putrid places where vultures and other foul-smelling things are said to
live. Perhaps this is why the skunk is the key to the underworld—
the skunk is foul-smelling all the time, especially when, as the narrator describes, it pounds its feet on the ground.

A PERSON OF THE MILPA AND AN EVIL THING
AND A PRIEST AND A SMALL FRIEND

WELL,
afterward, there was a man of the MILPA,
the milpa then.
•

He has a small milpa,
one he made.
•　　•　　•

He goes to the MILPA every day.
•

When he arrives at his milpa
•

there is a friend
called Xtziciluulme.
•　　•

Because this XTZICILUULME, the friend,
guards
the corn bin of the milpa
•

so that it won't be eaten by RATS.
•

The thing is, XTZICILUULME is a real friend.
So when he is leaving the milpa, the man says to his friend,
•

"Hey, little SNAKE,
I think I'll go to my TOWN.
YOU STAY HERE to guard my BIN
so that the corn won't be eaten by rats."
•

Then he goes.
"TOMORROW
I'll come to see you again. I'll be going now."
Then he goes, that owner of the milpa,
he comes to his HOUSE,
•

he says to
his wife like this:
"If you want to SEE, TOMORROW, if you want.
We'll go to the milpa to walk AROUND,
because there at the MILPA
some 'grace' has ripened.
THE CORN is getting fat.
You know, we can go there to eat a little roasted corn in the
    milpa."
•   •   •

"Okay, we'll go."
Then the next morning
he carried a little food,
some good food to take to the milpa.
•

(*voice trailing off*) They went there,
they arrived at the milpa
•

where a hut is.
When he sees
his friend there,
(*higher*) "Hello, friend, what's happening? You were left here
    alone.
Were there any rats to catch?"
"Well, THERE WERE."
•

"Uhuh, okay."
Well, the man said to his wife, to his wife,
•

"REST yourself a bit,
a while.
I'm going to take a walk around the edge of the MILPA
to see if anything has happened to this corn."
"Okay."
"Well, I guess I'll be going.
Be careful not to go
into the corn.
Already the sun . . . the sun has set.
Don't go out, be careful not to be bitten by a *snake.*
•

You won't be left here alone.
There's a friend of mine here, he'll stay with you.
•

I'll be going. I won't be long."
"Okay."
"Fine then, my wife."
•

(*voice trailing off*) Again the man went on. The man goes.
He went with his rifle across his back.
He goes for a walk around the milpa,
he begins to walk AROUND the edge of the milpa
TO SEE if there is anything doing harm to the corn *in the
     milpa.*
Well, he went to the edge of the milpa.
The woman then,
she just steps out of the door of the hut.

•   •

She stands there; she stands there a minute.
She sees

•

a MAN appear,
a RICH MAN.
He SAYS, "Come here, woman,
come here.
I want to talk to YOU."
"No, I'm not coming

•

because my, *my husband isn't here.*
He is here, but he went to walk around the edge of the milpa.
It won't be long until he comes back. I'm not coming."
"Oh dear, come here. Let's talk here."
"What are you going to tell me?"
"There are *things.* Come here."
"Okay, then, I'll be coming to hear what you want to tell me."
The man—the woman goes to hear what he wants to say, the
     rich man.
The woman walks over.
(*higher*) "Well, here I am. What are you going to tell me? What
     do you really want to say to me?"
"Well, this is what I want to tell you:
you LOOK GOOD TO ME. If you want,
I'll 'go' with you."
(*suspiciously*) "NO . . . how you talk! I have my HUSBAND.
What will my husband say if I have

•   •

accepted you?"
(*with confidence*) "What else is there?"
"I don't know"—"Well, what do you say?"—"Well, okay."
"He won't know anything. He had to take a walk around the
     milpa; he won't come soon.
If you want, I'll tell you what, I'll give you a LOT of money."
"Okay."
The woman then

•

IS BEING TRICKED by the rich man, by the rich man.
Teeth of pure gold.
When he laughed
his teeth were *pure gold.*
Really a rich man, a handsome rich man.
A PRINCE for the woman.
SHE LIKED HIM.
Well, he fooled the woman, he TRICKED HER.
"If you WANT TO,

•

bring yourself closer here. I will hug you.
What do you say?"
"Bring yourself closer, I'll hug you, I'll kiss you. What do you
     think?"
"If you come with me,

•

I'll give you money."
"Okay" then. She came closer.
She was hugged by the rich man.

•

She began to be kissed by the rich man, she kissed the rich
     man too.
When she realized that she

•

was hugged by the rich man,
when she realized it, the RICH MAN had already transformed
     himself
into a *large serpent.*
The woman changed her mind—she said, "Sweet Virgin Mary,
     what am I doing?
The man, by God, isn't human, it's an EVIL THING, by
     God . . .
well, what more?
It is done.
I'VE BEEN TRICKED!"
She began to scream.
The little snake, Xtziciluulme, heard the woman scream.
He came running,
he transformed himself into a SMALL BOY.
Then the small boy came, the Xtziciluulme, the thing turned
     into a *small boy.*
Then the small boy came RUNNING.
The woman saw the boy in the milpa.
"HEY, BOY—GO AND DO ME A FAVOR: CALL MY
     HUSBAND,
because I'm being killed by a serpent.

I'm already wrapped up,
he's wound around me!
He's KILLING ME! Go find my husband!" "Okay." The boy
    went running away to find the husband.
He came running to the edge of the milpa.
The man sees him at the edge of the milpa,
the man sees that a small boy is coming.
"HEY, BOY, WHERE ARE YOU GOING?"
"HEY, FRIEND, I came to talk to you.
Your wife
is being rolled up by a large serpent."
"WHAT ARE YOU SAYING TO ME?"
"Just that." "Let's go see."
They went. The man arrives. "Where, boy?"
"THERE."
They went on.
The man sees that his wife is really wrapped up with a large
    serpent.
"My sweet Virgin Mary. My beautiful wife, *look how you're
    ending with a snake:*
eh. There's no saving you." "WHAT WILL YOU DO?"
"I'm going to run to town. In a minute I'll tell the priest."
"Okay" then.
He left, running to tell the priest.
He came running to the priest.
"Hey, PADRE. If you can believe it, like this, like this
    happened to my wife.
Let's go so you can see how she became wrapped up with a
    serpent."
"What are you saying?"—"Let's go padre."
Well, the priest went. The man brought the priest there to the
    MILPA.
The man and the priest arrived in the milpa, he was brought to
    see
the place where the snake and the woman were.
"There, padre, look how my beautiful wife is!"
"Is it possible? Look, son!
Well, son, what more is there?
It's happened, the sin is already
made with this,
this thing.
Finished, I guess.
Let's make a . . . a prayer over her."
They began to make a prayer.
They began to pray, the priest began to pray.
Then he said, "Here's the prayer I'm going to make:

do you repent, son, for her?" "I repent for her, padre, because
    my wife is not of this world. She's gone to the
    underworld."
Then the priest began to make a blessing.
Then the earth OPENED UP. AWAY they went, the woman
    and the snake.
The woman went away with the snake. *The earth closed up
    again.*
Then he blessed it, the place where she went,
that woman and the snake.
He blessed it.
"Well, SON, take account of this.
Today you are without a WIFE. Your wife went into the
    UNDERWORLD."
"What?" "Let's go." "Okay, padre."
They went. They returned. (*voice trailing off*) They went on,
    they went on to the town.
Well, the padre came to the CHURCH.
Well, the man went to his HOUSE.
The small boy was left in the MILPA.
Well, LATER, the man came back.
He came and said, "Friend, listen, friend."
"You've come back." "I've come back, friend.
What shall I do, small friend? My wife was CARRIED AWAY.
My eyes are sad since it happened."
"WOULD YOU LIKE TO GO SEE HER?"
"I'd like to go see so I could find where she is."
"Good, fine. *You'll have to go to see*
BUT there is a WAY to see. You are going to SEE, friend.
THERE IS A . . .
    •
there is a . . .
    •   •   •   •   •
there is a skunk there on the ROAD.
A skunk on the ROAD.
That one is a KEY to the PLACE where you'll go.
It's also an 'Evil Thing.'
Here's what you have TO DO.
You have to find, YOU OUGHT TO MAKE about six SACKS of
    GROUND, BURNED CHILE, you have to PREPARE IT to
    bring with you."
"Why will I need it?"
"Well, it's not for you.
When you arrive at the edge of town,
when you arrive where you have to go,
you will see a skunk COMING

to BITE YOU.
GRAB the ground chile, THROW IT in its EYES.
While you are THROWING IT in its eyes, tie its throat, then
  go with it.
It will . . . it knows the road where you will be taken."
"Oh, okay."
"When it PAWS the ground to take you or to lose you, THROW
  MORE chile into its eyes.
MEANWHILE, tie it up.
You will go with it. You will be on the road.
The place that you go will be where your wife is."
"Okay."
"But BE CAREFUL not to FALL there."
"Okay, friend."
Well, the man went to his town.
He arrived in town.
He says to his sons, "Like this, like this, I will do.
BURN me six sacks of chile.

• •

so that I can take it
and I will buy one

•

CORD
to be blessed by the
padre."
Then he went to the padre to ask him if he would go to find his
  wife.
The padre says, "Okay, we'll go and find her.
The only thing,
is the CHILE prepared?"
He said, "The chile is ready to be carried.
Since it is dangerous, there is only one thing to defend
  ourselves with, the CORD.
Padre, you have to BLESS IT with holy water so we can take it.
We also need a crucifix to bring with us."
"We will go, son."

•

Well, EARLY IN THE MORNING
they left to go.
They got the chile and *began to go.*
(*voice trailing off*) They went on.
They walked to the edge of the town where it was said there
  would be a small skunk coming toward them.
You see, the SKUNK is the KEY to the *Putrid Things.*
Then,

•

they just see the SKUNK COMING.

They grab the bag of chile, ground chile, and throw it into the
eyes of the skunk.

They tie it with the blessed cord.

(*voice trailing off*) Then they began to go. They went on.

They were taken along by the skunk who led them.

(*voice trailing off*) They went on, they went on, they went on,
they went on, they went on.

When the SKUNK entered, when it squatted and pounded the
earth with its foot like that,

THEY THREW MORE CHILE IN ITS EYES.

(*voice trailing off*) They went on again, they went on, they
went on, they went on, they went on.

When it squatted again to stomp the earth so that the people
could be led off another way, more chile was THROWN
into its eyes.

They began to go on again.

Then they arrived at the FIRST PLACE.

It was over that place. As they went they saw the

•

world had already disappeared.

Then they went underground. They went through a CAVE to
go on.

The first place they ARRIVED at then was the *house of the
little Putrid Things.*

The house of the little Putrid Things was the first place.

The house of the LITTLE PUTRID THINGS.

Well, naturally the little Putrid Things went with the little
SKUNK.

Well, they gave it some chile,

then they began to be carried off.

They went on.

They were close to the little Putrid Things,

the little Putrid Things, not TRUE BAD THINGS.

Those ones were still very little.

Then they said to the skunk,

"Let's go to another place."

•

Well, *they went on.*

That little skunk is also a Putrid Thing, a key to the door of
the house of the Evil Things.

Well, that little one wanted to stomp on the ground to carry
them away to the underworld,

so they use the chile formula.

It rubs and rubs its eyes

and doesn't go.

Meanwhile he puts more in its eyes and that one CARRIES
    THEM AWAY.
Then they get to another little TOWN, a town of PUTRID
    THINGS.
Not very big Evil Things, LITTLE ONES.
Well, they PASS THROUGH the entrance and go looking for
    the wife.
(*higher*) She isn't found there.
Those Evil Things come, a bunch of them come, grouped
    together like that.
They come in a bunch then.
They come.
They CLOSE IN on them.
They are next to the HUMANS to do *evil*
to those people.
Well, the priest says then, (*higher*) "Ave María Santísima—here
    come the Evil Things, those pure Putrid Ones."
"Pray, padre, do a 'creed.'" He begins to pray.
The thing is, the padre is too frightened to pray.
He says, (*higher*) "Pa pa pa, ta ta ta ta, pa pa pa."
(*higher*) He isn't able to start a prayer. HE'S SCARED.
"Padre, pray! Don't be afraid."
(*higher*) "Titititi, papapapa." "Pray padre!" "Titititi." "PRAY!"
The padre was scared.
Well, the padre began to pray even though he was so scared.
Well, True God looked down. The Evil Things left and they
    were among the little Putrid Ones.
"Well, then, I have to go to ONE MORE TOWN
in the earth to see if my wife is there."
They start going there.
Well, while they're going, the little Putrid One, the skunk, the
    one who DANCES on the earth, it begins to carry the
    people into the UNDERWORLD.
That one THROWS THE CHILE into its eyes. It SHAKES and
    pounds on the ground again.
THEY GO ON.
   •   •

While they are going, they go on, they go on like that.
Then they arrive
at the edge of a town,
the entrance to the great Putrid Ones.
Well, the old man says, the husband that is, says,
"Hey, padre, we've
arrived where you told me, my FRIEND."
The Evil Things are so very large here, the Putrid Ones are so
    very large at this place here.

"Well, let's go."

They go in, but the thing is, those Putrid Ones look
    frightening.

That small Putrid One, that key, the key of the Evil Things is
    grabbed.

Well, (*voice trailing off*) they go on.

They come to the center of the town,

so he says, "Well, we've come all the way."

A great bunch of Putrid Ones come toward them,

a great BUNCH of Putrid Ones.

A GREAT BUNCH of Putrid Ones come; the Putrid Ones
    COME all bunched together.

They bunch together, they want to suffocate them.

Well, the PADRE is SCARED.

The PRIEST is SCARED.

"Padre, don't be afraid,

PRAY!"

(*higher*) "Titi, papa, tititi, A . . . A . . . A . . . Our Father,
    tatatata Santa María."

The prayer doesn't come out of the padre.

"Pray! We'll be squeezed to death."

"Tatatata here's the crucifix!"

The padre is SCARED.

WELL, all of the things move away,

the EVIL THINGS.

They go on to a small PARK.

"Let's go there to the small park to see if my wife is there."

"Let's go then."

They go and TURN to the PARK.

They come to the PARK.

He says, "She's NOT HERE; my woman ISN'T HERE.

Nobody's here; it's deserted."

"Well, LET'S GO BACK."

They start to return, they begin to go back.

Well, while they're going, the man says

to the priest,

"Hey, padre, here comes a group of women and men."

"Where?" "Here they come."

"I think your wife's there.

Let's move closer."

They move closer and see all the people passing by.

THEY ALL have their heads down so they can't see anything.

They go along with their heads down.

"My wife isn't there. That one could be my wife, but it isn't.

She's not here, so let's go over to that church of the Evil
    Things."

He sees that indeed it is his wife.
They go over there to the side of the church and shout at her.
He, ahh,
he waits for the people to come out of the mass.
Well, the people COME OUT. They come out in a group.
THEY COME OUT.
Well, while they are coming out, the people are talking.
The man says, "Padre, there's my wife . . . there's my wife!
Should I speak to her or not?" "Talk to her."
The man shouts to his wife,
he yells to her.
THE WOMAN leaves the group and comes over to her poor
    husband.
"But
my beautiful husband!
What are you doing here? Look at me, my beautiful husband,
    I'm among the Evil Things.
I'M AMONG THE PUTRID ONES.
What are you doing here? Look out, you might get caught here
    too.
What will you do? What can you do? You know it is
not good here.
The things here are pure Evil Things here.
Putrid Ones are here.
I . . . I'm stuck here, no matter what I say, I have to stay here."
"But I've come to take you away.
We have to go—come on!"
"Well, my husband, I'll come.
I have to say to you clearly, you have to hold me NEXT TO
    YOU, okay?"
"Then let's go!"
The Putrid Ones see the poor wife going away with her
    husband like that.
They ALL COME TOGETHER, ALL OF THE EVIL THINGS
    all come together again.
The people are going away with the priest in the MIDDLE
    LIKE that.
The man says,
"Hey, padre, pray, here come the people."
"I will, si si si tatatata papapapa but I . . . I . . . I'm scared!"
"Well, pray, padre!"
(*higher*) "Titititi Ave María s . . . s . . . s . . . s . . . Santa María
    ca . . . ca . . . ca . . . credo."
The prayers won't come out of the padre.
Well, the man sees that without prayer they won't have any
    way to keep from getting caught.

"Ca . . . ca . . . crucifix, ca . . . ca . . . ca . . . I'll show it to
 them!"
They all make the sign,
the Evil Things ALL MOVE AWAY.
"Well, let's get going."
(*voice trailing off*) They began to go on, they were going on,
 they were going on.
While they were going, this woman, that poor wife, as she was
 going away like that she was left without flesh.

•

Before she was very HEAVYSET but as she was GOING AWAY
 like that, she was LEFT without flesh; she got THIN.
While she WALKS ON FURTHER, she is among the living but
 she is SO VERY THIN.
"But wife, what's happening to you?"
"I don't know, my husband, how is it possible?
Look at me now!"
"Let's go, I have to get you out of here."
She is carried off.
When she is BROUGHT to the end of the town where the little
 Putrid Ones are, she's left without MUCH.
She is so very thin, just *bones.*
There, where she is about to be taken through the entrance of
 the cave, where they entered,
the woman became a SKELETON.
Almost all of her flesh had fallen off.
Then, as they LEFT the entrance of the cave, as they WENT
 OUT,
he says, "Well, my beautiful wife, we've made it! Let's go."
While he's saying "Let's go," he HEARS A FALLING SOUND:
 BENACH BENACH BENACH.
The flesh had fallen off the woman.
She was left without anything.
She became an Evil Thing because of the Evil Things, because
 of the Putrid Ones.
The priest says, "Look at that, SON, your spouse is not a real
 person,
she's an *Evil Thing* today. I guess I'll bless you,
I've got to throw holy water on you so that the Putrid One can
 be released.
The Thing has to be released, the woman has to be released."
The spouse was left as a pile of bones.
Piled up, couldn't be made right.

•

Well,
they go on,

THEY GO ON.
They arrive at their town.
The person goes to his HOUSE, the padre goes to the
      CHURCH.
"What did you do, papa?" "Nothing, son.
Your mother was turned into
an EVIL THING.
Her bones were left there at the edge of the cave where I
      carried her.
Well,
I think I'll go see the padre."
He goes to the padre,
"Padre what am I to do?"
"Nothing. You have to confess to me so you can become
      SAVED,
so you yourself can become SAVED.
•

Your spouse has become an Evil Thing.
Go to your house."
He goes to his house.
"Well, son, I think I have to go to the milpa to take a walk
      AROUND.
I've got to see how the MILPA IS DOING."
He goes to the milpa.
HE ARRIVES IN THE CORN GARDEN.
BIG WEEDS HAVE GROWN UP.
He sees his friend. "How have you been, my friend?"
That little snake has GROWN UP, his little friend.
But the CORN was growing in the milpa while he was growing
      too.
"How are you doing, my friend?" "Not so good, my friend."
      "Didn't I tell you your wife was brought to the
      UNDERWORLD? *She's an Evil Thing.*"
"Well, what more . . . it's over. I . . . I think I'll go back to my
      town. You wait here for me.
Live out your life here in this town.
Well, I'll be going to my town too. I won't come back to make
      another milpa."
This all happened.
When I passed by there earlier, the man was QUIET.
He was in his house.
His wife had gone back to the *Putrid Ones.*

Frightening Things and Wizards

The next two narratives were written down as they were dictated to me by Alonzo in Ticul. The story of the Xtabay or woman phantom is an anecdote that Alonzo told after he had taken me to see the giant ceiba tree of Ticul. Although the tree is not in a central area of the present-day town, it is next to a chapel and is considered sacred by the townspeople. The ceiba was the "tree of life" of the ancient Maya; in Yucatec Mayan its name, *yaxche*, means "first tree." According to J. E. S. Thompson,

> A giant ceiba tree, the sacred tree of the Maya, the *yaxche*, "first" or "green" tree, stands in the exact center of the earth. Its roots penetrate the underworld; its trunk and branches pierce the various layers of the skies. Some Maya groups hold that by its roots their ancestors ascended into the world, and by its trunk and branches the dead climb to the highest sky. (1970: 195)

In Ticul, this elaborate symbolism of the ceiba has been lost, although the ceiba is the place where the Xtabay phantom awaits her victims at night. In X-cacal, a young ceiba tree is cut down every year at the new year's ceremony and put in the ground in the center of the shrine area, where people anxiously hope that it will take root and in this way portend a successful year.

JUST THINGS THAT FRIGHTEN ONE

That phantom goes to a dark road.
When someone looks, they see a woman standing there.
When you walk by she comes to embrace you.
So I said, "Where are you going?"
"I'm going to my house. It's far from here, won't you join me?"
"No, let me go by myself."
"No. Let's go together. I'll take you there."
When the man hears that he's captured by the phantom.
The man says, "Let me go."
"I won't let you go until we get to your house."
The man tries to speak, but the phantom squeezes him hard.
It says to me, "Show me your face, I want to give you a kiss."
When it loosens the thing on its face, and the man sees it,
he looks at the thing and is scared out of his wits.
The man says, "Let me go! You aren't a real thing! You're a
   putrid thing, by God!"
So the man begins to pray.

The Xtabay throws the man down.
When the man gets up, he starts screaming, "I've been taken
    by the Xtabay!"
It's over.

WIZARDS

There is a Maker
that knows how to cure illness. He knows how to cure
    sickness too.
For if there is a person who makes you sick or who makes you
    ill with things,
who hates you like that,
who is going to make something happen, who is going to cast a
    spell on you like that,
that person goes to a Maker and talks like this:
"How much will it take to get you to make that woman sick?"
"Well, what particular sickness do you want me to make?
Do you want me to make her sick for the whole year?
Do you want me to make her shit worms or piss blood? Or do
    you want me to make her shit snakes?
Or do you want me to make her shit big cockroaches too? Or
    do you want me to make her give birth to a gopher?
Or do you want me to frighten her?
There are phantoms of cats, there are phantoms of dogs too.
There are phantoms of pigs too. There are phantoms of goats
    too."
When one of these phantoms is desired, the Maker can do it in
    her house like that.
You've gone to a Maker.
Well, you talk like this,
"I've just now arrived here in your presence, old man, so you
    can advise me with your saastun.⁴
Is there anything wrong with me? I want to know what it is
    like that."
"Well, lady, let's see what sickness you have, what sickness
    brought you here.
I need a candle and a quart of liquor and a claw from a rooster
    too."
Well, he grabs the liquor and throws it in a glass.
Then he grabs the saastun, he puts it into the liquor too.
He puts the saastun into the liquor three times like that until
    it is done.

4. The *saastun* is the small round crystal with which a *hmen* diagnoses illness.

Then he grabs the candle, then he lights it like that.
Then he begins his work like this:
he begins to Talk in Secret. He says your name.
Then when he is done with the Talk in Secret like that, he
    pulls the saastun out for the last time.
Then he looks to see what will appear there in the saastun.
"Well, lady, here is what made you so sick: it is a sickness
    thrown on you too.
I'll have to cure it, I'll have to pull it out.
The thing that made you sick like that, it is a big cockroach in
    your stomach.
There is some medicine that will let you pass the big
    cockroach out. Wait here while I make up the medicine."
He grabs the claw and a red rose and breaks them apart in
    water. Then he puts all of it into a bottle like that.
It is to drink so that the big cockroach will pass.
Well, when he is done with that,
"I'm going to prescribe an herb bath too." Some of the herbs are
    "albajaca," "siipche," "sinanche," "ruda."
He tears up the herbs like that on Friday and Tuesday.
That's how Makers work.
There are phantoms of bats too. There are phantoms of snakes
    like that.
They can be brought into a house like this:
he puts water into a trough, he puts a chhom flower in.
Then this is poured over a person's head.
Then when someone wakes up like that, when they lean over
    like that,
then their head will fall off like that.
Perhaps the husband is watching what happens,
when she is seen, when the wife is looked at,
when the head is seen like that, then the head falls off.
The eyes on the head just roll around like that.
You grab the head like that.
You put it into some lime powder. You put the head in like
    that.
When it comes out, when the wife comes out like that,
then she wants to grab the head but can't.
Then tears begin to come out of the eyes like that.
"Oh my husband, give me my head.
Oh my husband, you don't love me. Give me my head right
    now."
He doesn't give her head back like that.
He grabs the body, he puts it in a house.
Then he grabs the head and puts it in a box like that.
After that the husband isn't left alone because of the head.

When he looks at it it is looking cross-eyed like that.
The head is watching him like that. The head of the poor wife.
When the husband looks at it it is looking cross-eyed like that.
"Oh my husband, give me my head. You don't love me," it
    says, "poor me." The husband is made to think all of this
    by the phantom.
Because he had been watched by his wife who is a phantom.
    Because she is the return of the evil things like that.
She came to look for her husband so that she could take him
    too.
When sickness like this comes about, the husband begins to
    hop like an armadillo,
until he is killed.
There it ends.

5. STORIES

By far the most common use of narrative art in Yucatán is for entertainment. Stories or *cuento'ob* that are told for diversion and enjoyment range from narratives about tricksters or animal fables which may not take more than five or ten minutes to relate to long, complicated epics which can last two or three hours. Stories for entertainment are told in the evening, either out in the milpas (see chapter 6) or in the towns. In villages and towns, stories are told on benches in the main square or in people's houses. When a well-known narrator tells a story such as the last narrative of this chapter, "The Seven Towers of Marble," up to thirty-five people may crowd into a small house. When "The Seven Towers of Marble" was performed in our fifteen-by-thirty-foot house, people crowded in, some sitting four and five to a hammock, others leaning against the walls, and others coming and going so that they heard only parts of different episodes.

Stories told for entertainment are expected to engender especially vivid imagery. Alonzo Gonzales Mó said that a good story will be so realistic in one's mind that it will seem like one is watching a film at the movie theater. To complement this aesthetic of realistic imagery, storytellers utilize a number of stylistic devices to weld the world of the imaginary with the world of everyday life. A narrator who tells stories for entertainment is always listening and watching for events or actions that can be referenced into a story. If a narrative takes place in the fields during the dry season, a narrator will strive to include several references to water and water holes in a story and in this way play on people's thirst. More directly, a good performer will use the immediate environment of a storytelling event to attach the story to the experience of the audience. In the story in this chapter about the man who disguises himself as San Antonio, the narrator slapped the table as he told how a character banged on the furniture of his house with his machete while he looked for his wife's lover. Gestures are also used in stories. Yucatec Mayan story gestures are restrained and carried out with considerable forethought. A gesture which describes something falling from the sky to the ground, for example, begins with an arm raised and one's eyes on the outstretched hand. The hand is brought quickly down to within a foot of the imaginary ground, which could be a table or a spot even with the edge of a hammock. The quick motion is then slowed down so that the hand lightly touches the spot which denotes the earth. The control of gestures and their highly stylized movement result in a majestic, dancelike quality that is fluid and understated, not sharp and forceful. A good narrator moves her or his hands more like a Javanese dancer than a Western orator.

The stories are often connected back to the everyday world by their ending formula. Most stories told for entertainment have a phrase at the end which not only signals the conclusion of the performance but also suggests that the narrator has personal knowledge of the main characters. A story normally ends with a two-part phrase: "when I passed by there earlier," followed by a comment about the characters, such as "they were sitting together in their house, very happy," or "the man's funeral was going on." Stories do not necessarily have to end on a happy note, but it is common for them to figuratively end the morning of the storytelling performance. While no one seriously believes that the narrator actually saw the characters, this formula serves both as a signal that the story is over and as a final touch of reality for the audience.

Stories told for diversion and entertainment include not only highly indigenous accounts of the Yucatecan natural world, such as stories of vultures and other animals; they also include plots of European and African origin. A favorite trickster story is that of Juan Thul or John Rabbit. John Rabbit is a trickster cut from the same mold as the Hare stories of West Africa, Bre'r Rabbit of the southeastern United States, or Bugs Bunny of Warner Brothers cartoons. Other well-known European and Middle Eastern stories such as that of Aladdin have come to be appreciated in Yucatán—with changes that allow for milpa agriculture to take precedence over other occupations and features of the Yucatecan landscape such as cenotes and rain forests to take precedence over the landscape of the Old World. "The Seven Towers of Marble" is included in this chapter as an example of a well-told narrative with an Old World plot.

Many stories told for entertainment are humorous. The story of Ahau in this chapter contains several plays on words in Yucatec Mayan which the antagonist, a Spanish priest, fails to understand. The slightly obscene plays on words are very much enjoyed by a Mayan audience, as such double entendres and other wordplay are common in everyday speech. Some of the other stories are more slapstick than intellectual in their manifestation of humor. The story of San Antonio has a hapless lover masquerading as a saint while people burn incense in front of him. "A Person and a Vulture" includes a human having to live like a vulture as a price for finding a good wife. After being asked to eat shit, the person decides that it is better to be single than to be married.

A Story about Mistaken Identity

"San Antonio" was recorded by Alonzo. It quickly became something of a hit with people from villages in east central Quintana Roo. As a story which contains humorous treatment of adultery, of saint's day observances, and of buffoonery, "San Antonio" was a favorite of other narrators, who delighted in hearing this performance from another part of the peninsula. The story was not known in the small villages around X-cacal; the closest thing to it was the satire on Spanish priests known as "Ahau." "San Antonio" dealt with religious practices which had not been regularly performed in the separatist villages since the middle of the last century, when the Caste War began. The villagers still knew of such things as saint statues and tabernacles, even if they did not have any such Catholic paraphernalia in their own religious system.

The story contains many long pauses at the outset and was recorded before I had come to appreciate the need for narrative conversations in performances. I found that, when the tape of the story was played to other audiences, invariably someone listening would join in, take the role of the respondent, and in this way complete the performance.

SAN ANTONIO

There is a PERSON
•   •
and his
•
wife.
•   •   •
This person and his wife
•
had a
San Antonio.
A real Sa—int.
•
Every time
that the day came,
the feast day of San Antonio,
they really celebrated it
with novenas.[1]
They celebrated San Antonio,
really made a celebration.
THEY WERE CELEBRATING
that Saint, San Antonio.
It happened then to that
woman.
There was a person
who liked the woman.
He fell in love with the woman—LIKED HER A LOT.
He spoke . . . he said to the woman
one DAY,
he spoke to the woman like this,
"Listen, woman,
if you believe it,
there's something I'm thinking about you.
I REALLY LIKE YOU.
If you want, I'd like to tell you
•
I'd give you a lo—t."
"No . . .
what do you mean?
I CAN'T because I have a HUSBAND.
Even if I did, my husband would find out and hit me."
(*higher*) "But why would he hit you?
If you don't tell him what we do . . . if we just know

---

1. Novenas are nine-day ceremonies of prayer and feasting.

that's how it will be." "But won't he know too?"
(*higher*) "Know? How?
I really like you."
"Okay, you may like me
BUT I've got to talk it over with my HUSBAND. I've got to
    talk to him and tell him what you SAID
to see if he says what you SAY is okay.
TOMORROW I'll tell you WHAT HAPPENED."
"No, lady, don't tell him, *don't let him know.*"
(*higher*) "Why shouldn't he know?
It's better if I let him know
so he can tell me what's going on.
If it's okay, well, I'll tell you that."
Later,
(*higher*) "Okay, okay, that's all right.
I guess I'll be going.
See you later."
Well, the woman stayed in her house there.
When the husband came in
the woman told him,
"Listen,

•

my husband.
If you can believe it,
a man told me this and this."
"Oh really? What did you say?"
(*higher*) "Well, that you would tell me if I should accept what
    he told me."
"Uhuh . . ."
"Then I said to him that I would talk to you to see if it was
    okay. If so, it would be okay with me
what he said.

•   •

He offered me money;
he said he'd give me something."
"Good. Put what he gives you in the box." "I don't know where
    it is."
"Okay, go and find it.
If you
ask him for
four thousand pesos[2]
and he gives them to you, ACCEPT HIM.
BUT when he comes here
to the . . . to the house,

2. This is a very large amount of money, equivalent to about 320 U.S. dollars in
1971.

put the money, the four thousand worth . . . take the money,
the four thousand,
and put it in the box. Then lock it and take the key.
When he says to you, 'Come here to my side,'
the first thing you say is, 'No, I can't because my husband and I
are not used to doing it like that. My husband and
I . . . when I do it with my husband together like that, first
we EAT, then after we eat we go into the house to BE
TOGETHER.'
Ahah, that's what you have to say to him."
"Okay, my husband."
"I'll be going into my milpa
but while I'm going, I'll just go to the edge of town and there
I'll wait for the time to come
when that man comes.
(*higher*) I'll be waiting for the man to come,
then I'll come."
"Okay."
Well, the husband
went.
He stayed at the edge of town with some food
and drink.
THE MAN came back lat—er, about six.
He came
and knocked on the door,
"Bah, bah, bah, bah" he knocked on the door.
"Who's there?" "Me."
"Oh good."
She opened the door for him.
(*higher*) "Come in."
"Okay." The man came in.
•

"Here's a hammock, rest a bit."
"Okay, then."
The man sat down there in the HAMMOCK.
Well, the man said,
"Come here, woman,
(*quietly*) come here, woman."
"No, I can't come over there
because I'm
not used to doing it with my husband so quickly.
We don't do it until we're finished bathing, finished eating.
Then we come and—SLEEP TOGETHER, my husband and I."
"Oh. That's what you want to tell me then."
"That's it."
"Tsk, girl, is that all?"

(*quietly*) Well, well . . .
the woman went to THE KITCHEN.

•

She prepared
the food,
the drink.
Then the woman said to the man,
"Let's go eat."
(*higher*) "Okay, then." The man got up and went to eat.
After they had eaten and drunk,
the woman cleaned up all the things there in the kitchen, then
    they went into the HOUSE
so they could sleep together.
The man . . .
the man said this,
(*higher*) "Come here, woman, come here so we can get
    together." (*quietly*) "I can't yet, don't hurry so much.
I'm used to doing it with my husband and we
TAKE OFF ALL OUR CLOTHES. We get naked. That's how
    I'm used to doing it too. We're used to sleeping without
    any clothes."
"Oh, that's what you want me to do?"
Well, the man got up
and took off all his clothes;
then he was left naked.
"Where are your clothes?" "Here they are."
She grabbed his clothes and put them in the box and closed it.
Well, then, (*higher*) "Come here, woman." (*quietly*) "Just a
    minute, man, don't hurry yourself."
It wasn't mu—ch longer when
they heard
BAH BAH BAH, they heard someone knocking.
(*quietly*) "María Santísima, my husband's come back!"
"Who's there?" "Me, your husband."
(*quietly*) "María Santísima, didn't I tell you, my husband's
    come back!"
(*quietly*) "What should I do? Where's my clothes?"
(*quietly*) "Hmmm. Tsk. What you should do, man," she said
    like this:

•   •   •

"Go in there
into the tabernacle.
Go in there to San Antonio's place.

•   •

Go and
take out San Antonio,

put him in the other house."

"Oh. Okay." He took out San Antonio and put him there in
     another HOUSE.

"Go there and pretend you're San Antonio—PUT ON HIS
     CLOTHES."

(*higher*) "Why?" "Because my husband will hit you."

(*higher*) "Oh. Okay."

He stood there like San Antonio

and she dressed him in his clothes.

She even gave him his SASH, tied the SASH.

Then he went in, "Get into the tabernacle."

"I'm in." "Good."

San Antonio got in.

"Here's the baby: hold it.

But the thing is, don't run away. Be careful not to ta—lk

because if you talk, if you make any noise there, *my husband
     will kill you."*

"No, I won't." "I'll have to put you in now. Be careful not to
     make any noise.

If you move you'll be killed."

(*higher*) "I won't." Well, San Antonio went in.

She turned

to the door.

"Woman, who were you talking to? Who was the person you
     were conversing with?"

(*higher*) "Oh my husband, there's no one here; I wasn't talking
     with anyone."

(*higher*) "Well, someone's here!" Then he drew out his

•

long machete and went about BANGING it on everything.

"TAH tah tah tah," he went around hitting things, making a
     cloud of dust.

Then he went to the table, "TAH TAH TAH," he hit the table.

He broke the table in half!

"Someone's here!" he went around looking here and there. HE
     HIT the table, HE HIT the door. Well, he went and made a
     mess of things.

Well,

•

meanwhile,

•

that poor man

•

was almost TREMBLING

with FEAR.

SWEAT was pouring out of him.

He was trembling there in the tabernacle,
but there was no way to escape, he was locked in.
The poor man says, "María Santísima, if he finds me here
this man will cut my head off!
I better stay here," said the poor man.
That other man went around banging his machete, hitting his
    machete. "THERE'S A MAN HERE, there's one here,
    there's one here! I heard him talking. If you don't tell me
    where he is I'LL KILL YOU."
"But my husband, NO ONE is here, no one."
"SOMEONE IS HERE!" "TAH TAH TAH TAH," he goes
    around banging his machete.
Well, he finishes doing that.
"Well, my . . . my wife,
you are right. You were correct, no one is here."
(*higher*) "I wasn't talking with anyone, my dear. You were
    just . . . just thinking
that there was someone here, but there wasn't anyone."
(*higher*) "Well, okay."
Well, then they left and went to the kitchen,
they went to the kitchen
to prepare the *dinner*.
They closed the house. MEANWHILE the wife said,
(*quietly*) "Did you know that the man came? I told him you
    were coming. I made him do what I did. Even I was
    frightened because I knew he was there in the tabernacle.
Well, I gave him the baby because he asked for it."
"Well, someone wants to buy that San Antonio.
I've been asked to sell it recently. I'll go and see if the man will
    buy it from me. If he will, I'll sell it."
"Okay."
The man left.
He went to see if his friend would take that San Antonio.
He went to see
if he'd buy it.
Well, he came to his friend's house
and said to his friend, (*higher*) "Listen, friend,
I'LL SELL that San Antonio."
"What did you say?" "I'LL SELL IT
if you'll buy it, I'll sell it to you." "I'll buy it, if you will . . ."
    "Well, LET'S GO GET IT." "Well, let's go get it."
"The only thing is,
you have to get an orchestra.
You have to get it with some musicians."[3]

---

3. A procession was needed to move a saint's statue from one house to another.

"I'll have to find
the people to PRAY,
I'll have to buy SKYROCKETS,
I'll have to buy CANDLES, INCENSE, PERFUME,
so I can take that San . . . San Antonio to my house where I'll
    have a FIESTA because that saint's day is almost here."
"That's good."
Well, a little orchestra was found,
he bought candles, he bought INCENSE, he bought
    SKYROCKETS.
Then he bought FLOWERS, people to pray were FOUND.
Then ALL THE PEOPLE, a lot of people came together and
    said, "Let's go!"
That's how he went to take that SAN ANTONIO;
there sure were a lot of PEOPLE.
Well, they arrived
at the house of the friend.
He opened the door, "Well, my friend,
here's that San Antonio on his
ALTAR there in the TABERNACLE.
There he is."
(*higher*) "María Santísima! My wonderful SAN ANTONIO, my
    wonderful master, look how lifelike you are!
Ahh . . . today is the day that your NOVENA will be made. I'm
    so VERY HAPPY that I've come to take you.
I'll pay the ransom for you."
Then San Antonio was *taken down so very slowly*.
The man said, "María Santísima, my Important Person San
    Antonio, you're REALLY HEAVY." That San Antonio was
    really heavy.
Well, he was taken down.
He was made ready to be DRESSED to be TAKEN.
Well, he was taken out of the doorway.
There at the doorway
they began to shoot off skyrockets, candles were lit so he could
    be TAKEN.
He was TAKEN and they burned candles, they lit
    SKYROCKETS,
incense was burned. San Antonio almost CRIED.
His EYES burned. His eyes got HOT from the incense and the
    SMOKE.
That San Antonio ALMOST DIED, he ALMOST BROKE
    DOWN because that wasn't the real San Antonio.
A person,
a MAN.
Well, the singing of the rosary was heard as they went

as well as a little dancing and some music.
Well,
they went on, certainly.
The poor man who took care of him
said, certainly,
he said, (*higher*) "Oh my wonderful San Antonio, they are
  taking you away.
What will I do? I've been caring for you in the house, I know
  you. I live here just to serve you. Every day I take care of
  your URNS, I clean out your TABERNACLE, I clean off the
  TABLE. I do it to get just a little bit of food; you were my
  only HOPE before.
But today YOU WERE SOLD. Well, what more is there, my
  true master? Well, I'll have to be left with what I can find;
  what I can find I'll have to eat."
The person who bought it said to him,
"Don't think like that, OLD MAN.
You will still attend my SAN ANTONIO.
So let's go, don't think like that."
The man was left happy. Then he was taken to attend the San
  Antonio.

•

Well, they started to go with the MUSIC, with the DANCING,
  SKYROCKETS WERE LIT, CANDLES were lit. They were
  all happy WHILE THEY WERE TAKING HIM.
San Antonio arrived at the house of the man. The altar was
  prepared where he was to be set.
It was hot because of all the people. SAN ANTONIO was left
  there.
Then San Antonio was brought to the house of the MAN. He
  was put on the ALTAR.
The man was almost dead. "San Antonio is really heavy. It will
  be a miracle
if I get him HERE."
Well, then they made a NOVENA.
Then San Antonio was raised
to the altar.
Then he was placed standing up in his tabernacle there on the
  altar.
Then the women said,
"Well, let's go to the novena for San Antonio
because they will make a FIESTA."
So then they came to *the novena, the novena of San Antonio.*
Then they began to make the novena.
While the novena was going on,
EVERY ONCE IN A WHILE they heard, "*Eh pech.*"

"María Santísima,
that San Antonio is really MIRACULOUS;
he knows how to 'eh pech.' He's really happy that there are so
    many people here."
Every once in a while, "Eh pech."
Every once in a while, "Eh pech."
"María Santísima, my Wonderful True God, look how much
    San Antonio loves us! Look how much he cares. He has a
    lot of love for us.
He's happy, he's *content*."
They made the novena.
They also made a FIESTA,
they made people happy.
After the novena
they brought in things,
THINGS to be given out at the novena.
They gave out things, really sweet things.
They gave out all the things little by little
after the novena was done.
After the novena and the gifts were given out
then all of the people went with the women
to the other room where they were making it,
the place where they were going to celebrate.
Well, then they made A REAL FIESTA.
They were all happy.
San Antonio looked to see
if anyone was there looking at him.
There were just a few old women who were left there in the
    house.
Every once in a while, "Eh pech." "María Santísima, look how
    real San Antonio is, he's really miraculous."
Every once in a while, "Eh pech."
"My Wonderful True God, my San Antonio is really real. He
    talks. You're miraculous."
It wasn't because he was miraculous, the man was almost dead
    because of the heat of the candles, because of the heat of
    the SKYROCKETS, because of the heat of the incense. He
    was almost DEAD because of the HEAT.
He saw that no one was there.
San Antonio JUMPED OFF running, San Antonio HOPPED
    OUT. Away he went, HA—ALAH. San Antonio WENT. He
    knocked over a chair, ha—alah San Antonio was gone.
The people said as he ran off, "THERE GOES THAT Saint,
    there goes that Saint, there goes that Saint, there goes that
    San Antonio. There goes that little fart, falling in the dirt.
    There goes that little fart, falling in the dirt."

"Hey, man, don't make fun of the saint. Don't you see he's
    miraculous?" "What do you mean 'miraculous'? There
    goes the little fart, there goes the little fart, falling on his
    ass." The people went running after San Antonio. San
    Antonio escaped.
(*higher*) "The little fart escaped!" "Hey, man, don't make fun of
    San Antonio. San Antonio is MIRACULOUS; he didn't
    like what you said.
The thing is, he heard what you said, it's that he wasn't used to
    the fiesta so he went, he escaped."
Well, San Antonio left.

•

Meanwhile
the next day
the man who was the owner of San Antonio
brought San Antonio to the edge of town.
It was the real San Antonio that was taken to the edge of town.
Then he came back again to his house.
The man who bought San Antonio came by the house.
He said, "Hello, my friend." "Hello. Did you find another San
    Antonio?" "I bought another one."
"That other one, the other San Antonio I sold to you."
"Hey, friend, that San Antonio you sold me, it escaped; it
    went."
(*higher*) "How did it go?" (*higher*) "I don't know, my friend, it
    went, it escaped."
(*quietly*) "María Santísima . . ."
"Let me . . . let me tell you, my friend, that San Antonio was
    really miraculous. It escaped. It got up and LEFT!
Well, I had to buy another one.
I have to make another novena
to inaugurate it.
I have to make the other one happy in my home."
"Uhuh, okay, then."
The man went
to his house.
Then he said,
"Well, what can I do with my San Antonio? Well, what can I
    do, I sold it to you but it left. Perhaps you did something it
    didn't like?"
"Yes, but I didn't do anything. I just made it happy;
I just made a fiesta, nothing more."
Well, that next night
another novena was made. A new novena was made for that
    new San Antonio during the night.
They made a fiesta again.

When I passed by there,
there was a new San Antonio.
They were giving things out, they were dancing.
That's how it ends.

A Story about a Trickster and a Priest

The story of Ahau pits a traditional trickster against a Catholic priest. Ahau, the name of the boy trickster, was both a traditional Mayan name for royalty (Cruz 1970: 99) and a name from the ancient Mayan calendrical system. It is not used as a common name in Yucatán today; the narrator knew only that it was a name from the "old days." The priest has difficulty making his way through the Mayan world away from the town where he is supported by the Spanish-imposed political system. Out away from town the priest has trouble understanding Mayan, and he falls and breaks his leg when his horse loses its footing. Back in town the priest confronts Ahau and charges that he has been cursed by the small boy.

The story of Ahau was told in one of the X-cacal villages by Pascual May, a narrator who was also a traditional musician. Pascual May was a very intelligent, introspective person. He had bought a grammar of Mayan published in the early 1950s and took great interest in teaching me many traditional aspects of Yucatec Mayan culture. He often came to serve as a respondent to narratives that I recorded. This is one of the few that he volunteered.

AHAU

There was a man who was married,
•
first child, a GIRL,
the other one, a BOY. Truly, there were two.
•
Well, the father began to make a milpa. Well, he taught him to
    make a milpa too.
Well, they began to make a milpa like that.
•
The name of the small boy, (*higher*) AHAU.
(*higher*) Ahau.
•
Well, then he made a milpa—he PLANTED all sorts of things
    in the milpa. He PLANTED SWEET POTATOES, he

planted all sorts of things like that. Well, the SWEET
POTATOES began to grow.
He began to . . . COOK them to be eaten.
One time he just cooked the potatoes EARLY and returned
with the sweet potatoes one sackful of cooked sweet potatoes.

•

Well, he came upon a PRIEST
on the TRAIL from the milpa.

•

He said to him like this,
"Hello, AHAU," he said to him.
(*quietly*) "Hello, mister," he replied.

•

"What are you carrying, AHAU?" he said to him.
"Well, (*quickly*) it's a yam, hug it—it comes," he said to the
    priest.[4]
Well, the priest heard that.
STRANGE way to be answered.
Then the priest said to Ahau,
"What's your mother doing, Ahau?"
"Well, she's twisting her asshole."[5]
"Ahah," . . . he said to him.
"And what about your sister?"
"Well," he says, "we ate her out yesterday," said Ahau.[6]
"Ahah, well, what about your papa?"
"My papa's gone to the rear of what he LIKES," he answered
    the *priest.*[7]

•

The priest heard all of that, a BAD way to be answered by
    Ahau.

•

He says, "Well, fine . . . what time will I get to town to say a
    mass, do you suppose, Ahau?"
"Well, mister, if you go SLOWLY, you'll get there right on time
    to say mass;

---

4. This and the other answers which Ahau gives the priest are spoken very
rapidly and are barely intelligible. In this first answer, one-half of the phrase is in
Spanish, the other in Mayan: "*Es camote, lota tali.*" The double entendre includes a
reference to masturbation.
    5. In Mayan, "*tun haax tu yiit.*" The verb *haax* describes rubbing something on
one's leg. When sisal twine is made by twisting the fibers, the person making it sits
on the completed portion to keep it out of the way.
    6. In Mayan, "*huchh t-haanta'ah holiac*" or "the dough was eaten by us yester-
day." When I asked why this was a play on words, respondents said only that it
sounded bad.
    7. In Mayan, "*in papahe, biha'an ti u pach u gusto.*" The pun here refers to rear
entry in sexual intercourse.

but if you HURRY, you won't get there today," Ahau said to
   him.
"Ahah . . ." The priest heard EVIL in what he heard.
Well, he turned around,
he

   •

whipped his horse like that, he "stepped on it," and the horse
   left. The horse WAS OFF JUMPING. Well, he went FAST,
   so he would get there QUICKLY.
The horse SLIPPED in the . . .
MUD, and the priest FELL.
He broke his LEG,
his leg was BROKEN.
(*higher*) He stayed there, he couldn't go.
There he was. There he was.
Meanwhile, the older people of the town where he was going
saw that it was already late, but the priest hadn't arrived.
Well, they started out to see *where he had ended up.*
They got to where the priest was;
there he sat, his leg broken—NOT ABLE to get up.

   •

Well, they carried him to the town. The priest arrived there,
and he went—was carried—to the . . . the MAYOR of the
   town. He complained.
He said like this, "Well, I have been cursed by Ahau. He threw
   a curse on me.
He cursed me like that;
well, an evil thing HAPPENED TO ME like that."
"Ahah."
"Well, I beg you, mister . . .
you ought to talk to Ahau;
punish him—lock him in JAIL
because he cursed me." "Ahah, okay, why not, I'll summon
   him."
Then he

   •

summoned Ahau:
"Go, have him arrested by two police,
immediately
because he said such a BAD thing."
They arrived and Ahau was arrested. He was brought in.
He was handed over to be locked up in JAIL.
Then Ahau said, "Mister?

   •

Pardon me if possible . . . but what have I done?"
"Well, this is about your curse on that priest. That's why you
   have to go to jail."

"Well, mister, has it happened that one is not able to speak?
Even if you're going to kill a pig," says Ahau,
"it ought to be given water, then afterward, it is killed.
How about me? I've killed no man."
"Ahah, your word is true," replied the mayor of the town.
"Well, how do you respond to what the priest said? You said to
    him ALL OF THOSE BAD THINGS."

   •

That priest said,
"Well, the first thing he said to me, mister, when I asked him,
'WHAT is he carrying?' he answered me, 'It's a yam—hug it—
    it comes';
this is what Ahau said to me."
"Ahah, like that, huh?
(*higher*) Ahau, do you hear then what he said?"

   •

"It's true, mister; since I'm poor, I don't know the words.
Well, the words I made weren't BAD," answered Ahau,
"I said to grab it and eat it—how else are cooked sweet
    potatoes eaten? That's what I said."
"Ahah, very well."
"Well, the other thing he said to me, mister," said the priest,
"I asked to hear from him
what his mother
was doing. Then he said, 'Twisting her asshole.'
Well, BAD . . .
a BAD THING to say about his mother like that."
(*higher*) "Well, mister, I really said that. Why not?" replied
    Ahau again.

   •

"Well, she sits on the string that she's twisting,
my mother does. She twists the string like this.
Well, there isn't any other way it can be said; that's what I said
    like that."
"Very well, okay."

   •

"Since we're poor, we don't know how the words go. Well, I
    told him like that; I don't know Spanish, I just measure
    out the words like that,"
he said.
"Ahah, okay."
"Well, the other thing that he said to me," said the priest; he
    explained his statement to the mayor of the town:
"I asked to hear from him what his sister was doing. He said to
    me, 'We ate her out yesterday.'

   •

There. You hear it," he said to the mayor.

(*higher*) "Well, mister, his words are true like that about what I
said to him. But it's because
my sister made dough from borrowed corn. Today she grinds
some other to return.
I said it like that, only very quickly."
"Ahah, very well."
"Well, another time he said to me,"
the priest continued to state what he had said to him:
"Well, he said another thing,
the other thing he said was when I asked him like this: 'What
was his papa doing?' I didn't ask him to tell me 'He's
GONE to the rear of what he LIKES.' He said a BAD thing
like that."
(*higher*) "His word is true, mister, why not?
I said the truth to him, you see,
my papa went to his milpa; when he just gets there behind the
CORN PLANTS which are so WONDERFUL, he's so
CONTENT. Well, isn't that being BEHIND what he likes
like that?
Truly, I told him the correct thing. The thing I said to him
wasn't a big thing."
"Ahah, okay." Ahau was answered. He was . . . he was justified
like that.
"Well, he told me another thing, mister," says the priest to the
mayor.
"He said to me,

•

when I asked him what time would I arrive to say mass here,
he said to me, 'If I come SLOWLY, I'd get here right on
time to say *mass*,
But if I go QUICKLY, I wouldn't arrive today.' There. I heard
EVIL in what he said to me.
Well, when I heard that,
I jumped on my horse, I 'STEPPED ON IT' so that I'd get here
QUICKLY.
Well, my horse tripped in the mud and I fell. I broke my leg.
A *curse* like that."
Ahau answered again,
"Ahah, his word is true, mister. I said it to him, why not?
(*higher*) But isn't what I said straightforward? Didn't I give him
true advice? If he came SLOWLY with the horse, how
could he fall?
Isn't it right what I said to him?
(*higher*) No, I didn't curse him. I told him the truth—the thing
is, he didn't UNDERSTAND.
Well, I told him the TRUTH. I told it to him, why not? If he
came slowly, nothing would happen to him."

"Well, then, Ahau, *your word is true,*" he said . . . (*quietly*) was
      answered by the mayor of the town.
(*higher*) "Well, mister, if it is just about this, then I
haven't done anything to him,
. . . said anything to him that was bad.
Neither did I
curse him."
(*higher*) "Well, your word is true, Ahau, (*higher*) YOU ARE
      FREE."
Well,
Ahau left. He was set free, not LOCKED UP.
It ENDS like that,
HE SAVED HIMSELF.

A Story about a Vulture's Clothes

This next narrative was performed by Alonzo Gonzales Mó in Ticul
late one afternoon. The narrative was short; it took Alonzo only
twelve minutes to complete the story. The plot concerns a vulture, a
disgusting bird in Yucatec Mayan thought, who attempts to learn a
magical formula from a small dove. Doves are prized birds among
the Maya; many are kept as pets in small cages in people's homes.
Vultures, on the other hand, are carrion eaters who efficiently clean
up not only the corpses of animals but human excrement as well (see
the next story, "A Person and a Vulture").

In the story the vulture loses his clothes. Clothes are a very important way that Yucatec Mayan people communicate with each
other. A man's hat, the type of sandals he is wearing, and the type of
shirt all indicate first whether he is Mayan or non-Mayan and second what social class he belongs to within the Mayan conception of
"rich people," *dzulo'ob,* and "poor people," *otzi maaco'ob.* In addition, within these categories, clothes also indicate where a person
lives. Although Yucatec Mayan clothes all look the same to an outsider, for a person living in the culture the slight difference in the
stitching of a hat is a clear and unambiguous sign which communicates a man's social and geographic place to all who see him. Likewise, women's clothing also communicates a clear message to the
world. The particular designs on a woman's *huipil,* the elaborate-
ness of the embroidery, the length of the garment, the kind of slip
that is worn under it, the amount of gold jewelry worn around the
neck, and the relative fineness of the shawl imported from central
Mexico all combine to show a woman's hometown, status, wealth,
and ethnic identification.

Although the following story is not consciously considered an allegory by the narrator, it does derive its meaning from the importance of clothes as social indicators in Yucatec Mayan life. Without clothes the large vulture is left helpless and is kicked around by the other animals.

A VULTURE, A DOVE, AND A SQUIRREL

There is, then, a little Dove here.[8]
•   •   •   •   •   •
It says this,
•   •   •   •
there on a branch
of a tree.
•   •   •   •
Then it says this,
•   •   •   •
(*sung*) "COME my feathers; COME my feathers; COME my
    feathers."
•   •   •   •
It is playing like that.
Then there is a Vulture here,[9]
there on a branch,
a little higher than the little Dove like that.
•   •   •   •
It's that this Vulture . . . sees . . . what . . . the little Dove . . .
    is doing, there below.
•   •   •   •
The little Dove says this,
(*sung*) "GO, GO, GO, GO my feathers;
(*sung*) COME, COME my feathers."
Well, the feathers return,
those feathers return.
Well, Vulture sees it.
Vulture said this, "Listen, little Dove,
the thing you're doing
looks good to me!"
(*higher*) "Looks good to you?"—(*normal voice*) "Looks good to
    me."
(*higher*) "You'll learn it?"—(*normal voice*) "I'll learn it."
"Okay, then."
•   •   •   •

8. *Chan mucuy* or the common Ruddy Ground-Dove, *Columbigallina talpacoti.*
9. *Chhom* or the common Black Vulture, *Coragyps atratus.*

"Do it so I can see again—I'll see how it is . . ."

•   •   •   •

The little Dove said this,
(*sung*) "GO, GO my feathers; GO, GO my feathers. COME,
    COME my feathers; COME, COME my feathers."
Well, the little Dove's feathers go . . .
they return again.
The little Dove's feathers go—they return again.
"Did you see it?
Will you learn it?"—(*higher*) "I'll learn it."
"Good, okay, then."
Then Vulture said this,
"I guess I'll see if I can say it too." (*higher*) "Okay, then."
(*sung*) "Go, go, go my feathers; come, come, come my
    feathers," says the Vulture.
"How does it look?

•   •   •   •

I'll learn it, huh?"—(*higher*) "You'll learn it."
"Sure!"—"Okay, then, I guess I'll go . . .
keep at it!"—"Okay." Little Dove goes. Big Vulture is left . . . is
    left.
Well, big Vulture says this,
(*sung*) "GO, GO, GO my feathers;
(*sung*) COME, COME, COME my feathers."
Well, the big Vulture's feathers return again.
They return—(*higher*) he sees that the feathers return.
Well, he says this
again—he's playing around like that; he's playing like that—
    he says this, (*sung*) "GO, GO, GO my feathers;
(*sung*) COME, COME, COME my feathers."
Well, the feathers go, the feathers return again. The feathers go,
    the feathers return again.
Well, he says this
another time, "GO, GO, GO my feathers . . . ," well, the
    feathers go away.
Just then a storm raises itself up. But the storm
it really comes!

•   •   •   •

Didn't the feathers go?
The storm
begins—but a REAL STORM—REALLY YELLOW WATER!
Well, poor Mr.
large Vulture—like without his feathers—without his
    CLOTHES.
When the rain has PASSED—that YELLOW RAIN,
when he remembers

to seek his feathers,
he begins to seek, (*sung*) "Come, come, come my feathers."
    Well, the feathers don't return.
The feathers don't return. (*sung*) "Come, come, come my
    feathers."
The feathers don't return—well, he TIRES of asking the
    feathers to return.
The feathers aren't returned, and the feathers do not return.
    The feathers have a—ll been carried off by the rain.
Well, he tires like that, he is left—without his CLOTHES,
    PINK-SKINNED NAKED.

•   •   •

Well, whatever comes
there on the road where he is KICKS HIM OVER.
Whatever comes to the road kicks him over. Why? Because he
    is without feathers to defend himself. Pink-skinned naked.
Then all the water comes over him. He is SOAKED—without
clothes.
(*quietly*) Without clothes.
Well,
then the rain has passed.

•   •   •

Little Dove appears. Poor Vulture is there without his clothes.
    He is spoken to by little Dove,
"Hello, friend!
What happened to you?"
"Nothing happened to me; I'm without clothes!"
"How without your clothes?"—(*quietly*) "Without my
    clothes."
"What then happened to you?"
(*quickly*) "WELL, WHO . . . I say like this, 'Go, go my
    feathers,' the feathers go, when the feathers go . . . but a
    storm began— a large storm . . .
Well, the RAIN started,
(*quietly*) the rain started.
When the rain passed, I sought my clothes,
(*sung*) 'Come, come, come my feathers; come, come, come my
    feathers,' well, now then? It's that my . . . my feathers
    were carried off by the rain.
It's that . . . then how can my clothes come? I've none—
    carried off by the rain!
Well, I was left pink-skinned naked like this. It's that whatever
    comes then today where I am KICKS ME OVER.
I've no way to defend myself. I've no clothes.
(*quietly*) I sleep pink-skinned naked."
"Ahah."

•   •   •

As he is just doing this,

•   •   •   •

a flock of BIRDS COME

•   •   •   •

(*quietly*) like this:
a flock of birds come.

•   •   •   •

They said to the large Vulture,
(*higher and quickly*) "What happened to you like this,
large Vulture?"
(*quietly*) "Hmmm. What happened to me?—I've no clothes."
(*higher*) "How is it you have no clothes?"—(*quietly*) "I've
     none . . . carried off by the rain.
It's that I began to look, look, look like I did before like that,
asking, 'Come . . . return, return, return my feathers; return,
     return my feathers'—didn't return—made away—carried
     off by the rain. Well, I was left pink-skinned naked,
     without clothes." (*sung*) "Ha ha ha ha . . .
ha ha ha ha ha.
Then your feathers were carried off. Then you're without
     clothes."
(*quietly*) Well,

•   •   •

well, then . . .

•   •   •

then the birds said this,
"THEN LET'S GO TODAY. HE WON'T COME.
You certainly won't catch up today."
(*quietly*) "Good-bye, I won't catch up to you today,
today I am not ABLE. I've no CLOTHES. I'd fall for sure."
(*sung*) "Ha ha ha ha," then the birds say like this. He is
     LAUGHED AT like that.[10]
There
appears then a little Squirrel, running.[11]

•   •   •   •

Little Squirrel says this,
(*higher*) "Hello, friend, Mr. Vulture,
so what happened to you like this?"
(*quietly, lower*) "Hmmm. What happened to me?
My clothes were carried away by the rain." (*higher*) "How did it
     happen that they were carried off?"
(*quietly, lower*) "Because I said like this, (*sung*) 'Go, go my
     feathers; come, come my feathers. Go, go my feathers . . .'

10. Eugene Hunn (personal communication) notes that flocks of small birds
often attack larger birds.
11. *Cu'uc* is the Common Squirrel, *Sciurus yucatenensis*.

When I said, 'Go, go my feathers,' then a large STORM
    arose.
But the storm arose. It's that the rain came.
(*quietly*) Jesus, it's that a big storm began.
When the big storm had passed, I sought my clothes;
(*quietly*) I began to ask, (*sung*) 'Come, come, come my
    feathers; come, come, come my feathers . . .' Well, my
    feathers didn't return.
Then,
I was left. My clothes didn't return.
Gone.
Well, I am left like that."
Large
Vulture
was just
seen CRYING. (*quietly*) He weeps because he has no clothes.
"That's why you tell me you have no clothes?" "That's why.
You have your clothes, but I, I have no clothes; how can I go on
    then?"

•   •   •   •

"Ahah, but for *that you pay.*
(*quickly*) Why do you say, 'G . . . go, go, go my feathers; come,
    come, come my feathers'? Who left you so stupid?
Who left you so stupid!"
"Well, that little Dove, it told me that . . . that they go. Since it
    was playing,
there on a branch like this, I saw what it did. I see what it did,
    (*sung*) 'Go, go, go my feathers; come, come, come my
    feathers.'
It's that I see that all its feathers go, it's left pink-skinned . . .
then it asked its feathers to return again, (*quietly*) as is natural.
I said that it LOOKED GOOD to me.
It said to me that I could learn it.
Well, I did it too, I LEARNED IT TOO, (*sung*) 'Go, go, go my
    feathers; come, come, come my feathers . . .'
It's that the thing is, I FORGOT, and that's why when I said,
    (*sung*) 'Go, go, go my feathers,' a large storm came up. The
    rain really came.
It's that it began to RAIN—(*quietly*) a large storm!
When the storm had passed,
my feathers were gone. I began to call again so they
    RETURNED; I was left pink-skinned naked."
(*sung*) "Ha ha ha ha; then you've no clothes there today!
(*sung*) Ha ha ha ha; then you've no clothes there today!"
(*quietly*) The poor Vulture was laughed at.
"Sure, let's run then,

'catch the one behind.'
Let's see who runs fastest.

 • • •

The one who is left on the road,
who falls, will be HIT."

 • • • •

"Well, let's go then."

 • • • •

They
began to go like that, running like that. Since the poor Vulture
  had no clothes . . .
he began to go running, running. Piclic, piclic, they all went
  running like that.
Wasn't it then that the big Vulture fell, his throat to the
  ground, followed by the birds? Afterward, he began to be
  kicked around.

A Story about an Unusual Marriage

This is a story, also told by Alonzo, about a marriage doomed to fail-
ure. An old man jokingly asks a vulture that sits in a tree near his
house if it would bring its sister so that the man would not have to
be alone all the time. The vulture's sister comes in the form of a
beautiful woman, but, as expected in traditional Mayan marriage
agreements, the man must go and do bride service at his new wife's
home for a few weeks. Bride service in a cave full of other vultures
proves disastrous for the old man and his marriage to the beautiful
woman.

  The humor in the story is blunt. Like the previous vulture
story, this narrative includes a storm sequence which nearly kills
the poor man, who has been transformed into a vulture. The man's
misfortune becomes even more humorous when he is faced with a
distasteful decision: should he eat human excrement or stay weak
and hungry? Because of the difficulty in digging through the limestone which lies a foot or less beneath the surface throughout most
of Yucatán, and because of the danger of polluting underground
aquifers, human waste in Mayan villages is left on the surface. Every
house has an area reserved for toilet activities in the backyard. The
reserved place usually has a four-foot-high stone fence on two sides
for privacy. Vultures commonly come and eat the excrement, thus
keeping the area relatively clean. Because of this association with
human waste, vultures are also associated with disease and misfortune. A particularly dangerous fly which causes a festering wound

which can eat away a person's nose or ear is common in the southern part of the peninsula. This insect is known as the vulture's fly
and is said to fly with these carrion eaters. This, in addition to vultures' general disagreeable activities, was stated as a reason to keep
away from the birds.

A PERSON AND A VULTURE

Well,
there was a
person.
That person
was an old man; he didn't have a woman.
When he went to his milpa,
when he returned *later*,
well, he made his own food to eat.
He made TORTILLAS, he made the dinner so he could eat in
    his home.
There to one side of the house on the branch there
was a vulture, just sitting on a branch there.

   .   •   .

When that man came to the door of his house
the vulture said, it talked every once in a while: "Uus,"
it said, "uus." He said to the vulture,
(*higher*) "Hey . . .
hey, brother-in-law,
if you would bring your sister here, if I could see her TODAY,
perhaps she would work with me.
You know I'm all alone.
I want to see your sister,
brother-in-law.
If you could, could you bring your sister here to work for me?"
It's that the man
sees the vulture there every day.
He ASKS about the sister of the vulture.
The vulture listens to it all;
it hears him say, "Hello, brother-in-law,
if you bring your sister today, I would be happy."
Well, one of those DAYS . . .
one day the man goes to work,
as always he goes to his milpa.
Well,

   •

when the man comes
back to his house
there is a woman

just sitting there in the house.
She had finished sweeping the house, she had swept out the
     kitchen.
She had finished fixing the table and had put a new tablecloth
     ON IT.
She gave him
a napkin full of TORTILLAS. They were the tortillas she had
     made; she served them in a gourd.
She put the dinner
on the table.
That woman
had a white dress on while she worked in the kitchen.[12]
Well, when the man got there and saw that there was a woman
     there in the kitchen, he was VERY HAPPY.

   •

"But woman, (*higher*) what are you looking for here?"
(*higher*) "I'm not looking for anything here.
Didn't you ask my brother for me every day?
Every day when you came out of the house you asked,
'Brother-in-law, can't you bring your younger sister
or your older sister? It would be good
because I'm here all alone. I don't have a woman.'
Well, it's my brother,
so one day it came to my house and said to my mother, 'You
     know, mama,
there's a man who needs help every day. Every afternoon he
     says, "Hello, brother-in-law."
He says, "If you can bring your sister today
to work, or even your younger sister, to help me out, I would
     be so happy.
I'm all alone here in my kitchen."'
Since you said that over and over,
well, my brother said, 'I'll have to bring my younger or older
     sister.
Let's go, sister, let's go.'
It took me here,
brought me into this house."
Then,
well,

   •

the man
said, (*higher*) "Who brought you here?"
"My brother brought me, no one else. You asked it every day
to bring me to work for you, to stay with you.
How do you like it?"

12. This is a sign of cleanliness.

"How do I like it? I'm happy that you came to work with me
     here
because I don't have a woman.
Now you can help me."
(*quietly*) Well, the woman stayed there.
In other words, she was a *wife*.
Well,

•   •

the next day he went again to his milpa
to get some food.
He went along
very happy because the woman was VERY PRETTY, VERY
     BEAUTIFUL.
Well, he went on.
LATER
when he returned,
the table where they eat was CLEAN. The napkins were
     WHITE. They were put on the table.

•

She had PLACED a napkin full of tortillas there; a new
     DINNER was all set for the *man*.
Well,

•   •

he was very pleased with the food.
"Well, then, woman, come here and eat.
Aren't you hungry?" "Yes, I'm hungry." "Well, come and eat."
Well, she gave him food.
He ate CHICKEN. When there wasn't any chicken, then he got
     MEAT. He ate well, he didn't just eat BEANS. Every day he
     ate meat. It was good, fine food.
Well,

•   •

the days went by like that.
The woman said, she said to her husband,
"Well, I've come here to your house;
we ought to go
to my mama's house too, my papa's house,
so I can show you to them, show that you're my husband."
(*quietly*) "Well, why not? Let's go. Let's go."
Then the next morning
she said, "Let's go, husband. Let's go, we have to go."
They went on.

•

While they were going on like that
they came to a *cave*.
They went in there.

"Well, let's go in there, my husband."
"WHY should we go in there?"[13]
(*quietly*) "Because my house is in there;
my mama's house is there."
Well, they
went in.
While they were going into the *cave*,
just while they were going,
he sees that they are coming to a little town.
He sees that there are a LOT OF PEOPLE there.
Well, while they are going
she says, "Let's go over there."
She brought him to the house of her father, the house of her
    mama, where her family was.
Well,
• •
she says,
"Well, papa,
here's my husband. I brought him to present to you, to show
    him to you."
(*higher*) "Good. Very good. I'm happy."
"Here is my husband, papa, here he is, mama, here he is,
    family."
He greeted her father, hugged him. They were all happy.
Then it was over.
Well, the man ate everything there. There were good tortillas,
    good meat, there was everything.
They gave him everything to eat; he ate a lot of good food.
Well, one day they said to him,
they really spoke like this,
"Well, today, brother-in-law,
we have to go and find
some good tortillas. We've finished all the good food.
We have to go and find some more. I'll bring you along."
"Okay, why not?"
That person looked like a real person, a human being.
"Okay, that's good."
Early the next MORNING they LEFT.
He said, "Let's go." He said, "Let's go." "Okay, let's go."
Well, they left.
As they were going out of the cave,
while they were going, he was changing
as they went along, he was changing.

13. Caves are also understood to be the entrance to the underworld, as noted in
the Xtziciluulme story of the previous chapter.

He had turned into a big vulture when they passed through the
mouth of the cave.
A Black Vulture.
"Well, let's go, brother-in-law."
"Where are we going?" "To the sky."
They flew up and went off; they flew into the sky.
•   •

They TOOK THEMSELVES into the SKY.
They flew around the sky.
Then
they flew up in the sky, they WENT THROUGH the sky like
that.
They came down about eight or nine in the morning.
They landed on a *fence.* IT WAS ABOUT eight or nine in the
morning,
EARLY.
Well, they were tired of looking for good food. There WASN'T
ANY ANYWHERE. They looked everywhere for food, but
there wasn't any good food ANYWHERE.
They were FEELING HUNGRY.
Then they came to the fence.
IT WASN'T MUCH LATER when a person came over there
TO SHIT!
Well, the man squatted down and shit.
Soon another person came
to shit.
"Well, brother-in-law,
we didn't find the good food where we should have. There
WASN'T ANY.
Since we're so hungry, the only thing we can do is EAT THAT
SHIT."
"María Santísima," the man said.
"I've got to eat shit?
I don't really want to eat shit.
It isn't very good, it doesn't taste good. Shit isn't good."
"Well,
let's go."
They flew up and left.
They landed in a tree.
IT WASN'T MUCH LATER when a
STORM came, a storm with STRONG WINDS that BLEW
with lots of RAIN.
It blew the tree around.
He said, "Oh, what will I do? I'm about to die." The poor man
wasn't used to it.
"I'm going to die . . ." YIIN YIIN YIIN the tree was
SWINGING there where they were.

The storm went on for about AN HOUR AND A HALF.

Then the wind died down and the rain stopped.

"Well, let's go." They went on looking for food.

Then they came to the mouth of the cave, they left their
    feathers there.

When they got to the door there, they were PEOPLE, human
    beings.

"How did you two make out?"

"Not too good. We didn't see anything, there wasn't anything
    to eat, no meat."

"Well, my husband, how did you make out?"

"Oh woman, the thing is, I can't eat any of that shit.

I couldn't eat shit today, no. I'M NOT USED TO THESE
    THINGS HERE.

It's that

IF THINGS GO ON LIKE THIS . . .

(*higher*) let's go back to my house.

At my house we don't eat shit. There is good food, good
    tortillas, there is a lot of food there.

LET'S GO to my house. I can't continue to STAY HERE. I can't
    continue eating those things,

foul things like that."

"Well, my husband, okay, let's go."

Everything is prepared for the journey.

"Well, papa, mama,

I have to get ready to go with my husband.

I won't be back for a while."

"Okay, daughter, take your husband away then.

But son, why are you going?"

(*higher*) "Well, papa, I have to go. I'm not used to eating them.

Even though I'm a poor man, at my house we have good food.

There are tortillas to eat every day.

I'm not used to these THINGS here."

"Well, okay, then. Girl, take your husband."

She began to take him but he sees that she's a VULTURE, not a
    PERSON.

There, where they were, she was a person

but when they went out he saw that she

was a vulture.

He didn't know it.

"Well, what can I do?

What am I going to tell my

friends?

Tell them my wife's a vulture?"

They went on.

"Okay, okay,

my wife.

If I take you out there you're going to be a vulture.
You have to go back."
Well, as they were going he lost his feathers.
As they were going out, he left his feathers there.
When he got to the mouth of the cave
he was a *person*, a *human being*.
"Come on, my wife."
"I won't come. I'm not used to things at your house either."
So the woman went back.
The wife went back to the cave, to her house where she wanted
    to go.
He went back to his house.
When he came to his house, his friends asked him,
"Where were you, neighbor?"
"Hmmm. What do you mean? I went away. I went away to find
    a wife.
But my wife was a LADY VULTURE. I didn't know my wife
    was a Lady Vulture because when she was here, she was a
    woman, a REAL BEAUTIFUL PERSON.
But she was really a Lady Vulture.
They even made me eat SHIT.
I wasn't used to that, not one bit.
I couldn't stay there so I came back."
"Hey, friend, what happened to you when they told you to eat
    shit?"
"There wasn't much to eat there like there is here; we don't
    have much meat but we eat every day."
"Thank God you came back from where no one has ever lived,"
    he said.
When I went by there earlier the poor man
was sitting in his house; he was happy.
She didn't come back, that
LADY VULTURE.

A Story about an Attempt to Ward off Death

The Maya of Yucatán have adopted the Spanish custom of forming ritual relationships through a sponsorship system common in much of Latin America. The compadrazgo system is centered around a child to whom parents ask friends or relatives to be godparents. The particular time at which coparents are selected can be a Catholic baptism or a traditional Mayan ceremony for young children, the *hetz mec*. The *hetz mec* ceremony is carried out when an infant is first carried astride on the hips. Like Catholic baptism, the ceremony includes naming two godparents or compadres to the child, who give him or her small models of tools which reflect male or female roles. A baby girl receives a small needle and some thread while a baby boy receives a small water gourd and machete during the ceremony. Prior to the *hetz mec*, Yucatec Mayan children are dressed in small huipils regardless of their sex and are affectionately called "small people," *maaco'ob*, rather than "boy" or "girl."

In this story, told by Alonzo, a poor man convinces Saint Death, the person who fetches souls from the earth when they die, to become his compadre. The relationship is clearly based on *interés*, not on *amistad*. Saint Death emerges as a hapless victim of the relationship as he becomes caught between the orders of his superior, True God, and his contract with the poor man when the time of the man's death approaches.

SAINT DEATH

Well,
•
there is a
poor man,
so poor.
He says, "Since there will be a *small son* in our family,"
he says this to
his wife, "if you *want,* I . . .
what we have to do here
in this world
•   •   •
I think that . . .
if one was to go and get as a compadre
Saint Death,[14]
(*higher*) then a person wouldn't die because when Saint Death
        would come here to earth,
to grab some people, dead ones,
(*higher*) to carry off to True God,
he would do it.
I want to be a compadre with him.
ISN'T THAT A GOOD IDEA, WOMAN?
•   •
The thing is, my words are good, aren't they?"
•   •   •

14. The words used here were "Santo Muerte," Spanish for the angel of death.

Well,
when the child was born,

•   •

the man said,
that man said,
"Well, woman, the child has been born. What do you say?
    Should I go talk to Saint Death?"

•   •

(*higher*) "Why not?

•

(*higher*) But where will you talk to Saint Death, where WILL
    YOU SEE HIM?"
"Well, don't ask where I will find him. I know where I'll see
    him."

•   •

"Well, okay."
Well, during those days,
at night,
he says,

•   •

"*Hey, Saint Death, where are you?*
In the name of True God I'M CALLING YOU."

•   •

Well, he does it over and over like that.
He was asking like that.
Well, one day
when he just went there to his milpa,
as he was going down the path,

•   •

(*higher*) he asks, "Saint Death, where are you?

•   •

Saint Death, (*higher*) I want to talk with you."

•   •   ·

Saint Death just appears over there.
It was about TWELVE NOON.
Well, Saint Death says to him,
"Listen, big man,

•   •   •

many days have gone by
with you calling me.
What happened to you?"
(*higher*) "Well, nothing happened.
There is something, though,
Saint Death.
You know I,
(*higher*) I've been thinking
that I should talk to you

so you could be my compadre."
"*Uhuh.*"
(*higher*) "Do you like this idea?"—"I like the idea."
• •
"Ahah,
okay, then, okay.
If you think it's a good idea, great."
•
"Well, where are you going?"
(*higher*) "I'm going into my milpa."
"Well, don't go into your milpa,
LET'S GO BACK
RIGHT AWAY so you can show me my godson."
(*higher*) "Okay, then."
Well, they went back.
They came
to the house.
He said to his wife, "Well,
• •
my wife,
here comes my compadre, I FOUND HIM."
"Uhuh."
"He will carry the child
there for the
baptism."
"Okay."
•
"What day will you baptize it?"
"Well, if it's all right with you, we can do it TOMORROW,
so we can
baptize the child."
(*higher*) "Well, okay."
• •
Well, the next day,
very early, they woke up.
They got everything they were supposed to.
Saint Death came.
"Well,
compadre, I've come. Let's take the little
boy there to be baptized."
"Let's go then."
Well, they took the child to be baptized.
Then THEY CAME BACK.
Well, "So, my compadre,
thank you so very much. (*higher*) When will you come back to
    visit your godchild?"
"I don't know. *Whenever you want, call me and I'll come.*

I don't know when True God will send me back here to earth
     again.
Since you sought me out over and over,
Wonderful True God said to me,
'Hey, SON,
go and find out what that one wants
there on earth.'
'Okay, my master.'
That's how I happened to come here to earth, just to hear what
     you wanted."
"Uhuh, okay, then, I'm happy." "*I guess I'll be going.*"
Well, one day . . .
since Saint Death
comes to a house or wherever, perhaps a street,
he is sent TO GRAB
the person whose
time has come.

•   •

Well, he goes.

•   •

That poor man, this compadre,
when his time comes, his day like that,
HE'S SO SICK.
He's so sick. He's about to die.
He's just a little, just a . . .

•   •

HE'S BREATHING HARD;
he's suffering.
Well, True God says
to Saint Peter,
"Listen, Peter,
I guess Fulano has to die.
Go tell Saint Death to go and grab Fulano.
FULANO."
"Okay, my master."
So SAINT PETER says,
Saint Peter talks, "Okay, then, my master, I'll talk to him as
     you say."
"Listen, come here, Julano.
You have to go and grab that Fulano
there in the land of honey."[15]
(*higher*) "Okay, then, my master. What you say I WILL DO."

15. A common phrase for the earth in Yucatec Mayan is *yoko cab*, which means "over the honey." Yucatecan honey has been prized for its taste since pre-Columbian times.

Well, he went to go and grab the man WHOSE TIME HAD
COME.
He came down here to earth
and sees that it's his compadre.
He's not about to grab him.
He finds another man WHOSE TIME TO DIE ISN'T FOR A
LONG TIME.
He was obligated to become a dead person, even though the
day of his death hadn't arrived.
He had to die and WAS CARRIED OFF.
•

Well, he arrived there
in heaven.
•

"I brought you your man, Saint Peter."
•

"Oh no, that's not him. I told you,
SAINT DEATH . . .
this isn't the one I told you, not this one.
Well, you have to go back."
So that man went back again TO EARTH because of Saint
Peter.
Yum Saint Peter brought the charge to Wonderful True God,
"Oh my master,
(*higher*) the thing he did . . . I told him but he didn't do it right.
I sent him to grab Fulano, he brought me SOMEONE ELSE.
What can I do? He doesn't do what I ask. He should do it.
He didn't do it; he brought some other person.
I tell him to grab Fulano but HE GETS SOME OTHER
PERSON."
"JULANO! YOU DIDN'T BRING ME THE PERSON WHO
WAS DYING. Bring him to me.
Not that other one."
"Okay, master."
Well, Saint Death goes down again, he comes back to the earth.
Well,
meanwhile that compadre is going fast.
He's barely breathing, he's just breathing little by little, he's
only got a few hours left.
STILL HE DOESN'T TAKE HIM.
He finds some other person with a lot of time to go.
Who knows where he took him, SINCE THERE WAS A LOT
OF TIME BEFORE HIS DEATH?
He made this other man DIE.
His time hadn't come.
He took him.
•

He went back to heaven

•

and said,
(*higher*) "Well, here's the man I've brought you, my master."
"But MAN," says Peter,
that's not the person I told you to bring me,
this man HAS A LONG TIME TO GO BEFORE HIS DEATH.
WHY DID YOU BRING THIS MAN HERE?"
(*higher*) "Well, master, he died and I brought him . . ."
    "THAT'S NOT TRUE.
Don't kid me. That isn't him.
Well, PUT THAT MAN BACK. Go and get the ONE I told you
    TO BRING ME."
Well, the man is brought back again.
Meanwhile, the man was being waked.
He was laid out over the table even though it hadn't been time
    for him to die.
He was taken away.
He died, he was made to die like that.
HE WAS BEING WAKED,
laid out on the TABLE.
Well, it was about midnight I guess
when the man returned with Death.

•

When he returned, he was alive again.
His spirit had been taken away;
his spirit now came back again here on earth.
Well, it came back again, it came back to its corpse, the body
    like that.
Well, he ROSE UP again.
He SAT UP like that.
"SACRED MARY!" said the people at the wake,
"THE DEAD ONE IS ALIVE!"

•

THE PEOPLE WERE SO SCARED THEY JUMPED UP AND
    RAN AWAY.
The man got up, a dead body GOT UP.
"SACRED MARY! The . . . the . . . dead one lives."
They jumped up and ran away.
The man says,
"What are you doing here? Why have you come here?"
"Oh father, you are dead."
(*higher*) "How can I be dead?" "Well, you're dead.
But you're not dead.
You were dead."
"I was dead?"

"Well, *we knew you were dead.*"

"Well, I'm not dead. What did you put on this table: look at all
these candles!

What are you doing?"

Well, the man got down off the table.

That man had a long time to go before he died.

He had just been sick for three days when he was carried off.

Death made him die.

Well, it was over.

The candles were put out.

The people left. They didn't get drunk at all because they
didn't even drink the LIQUOR.

Well, they left.

Well, poor Saint Death said,

"Well, master, I've got to bring in my compadre I guess.

There's no other way;

you want me to bring my poor compadre here.

I shouldn't BRING HIM,

THE POOR GUY.

If I BRING HIM, who's going to take care of my poor godchild?
Who will watch out for him?

NOBODY.

Well, I've got to go get him, I guess."

"Well, COMPADRE,

even though

it hurts my heart so,

even though it hurts you too,

I've got to take you."

"Oh compadre, you're really going to take me?

You're really going to take me? Leave me here on earth!

The earth here is so beautiful!"

(*higher*) "Well, there's nothing I can do, compadre. I have to
take you,

because I . . .

I was told to TAKE YOU.

I took TWO or THREE before you but they DIDN'T GO.

I had to come back again.

Well, I have to do it so that I won't lose my job

there in heaven.

(*higher*) Well, I have to take you."

"Oh compadre, leave me, I'm so poor.

Leave me, I'm so poor.

(*higher*) Don't take me.

(*higher*) I don't want to die.

(*higher*) The world is so beautiful.

(*higher*) I don't want to go."

(*higher*) "Well, I've got to take you."
"Oh compadre, tell me the truth: do you have to take me?"—
    "I've got to take you."
"How will my wife make it
with my children?"
"Well, compadre, perhaps it won't be too long until she finds
    ANOTHER
to take care of your CHILDREN."
"Well, I don't like the idea that there will be ANOTHER
    •   •
to be the father of my children."
"But who will care for them? That's why she has to find
    another."
"COME HERE, WOMAN."
The poor woman comes over.
"What . . . what do you want, compadre?"
"Well, didn't I tell you long ago that since he is my compadre I
    had to take him?
I was ordered to take him there to heaven. True God told me
    that I have to take him.
Well, I have to take him."
    •   •
(*with sorrow*) "Oh, no!
Oh compadre,
leave him here.
How can I make it with my small children if you take
your compadre?
When? When will I ever see him again?
He's truly my equal.
He's my LOVE. HE LOVES ME.
How will I make it?"
"Well, there's no other way. I have to take him."
"Well, compadre, okay."
He took the poor compadre.
They came to the house in heaven, the house of True God.
He said to him, "Well, my
master, I've brought this person."
"THIS ONE, this is the one I TOLD YOU TO BRING ME,
    THE ONE I TOLD YOU TO GET BEFORE THAT YOU
    DIDN'T BRING."
He was brought there. The wife was left, the poor wife was left
with the children.
When I passed by there the children were crying.
They asked for their father but they didn't have a father
    anymore.

A Story about Heroic Adventures

This narrative was performed by Santiago Chan in one of the villages of the X-cacal center in east central Quintana Roo. Mr. Chan was a narrator who was well known in the region. He specialized in stories about princes and kings and epic adventures involving giants and maidens in distress. This story describes the adventures of a boy who sets out from his home on an odyssey. He marries a dove woman but then loses her; he must find her and win her back from a giant. Throughout the story the boy is helped by magical animals who allow him to transform himself into different shapes and sizes in order to win the battles against the giant, who can also take on several different forms.

"The Seven Towers of Marble" is an exotic story for Mayan people. Princes and kings, giants and the adventures of the boy are uncommon ideas in contemporary Mayan society. Still, stories such as this are greeted with great interest by audience members. While it might be expected that stories such as this one, with its strong European and Middle Eastern motifs, would be found in the acculturated villages close to the capital of Mérida, with its international ambience, in fact this and other stories like it were common in the more distant, more isolated villages.

This is an important story because it incorporates a European plot into a Yucatec Mayan mold. The expert narrator used more vocal qualities than others and sustained interest in the story for the forty minutes of its telling by changes of pace, intensity, and pitch. The story contains marvelous transformations of people into animals and animals into different forms. Metamorphoses like these resonate with those in stories like "A Person and a Vulture" and with real-life descriptions of sorcerers who can take on different shapes. Like other Mayan narratives, this does not have smooth junctures between succeeding scenes and episodes. Instead, these are marked by more pausing than is present within episodes. The narrative is framed in the same way as other stories. It begins with a stock phrase, "it will have been completed," and ends with a formula relating the story to the real world, "well, boy, when I passed by there this morning, they were sitting together in their house."

When the story was told in our house in Señor, thirty-five people crowded in to hear this respected narrator. Children sat together in hammocks, teenage boys and girls flirted with one another, and adults leaned against the walls to listen to the story. Such a large audience was not common in storytelling sessions. In this case it illustrated the high esteem that Mr. Chan had as a craftsman of words.

THE SEVEN TOWERS OF MARBLE

"Seven Towers of Marble,"

•   •   •   •

well, that's its name.

•   •

Well, it will have been completed, there was a KING,
there was a SON too.
That son there went, he began to go to school. He began to read
    a little, he began to read a little. He reached the age of
    ELEVEN YEARS; he was ELEVEN YEARS OLD.
He went and said,
(*quietly*) "Hey, papa," he said,
"I'm going again today for a little WORK. I'm going to get a
    little money from the rich people."
(*higher*) "But son, the thing is, you don't have anything.
You don't have food, you don't have drink,
you don't have . . . clothes, shoes, a hat, all of those things."

•   •

"But father, if you died tomorrow,
how would I find my life?
That's why I want to do this."
(*higher*) "Okay, son, if that's what you want to do, DO IT.
Well, for my part, if you get in trouble, I'LL PAY FOR IT. As for
    the money you'll make, fine."
He went and took FI—VE mules
and began to work.
But there where he went to get the loads was a little lake.
Well, he went carrying the loads, carrying the loads with the
    saddles like that.
Afterward, going on,
he doesn't see anything.
But just as sure as he goes he saw three *doves* coming.[16]
They go and settle on a branch of a TREE.
Afterward, they go and throw themselves into the lake, they
    begin to BATHE.
After bathing, they rise up and settle.
(*higher*) Right after they settled, the first child
said to them like this:

16. The word used here was the Spanish *paloma* rather than the common
Mayan name for dove, *mucuy*. Perhaps the use of Spanish for this character as well as
all of the other main characters in the story is a device which functioned to take the
narrative out of the everyday world where exact Mayan names would have been used.

(*higher*) "Jesus," she said, "If Príncipe Moreno wanted to marry
    me, I would make a house, of *pure gold*."[17]

•

Well, the middle child answered, "Well, not me,
if Príncipe Moreno wanted to *marry* me, I would make a house
with SEVEN TOWERS OF MARBLE."
The youngest answered, "Not me, if Príncipe Moreno wanted
    to marry me, I would just make a suit of clothes, only out
    of DIAMONDS,"
said the youngest, just smoothing her feathers there above in a
    branch of a tree.
Just after they went and said this,
(*quietly*) they rose up and left.
The workers finished tying the loads on the horses and went.
They came to the rich people.
They said that there were three doves that came there. There
    hadn't been any seen for a long time.
"Okay, if it is done there,
well, okay.
If you're going there, prepare my horse
again."
(*quietly*) "Ahah, okay."

•   •   •   •

Well, then the workers went there and prepared the horse of
    the rich man. "Well, let's go then."
(*quietly*) "Okay." They went,
THEY WENT ON.
They came there . . . to a ranch where the things were taken.
They went with the mules.
(*quietly*) They arrived, they tied the horses, which began to
    drink WATER.
The horses finished.
That Príncipe, he was there hidden in the bushes so he
    wouldn't be SEEN.
Hmmm. The doves come and settle there.
(*quietly*) They go into the water.
They entered, they came out and settled again there.
The first child said like this:
(*quietly*) "Jesus," she said, "if Príncipe Moreno wanted to
    marry me, I would make a house of *pure gold*."
The middle child answered, "Not me,
I would just make a house with seven towers of marble."

17. "Príncipe Moreno" is a Spanish phrase which would literally translate as
"Prince Dark Hair." I have left it untranslated because it helps retain some of the for-
eign flavor of the story.

"Well, not me," said the youngest,
"if Príncipe Moreno wanted to marry me,
I would just make a suit of clothes, only out of diamonds," she
    said.
They're sitting like that; after sitting there, they rise up and go.

•   •

That Príncipe Moreno saw it.
He WENT to his town.
He came to town. Well, (*quietly*) he took the saddle off the
    horse, he put it away, he hung up his hat, he left.
When he LEFT, he didn't go to his house to sleep.
He slept there in the street.
(*quietly*) Passed, passed . . . (*normal voice*) eight days passed
    with him in the street.
He slept there, he woke there.
Going on, just one morning there, an old woman came, going
"chici-tomin chici-tomin chici-tomin" she came with her
    cane.[18]
Well, she goes on saying, (*higher*) "Is it possible, Príncipe
    Moreno," she goes on saying,
"what do you really think?" she says.
"Even if I told you, old lady, just what do you know?" he says.
"Eh? Don't you know? You see, old women know a lot of
    things," she goes on saying.
(*higher*) "Well, then, say it!" he says.
"Okay, if you want to know;
there are three doves that come to a water hole there to sing,
where they say, 'If Príncipe Moreno wanted to marry me, I
    would make a house of pure gold.' The middle child
    answers,
'Well, not me. If Príncipe Moreno wanted,
I would make a house, but with seven towers of marble.'"
(*quietly*) "Ahah, like that."

•

"The youngest: 'No,' well, she answers, 'I would just make a
    suit of clothes, only of diamonds,'" she says.
"Ahah, okay."
"Isn't that what you were thinking then, Príncipe?"
"Well, that's it."
"You—stop thinking. You have CHILDREN. Go and tell them
    to go to all of the houses in town to find glue.
SIX POUNDS of glue.
NOT ANY LESS, NOT ANY MORE,"

•

18. The words "chici-tomin" describe the sound of her walking with a cane.

she said.

"Okay."

Well, then, he went QUICKLY to his house. He got there and began to

say to the children like that . . . well, the children of the
    workers,

that they GO.

They began to go and look for it, they went looking for it.

Then they found the glue.

They went through the WHOLE town. They *bought it* and
    weighed it out—SIX POUNDS, no more, no less.

•   •

"But you will stick it WHERE THE YOUNGEST WILL
    LAND."

(*higher*) "That's fine, okay." Well, he left. He came to the edge
    of the water hole,

(*higher*) he knew where the youngest would land.

He climbed up quickly and stuck the glue there. After this, he
    hid himself in the bushes.

Hmmm. There he was hidden in the trees.

•

Not much later, (*higher*) HE—IN, the doves passed by the edge
    of the tree as they went directly to the water hole.

After they had bathed, after bathing, after they were done,

they arose and then settled there on the branches of the tree.

THEY BEGAN TO SMOOTH THEIR FEATHERS.

After they had smoothed their feathers like that,

the first child said like this:

"Jesus," she said, "if Príncipe Moreno wanted to marry me, I
    would make a house of *pure gold.*"

(*higher*) "Well, not me, if Príncipe Moreno wanted to marry
    me,

I would just make a house, but it would have *seven towers* of
    marble."

"Well, not me," said the *youngest*. "If Príncipe Moreno wanted
    to marry me,

well, I would just make a suit of clothes, the only thing is, out
    of DIAMONDS," she said.

•

"Ahh, that's good." After they had SMOOTHED THEIR
    FEATHERS, after they were done like that,

the doves ROSE UP like that to go.

But the youngest was stuck. She wanted to rise up but didn't
    go.

She was left there on the branch of the tree.

She saw Príncipe because he came out running.

He grabbed the tree trunk, COOXO, he went up it.
Just as he was about to REACH, to grab the branch of the tree,
 PUC he fell to the ground.

 •

He sat on the ground. He sat up again and felt that nothing had
 happened to him,
so he quickly climbed up again. He was about to REACH, to
 GRAB THE TREE BRANCH, when he slipped again.
POH-XOOM he fell.
He sat up again and felt that nothing had happened to him.
Well, man, he got up running again and WENT up again. He
 came to where the youngest was, he grabbed her.
He grabbed the youngest, he pulled her from that glue.
"Is it possible, Príncipe Moreno," she said, "I've fallen prisoner
 in your hands, I guess. (*higher*) What more?" she said.

 •   •

"Hmmm. Well, throw me down so we can go as equals."
(*skeptically*) "Ha! What do you think? How many times have I
 fallen for you today? If I throw you down, YOU'LL
 REALLY GO."
"Ahh, no, sir," she said. "Let's," she said like that. "No . . ."
 "Let's. Throw me down."
"No, no, sir,"
he climbed on his horse and held her as he went like that.
(*higher*) As they went on, as they went on, he fell in love like
 that.
He was tired out. They went on like that then. Then she said
 to him that he should throw her down.
SHE TRANSFORMED HERSELF INTO A LITTLE GIRL.
But a regular little girl.

 •

They began to go on two by two.

 •

Well,
well,
ahh, the princess. They came there . . . there to the edge of the
 town.
"Tell me when we reach the edge of the town." "Okay."

 •

When they had neared the town, then he said to her, "Well,
 we've come to town."
"Ahah, already.
Is there some land there without an owner?" "There is. There
 at the very edge of town there is an old abandoned yard."
"Without an owner?
Ahh, that's good."

THEY ARRIVED THERE WHERE THE YARD WAS.
(*quietly*) They entered. There was a tall OAK TREE there.
They entered and the little girl sat down.
Príncipe sat down like that too. The little girl put her head on
    his lap like that and they went to sleep.
Ahah, they slept. After they slept, after they finished,
well, she made the house,
the seven towers of marble that she told him, she made it.
She told him to OPEN HIS EYES—there were the seven towers
    of marble. His house.
Before, it was just an old piece of land, full of trees, just thorns
    before.
•   •

Hmmm. "Well, here we are." "That's good."
"Today your papa doesn't know
that you've found a person." "Ahah, he doesn't know."
(*quietly*) "Well, you better go today and tell him.
Just as you get there, tell him, 'Good day.' Tell him that you've
    found a wife. He'll say to you, 'Well, son, why haven't you
    brought her into town?'
Say to him, 'The time hasn't come.
When the time comes, I'LL BRING HER TO YOU,
so you can meet her.'"
"Ahah, that's good."
•

Well, the days just went on.
•

As they went on as usual,
a paper came to Mr. King.
A revolution was coming against him, but a BIG ONE.
Then he called Príncipe
and asked if he would go and win the war.
He said, "Why not?"
He took it upon himself like that. He went to his wife.
He came to the little girl, he said, "HEY, GIRL, don't you know
    what I've taken on? I'm going to win a war."
"Is it possible, Príncipe, WHY have you taken it on?
The thing is, man," she said, "GO. If you've taken it on, GO!
The only thing . . . if there is love between your papa and your
    mama, nothing will happen," she said. "But if not, if they
    come here to look . . . well, if you have the patience, you
    won't see me until you see the SEVEN TOWERS OF
    MARBLE," she said.
(*quietly*) "Okay, that's good," he said.
The time came for him to leave. He went and left.
He could see the tower of his house over seven miles away.

Well, then he LOST IT like that.
He LOST THE TOWER OF HIS HOUSE as they went on. They
    came to where the war was going on. He began to fight.
He WON the flag and returned.
    •

Well, as he was returning from there like that, the mother,
she went from house to house in the town looking for the
    KE—YS. She found a WHOLE BUNCH of keys
so she could go and open the house.
They went on and came there.
Well, that king said, "No, we can't go in. If we do, we'll do bad
    to that little girl."
(*with disbelief*) "How could we do her bad? Besides, we don't
    even have the key." (*higher*) "Eh, you don't have it? But I
    have it."
She pulled out a whole bunch of those things.
"Let's go."
"Well, okay, if you say so, let's go." They went.
    •   •

(*quietly*) Didn't they go and get there? They began to open up
    the house.
They opened up the house, nothing!
They went and opened six of the rooms, (*higher*) nothing there
    —empty—there wasn't anyone there.
They came to the seventh room, they opened it, just a dove
    flew out. It flew in front of the mother's eyes and she fell
    backward.
Well, it really left.
    •

Well, sure enough, the boy was coming.
When he came within seven miles of the town,
he saw that, indeed, there wasn't a tower of his house.
(*quietly*) "Oh mama, I've been beaten."
Well, he came to the house of his father, he gave him the flag.
He gave it to Mr. King. After he gave it, after he was
    finished . . .
"Well, son," he said,
(*quietly*) "but is it possible that you don't know, son, that I've
    done you wrong?" "Ahh, you've done me wrong?"
(*pleading*) "But son . . ." he said.
"Before, I had a father. Before, I had a mother. But today, I'VE
    NONE.
    •   •

It's bad for you to see me here in town. You've done me wrong.
    Today I'm going only with the grace of God."
He said, he spoke,

"Hmmm, well, okay, what more? It's done. JUST BECAUSE
    YOU'RE MY FATHER,
nothing will happen. If it were not so, I'd hang you today," he
    said.
Well, he got ready and left.
He went, he went. Just to the mountains, just to the
    mountains, just to the mountains.
He saw that he'd gone over FIF—TY MILES.

•

He saw that he had gone over one hundred miles.
"Well, HUNTERS HAVE BEEN HERE." He continued to go. He
    continued to go. No man had ever gone through those
    mountains.
(*quietly*) "Man, here I'll be eaten, I bet,"
said Príncipe.
(*quietly*) He left and continued to go. Just as he's going, he
    hears echoes.
He went over one hundred and fifty.
Well, he went and quickly climbed up a tree.
As he climbed, the
things came.
A lion and a tiger.
Well, there at the tree they had overcome a big DEER.
After they'd KILLED THE DEER, after it was done, one of
    them said like this:
"Listen," he said,
"let's eat it."
"HUH? We can't eat it together . . .
I JUST KILLED IT BY MYSELF.
Well, I'll just eat it by myself," said one of them.
"What did you say? Don't you see, both of us killed it.
Well, both of us will just eat it.
Well, if you don't give it to me to eat, we . . . we'll have to
    FIGHT OVER IT,"
he said.
The BOY, he just heard it.
He just sat there and saw it then.
Hmmm.
Well, LAT—ER, they looked up and saw the boy.
"But is it POSSIBLE, boy, WHAT ARE YOU DOING THERE?"
"Well, nothing. I'm just listening to you fighting among
    yourselves over the meat."
"Oh really? Listen, boy, do us a favor and come down here
and divide this little meat for us."
"Huh? No, I won't. You see, you won't finish with that. When
    you're done with it . . .

if I come down there, you'll finish by eating me. Hmmm, no,
    sir!"
FEAR.
Ahah,
hmmm, he was afraid.
•   •

"No, boy, don't you see that we won't do you harm?
A FAVOR IS A FAVOR RETURNED."
"Okay, then.
But I have to ask you to go about twenty yards away, to move
    away. Then I will get down."
(*quietly*) "Okay, boy, okay." They went there and sat down.
Then the boy came down and began to cut it up.
He cut off the head and put it aside.
•

He pulled out the intestines of the DEER.
There was an eagle there then. (*higher*) "PI—IU PI—IU," it
    said. He grabbed it, (*quietly*) "Hi—in,"
he threw it up and it was caught in the air. It was eaten.
After that he was finished.
•   •

Well, those small ants, THEY HAD A HOUSE—the skull.
That head was a "stone house," FOR THE CHILDREN.
For the children.
"Well, man," he goes on saying,
"well, yeah, here's your meat. Come on and eat it."
"Okay."
The boy got on the trail and left.
As he goes, AS HE GOES THEN,
AS HE GOES THERE INTO THE MOUNTAINS,
they are there with the meat.
They want to eat, they want to eat, but they don't start to eat.
"Man, what we ought to do like that," he says, "we ought to go
    and give him some.
Tsk, go and call him."
•

When the tiger heard this, "Let's." He ran and said to the boy,
    (*higher*) "Wait for me, boy, wait for me!"
Then the boy heard the shouts of the tiger.
"Ha, mother! It's true, the thing isn't over. Now they'll be
    eating me," he said.
"Tsk, why should I run? It's certain," he said. He stopped.
He's stopped there. Soon the tiger comes running.
(*whispered quickly*) "Listen, boy, let's go back."
"Ahh, Jesus, if it's certain that you'll eat me, eat me here."
"No, you see, we won't do you harm. Let's go back."

(*quietly*) "No, no, sir! If you want, let's go with you in front. I'll
  come behind," said the boy.
They began TO GO. "Let's go." They went and came back.
(*higher*) "But boy, what happened?" he said. "You've done us a
  big favor. You've divided up the meat for us.
We just want to give you some to eat. Just watch.
Isn't this a little to eat?"
"Okay."
He took it.
The eagle is STILL UP THERE CRYING.
(*quietly*) "You're so sad, you're hungry," he said.
He grabbed the meat he was given, HE—IIN he threw it up—
  LAP it was grabbed. It began to eat it.
"I guess you've done us a big favor, boy.
Here is one of my fingernails, pull it off."
(*quietly*) He grabbed it and he broke it off. He put it in his
  pocket.

  •

"Me too. Here,
grab it too." He broke it off.
"Whenever you say, 'GOD, THE TIGER!' you'll be me," he
  said.
"Wherever you are."
"Okay." "Me too. Whenever you say, 'GOD, THE LION!'
  WHEREVER YOU ARE, I AM TOO."
"That's good, okay."
"Well, me too," the eagle said then.

  •

"Ahah. Well, here is one of my feathers too. GRAB IT!
Whenever you just say, 'GOD, THE EAGLE!' wherever you go,
  I'll be there too." "That's good, okay."
He grabbed it, he put it in his pocket.
That's right.
Well, then the little ant goes and says,

  •

"Listen, because you've given us a place, (*higher*) me too,
  you've done me a big favor too.
(*quietly*) Hmmm. Here's one of my little legs, take it."
"Hmmm. No," said the boy, "poor you. If I take your foot,
  you'll be left crippled. You won't be able to walk."
"But it's like this, boy:
you've given me a 'stone house' for the little children. Good for
  YEARS." (*aside*) That head.
(*higher*) "Okay, if you say so, okay."
He grabbed it, he took it. He put it in his pocket with the
  others.

Well, man, he began to go. He went, (*higher*) he began to go.
Just as he's going, he's going, then gone.
He just remembers, "How about those things that were given
    to me?
(*quietly*) God, the tiger," he says. God! What? He LANDED on
    all fours. Then he PAWED AT THE TREES.
After he had pawed the trees, after finishing, "Ahh, let's go."
    He leaped up with a jump,
WENT RUNNING. He went.
After he calculated that he had gone one hundred miles, he
    said, "God, the person," he said.

•

Well, he transformed himself. "One hundred miles I've run,"
    he said.
He transformed himself into a person again. He said, "God, the
    lion," he said again.
He THREW HIMSELF INTO THE MIDDLE of the forest again.
He ran, he ran, he ran. He went.
He figured that he went . . . he figured he went ONE
    HUNDRED MILES.
Then he said,
"God, the person," he said. His body came back.
"Well," he goes on saying, "well, there's one more," he says.
"GOD, THE ANT!" he says.
HE TRANSFORMED HIMSELF INTO a little ant. "Cooxol,"
    he leaped and went running, went running.
"I guess that's about one hundred miles I've run.
God, the person." he said.
He sees that he'd gone about sixty feet from where he started.
    Ha! (*quietly*) "Jesus, that won't do," he said.
Well, he goes on. He goes on.
"One more to say," he said.
"God, the eagle," he said. He went up, COOXOL HI—IN
    PI—IU he really went up high.

•   •

Man, he just saw it. Around four in the afternoon,
"I ought to come down to earth," he said.
"So I can rest a while to sleep," he said.
Okay, he began to come down, to come down, to come
    down . . .
man, he came down there to a tree branch like this:
he sees that he's there in another place.
Every leaf that falls from the tree is EATEN UP like that.
As a leaf, a dry leaf falls, it is EATEN LIKE THAT. *There are
    evil things there.*
There are evil things there.

"Then I've come to where it is really bad."
Well, then,

•　•

he sees that there is a big rock, about twenty feet around.
"God, the ant," he says. "Huuhurutz," he goes into the little
　　hole.
(*quietly*) He begins to go, he begins to go, HE GOES TO THE
　　MIDDLE OF THE BIG ROCK, where the hole ends.
There he lays down too.
As he said that,
there in the rock, just as the sun set over the land, there came
　　the growling of something. Even the rock began to
　　TREMBLE.

•　•

That evil thing was coming.
Man, when it became a little darker, NEH RET
it was biting off the rock: NEH RET it bit off pieces of the rock.
Jesus, as the night went on, it was eaten.
He began to feel the rock being rolled over. IT WAS
BECOMING SMALLER.
It was . . . it was falling apart like that.
Jesus, well . . . he was just smelling,
he smelled the odor. He smelled the ODOR.
Just as he was smelling it,
dawn came.
The sun came out.
When the sun came out, the biting stopped. The evil thing had
　　left.
He began to come slowly out of the hole in the rock.
It was just deserted like that. He didn't see anything.
He came out, "God, the eagle," he said. He really went up.

•

(*higher*) Well, he went on. He went on. AT MIDDAY he saw
　　something VERY WHITE AT A DISTANCE.
He said, "Well, I guess I'll go and see it," he said.
(*quietly and higher*) He began to go, he began to go, he began to
　　go, he began to go.
Around evening then,
WATER!
He saw the ocean.
Well, he saw a small *island there to one side.*
The thing he saw was really white:

•　•

the Seven Towers of Marble.
He didn't get there.
How did he get there?

At NOON he saw the day come.

(*higher*) He went but didn't arrive.

He came to the island but didn't become a human being.

He stayed an eagle and roosted in a tree.

EARLY THE NEXT MORNING, "God, the eagle." PIIU he flew
up in the sky.

When he had gone away up in the sky, he saw that the Seven
Towers of Marble were there.

He pointed himself that way.

He arrived about NOONTIME, he arrived at the Seven Towers
of Marble.

He arrived there and called, "Piiu."

The giant said, "IT'S BEEN A REAL LONG TIME since any
insects have come here; today one has come."

He grabbed his gun and went running.

"Peen," he shot him. He just fell from the sky behind the wall.

•

Well, he was killed like that.

BUT HE WASN'T KILLED.

When he was shot HE WAS TRANSFORMED INTO A SMALL
ANT!

When he fell behind there he came out running.

He went to look for the wife. That girl STAYED LOCKED UP.

He went everywhere there were keys, everywhere there were
keys he went UNTIL HE GOT THERE.

He came to the house where his

wife was in a room.

He saw that the DOOR IS NAILED SHUT; he wants to cry.

Well, he went around looking, went around looking.

He saw a little hole

there in the stone wall.

TAM he went in there. It was about this big. (*narrator shows
with hand*)

It was about a *yard long.*

"Well, here," he said,

"here's where I'll defend myself," he said.

Because Mr. Giant was there in the yard.

He transformed himself into a human being. He was a man
again.

He went to get the girl.

THE GIRL SCREAMED; she was scared.

•

The girl had been scared before she realized who it was.

HE HAD ARRIVED.

"HE has come, for sure," she said.

Then Mr. Giant came jangling his keys.

He came into the house, "WHAT HAPPENED TO YOU,
     DAUGHTER?"
(*quietly*) "Well, nothing, papa, I was just DREAMING.
(*quietly*) I was just dreaming," she said.
"Uhuh, okay."
The daughter got up and he began to LICK.
He began to lick, lick, lick, he really licked everything.
He LICKED the bed, he licked everything, he turned them
     upside down.
After everything was turned upside down, when he was done,
     he went out of the house.
He left the house; it was done so he left.
The boy came out then, the prince.
He said, (*quietly*) "How are you, girl? I've come to see you."
"You've come, prince?" "I've come."
"Boy, look what has happened to me.
I want to get out if I can. I'VE BEEN HERE THREE WEEKS.
     I'm about to die.

•

I'm being punished for staying with you before. That's what
     I'm paying for now."
"Uhuh, okay. Where did your papa go?"

•

"Every morning
he goes to a forest there to go HUNTING."
(*quietly*) "Uhuh, good.
I'm going to see if I can get you out of here."
(*quietly*) "Cooxol," he quickly ran away.
THERE WAS A TOWN THERE where a king was.
He went there to see if the king had any work for him to do.
He said THERE WAS. He could guard the cattle.
(*quietly*) He could guard the cattle.
Every morning he could accompany the cattle while they were
     taken out to the forest.
When the cattle got out to the forest
they would go around eating.
He sat in a jicara tree
to guard them. When he heard, ME'E'EH, ME'E'EH from the
     cattle, he said,
"God, the tiger." He jumped down running and growling
     COOXOL.

•   •   •

When he got there he couldn't see who had killed the cattle.
Neither who nor what.
A thing had eaten them,
IT KILLED THE CATTLE.

He grabbed it and they began to fight.

They fought, they fought, fought, fought, fought.

The giant learned to change into a tiger so he said, "God, the lion."

He *transformed himself* and they began to fight, they began to fight.

As they were fighting like that the giant says,

"PORCUPINE." He transforms himself.

"Caramba," he says. "If I can find a puddle of red mud

I CAN DRINK IT FOR STRENGTH.

I'll rip you into four parts."

"Not me," he says.

"If I can find a small glass of wine and a biscuit and the breast of a young girl to suckle,

I'LL RIP YOU INTO TWO PARTS," he said.

Well, nothing happened.

"You couldn't eat me.

Tomorrow, if you come with money in your pocket, you'll eat. If not, you won't," he said.

"Okay." He left.

The battle was over.

But there were FORTY CATTLE before. FORTY.

BUT NOW one more had been born, there were forty-one.

Well, he went along behind the cattle. He carried the calf as he went.

He came to the king.

He had THREE DAUGHTERS.

There were three daughters.

Those girls walked around

and saw the place where the cattle were being eaten and where a new calf had been born.

(*quietly*) It had been taken away.

"What happened?

No one could stay here guarding them all night.

No one could stay here to guard them.

That's why all of the cattle are gone."

(*quietly*) Well, they went. The girls see that THERE ON HIS BACK he is all scratched.

They said, "Listen, papa, you were almost eaten." They asked him what had been eating there in the field.

Well, the boy's back was all scratched.

(*quietly*) It was true.

(*quietly*) The boy took a bath. After his bath he changed his clothes.

Well, they came. They came to give him something to eat.

He began eating and while he was eating they said,

(*quietly*) "Listen, son, what happened there in the fields, what
    was eating them there in the fields?"
"Well, it was a PORCUPINE."
•   •   •

"What did it say to you?"
"Nothing. It just told me that if it could find a puddle of red
    mud to drink
it would rip me into four parts."
"And so what did you say to it?"
"I said that if there was a small glass of wine and a biscuit and
    the breast of a young girl, I would rip it into TWO PARTS."
•   •

"Uhuh.
What are you going to do?"
"Well, if I get those things I'll do it."
"Good." Well,
•

it happened like that.
There were forty-one cattle.
The next morning
he asked for a drink and something to eat.
After he had eaten, after it was done
he began to get the cattle.
He started off.
That FIRST child saw him leave.
She heard what had happened. She got a small glass of wine
    and a biscuit and wrapped them up.
She wrapped them up.
It was the lunch for the boy. She went along behind him.
THE ONLY THING WAS, SHE DIDN'T GO WITH HIM.
She went along about a half block behind him.
The boy WENT REALLY FAST.
Well, he came to the edge of the field.
He was seen climbing up the tree. The boy said,
(*quietly*) "Now I can see what happens."
Not much LATER he hears,
ME'E'EH . . . the cattle are moaning.
It was BREAKING THEIR NECKS.
He says, "GOD, the tiger" and transforms himself.
He ran off.
The girl sees that he's a
monster. She FAINTS on the ground, PAH CHAN.
It's over. What can she do?
Nothing.
He gets there and they begin to fight.
They begin to fight, to fight, to fight, to fight.

After he had fought as a tiger he transformed himself into a
  lion.
They began to fight again, they fought.
He says, "My God, give me a PUDDLE of red mud,
THEN I'll drink from it.
I'll rip you into four parts."
Well, they finished fighting.
He says,
"Let's go, my pets." He brings THE CATTLE together.
HE BRINGS the cattle TOGETHER. He goes around bringing
  the cattle together.
He sees that another calf has been born.
He carries it back in his hands.
HE STARTS OFF.
He starts off.
(*quietly*) He gets to the end of the field and sees one of the
  sisters lying there.
The shit had been scared out of her.
It was the daughter of the king.
He said, "Listen, girl. Open your eyes. Let's go.
(*quietly*) Wash off your clothes. Let's go."
So she cleaned off her clothes. Afterward they left.
Two calves had been born.
(*quietly*) Instead of being eaten, two more had been born.
Well, they were going along again.
The middle child said to her, (*higher*) "How did it go, sister?
  Did you give it to him?"
"How was I to give it to him? That boy is a monster.
When he transformed himself his mouth was this big! He had a
  big mouth," she said.
"Well, TOMORROW YOU CAN GO."
"If you couldn't give it to him, how will I?"
•
"Well, you have to give it to him tomorrow."
The next MORNING the middle sister GOT THE NAPKIN
  and wrapped it up.
Then after she had done that, she went after the boy.
She went after the boy, but she didn't catch up to the boy; she
  stayed about a half block behind him.
He went on, he went on.
She stood where THE OTHER HAD STOOD.
She saw the boy climb up a tree.
When he heard the cattle calling he transformed himself again.
Then he went on.
She fainted in a minute.
She fainted and fell down there.
Well, he got there yelling,

"Who, who ordered the killing of the cattle?"
Nobody answered. Then HE CONTINUED to guard the cattle.
"I'm talking to you!"
He wasn't answered.
Well, they began to fight, they began to fight, to fight, to fight.
After he had tired of the tiger, he transformed himself into a
lion.
They fought, they fought. Meanwhile the porcupine, since it
was only one thing,
it tired.
But it asked for a puddle of red mud.
It sought strength.
"Caramba," it said.
He could tell it was really tired out.
"Where's a puddle of red mud
that I could drink? I'll rip you into four parts."
"Not me," he said. "With a small glass of wine and a biscuit
and a breast of a young girl I'll rip you into two parts," he
said.

•

NO ONE GAVE IT TO HIM.
Well, they
finished fighting like that.
"TOMORROW," it said,
"I have to eat tomorrow, no matter what."
"You can if you pay for it with money from your pocket.
But if you don't pay with money from your pocket, you can't.
Don't think that just anyone is on guard," he said.
Well, it was finished. He went on.
(*quietly*) Three calves had been born.
Three little cows were born.
He came to the end of the field.
There the girl was lying down. He said,
(*quietly*) "Let's go." He lifted her up. She straightened out her
clothes.
She got ready.
Then they left.
When they arrived,
(*higher*) "How did you do? Did you give it?"
"How could I give it? That boy is a monster." (*quietly*) "Uhuh,
he is."
"Well, tomorrow the youngest is going to go."
"Well, since you, my sisters, didn't give it, I'll have to give it to
him."
(*quietly*) "We'll see. Get up EARLY tomorrow. Get up before
the boy," they said to the youngest.
She said, "Listen, boy, I have to come BEHIND YOU."

"Uhuh, you have to come.
Okay. If you have to come, well, we'll go. Let's get a drink.
    Let's eat."
"That's good."
They left.
She gave him his food and they left.
Then she folded up the napkin with a little wine and a biscuit.
    He took it.
But he didn't take it, he didn't, she did.
Well, they began to go, both together. He had to win.
When they came to the edge of the field
the boy climbed up into the tree.
SHE CLIMBED UP TOO.
They climbed up together, together until he asked if the girl
    would like to rest.
She said, "No, not yet.
I'M NOT FINISHED WITH MY WORK," she said.
"Wait for me, but be careful not to fall out of the tree," he said.
"Okay," she said.
She sat down. Just then he heard
"Me'e'eh . . . me'e'eh . . ." said the cattle.
"God, the tiger," the boy transformed himself. She saw it and
    jumped down behind him.
They left.
He arrived yelling,
"Who ordered you to kill cattle?"

•   •

He wasn't answered.
That giant was breaking the neck of the cattle.
He was hungry.
The boy hadn't let him eat.
They began to fight, to fight, to fight, to fight, to fight.
The tiger felt tired. "God, the lion," he said.
He transformed himself into a lion.
They began to fight, they began to fight.
The porcupine said,
"Ay, caramba, if I could just get a puddle of red mud that I
    could drink, I'd rip you into four parts."
"Not for me," he said,
"if I had a small glass of wine and a biscuit and the breast of a
    young girl to suckle, I'd rip you into two pieces."
"HERE, BOY."
She pushed him the wine and the biscuit.
Then she gave him her breast to suckle.
HE SUCKLED the breast.
He came running back to rip it in half. He tried to grab it
but it escaped as a large deer.

He grabbed it but it changed itself. IT ESCAPED as a
    tepescuintle.
He grabbed it but it changed itself. It escaped as a big
    rattlesnake.
He grabbed it but it changed itself.
It went into the sky as a dove and left.
He chased after it RIGHT AWAY.
He reached it just as it came to the edge of the sky.
It changed itself into two eggs.
Just a YARD BEFORE THEY HIT THE GROUND, HE
    CAUGHT THEM. They were caught.
Well, it was over.
He went back there to his cattle.

•   •

Well, he started to round up the cattle.
They left then.
They went together, two by two. They got there,
they came back, and they gave him some food and things.
(*quietly*) Well, after dinner, after all of that, the king said,
"Since you gave him your breast, my daughter, well, you will
    have to marry him."
(*quietly*) "Okay, king, okay. That sounds good to me."
"You'll have to set up house with him."
(*quietly*) "Uhuh, good, king. That's good, it sounds good to me,

•   •

but I'm not done with my work.
I HAVE TO GO EARLY TOMORROW.
I have to go see where the giant is."
"That's good, okay."
(*quietly*) He took three sacks of money that were given to him.
He said, "Why did you give me this money?"
"I gave it to you because you won it here. It is yours FOREVER.
IT'S YOURS."
He gave it to the girl, to the youngest.
The youngest one.
"Okay, boy, let's go into the room," they went into the room.
Well, EARLY THE NEXT MORNING,
HE LEFT.
The youngest WAS LEFT THERE when he left.
She asked him what day he would come back. He said,
    "WITHIN TWO WEEKS.
I'll be back within two weeks to marry you."
"Okay, that's good."
Well, he left.
He had to go and
BEAT THE GIANT.
Well, he came back and began to go in, he began to go in the

house, to enter the house. He went there where the key
    goes in.
He came inside the seventh room where the girl was.
Well, he transformed himself into a HUMAN BEING.
"Well," he said, "it's over.
It's time for the giant to lose his strength.
I have to do something to the giant. Where is he?"
"He's there in the yard." "He's there?" "He's there.
If it happens today,
if you can do it today," she said, "if you go and take him, his
    spirit will be finished.
But be careful not to throw anything into his mouth," she said.
"Be sure to PUNCTURE HIM when you throw it.
If you throw it in his mouth, HE'LL EAT YOU," she said.
"Okay," he said. "Tell him YOU WANT THE KEY.
If he gives you the key, grab it, because that will finish off his
    spirit."
"Okay," he said. (*quietly*) He left.
(*quietly*) He got there and said "Good day" to the giant.
He growled, "Here's a seat, boy, sit down."
"Okay, that's fine."
He sat down.
"Listen, boy, I was a strong man before," he said,
"but I'm not a strong man now; you're more a man than I am."
"Why?" he asked. "I'm done, MY SPIRIT IS FINISHED," he
    said.
"The thing is, I won't finish you off, but give me the KEY."
"Uhuh, okay. I won't give you the key."
"Well, if you won't give me the key I'll finish off your spirit."
"NO, YOU WON'T. No, you won't."
He heard Mr. Giant begin to vomit what he had swallowed.
He began to vomit.
He threw it up VERY HIGH.
"Well, Mr. Giant, lie down in your bed. Here comes the end of
    your spirit.
CLOSE YOUR EYES."
Mr. Giant CLOSED HIS EYES.
He thought that if it came in the mouth, . . . he thought that if
    it was thrown into his mouth he could catch it.
But he threw those two eggs there into his forehead.
He died.
Mr. Giant DIED.
Well, he grabbed the key and opened the rooms. He went to see
    the girl.
He opened the place where she had been held and she got up.
She said, "Well, what more? You've won.

•

Well, let's go see where the giant's money is," she said.
They opened up a room and saw it. God, there was a box full of
   money there.
"Let's go to the other room."
They went there; it was the same.
"Let's go to another." SEVEN HOUSES were full.
All full of money. There wasn't anywhere that the giant hadn't
   put money.
He just ate cattle.
Well, then it ended like that.
It was done like that. Well, they left.
"Listen," he said, "we have to do something. LET'S GO TO
   ANOTHER TOWN," said Príncipe Moreno.
"Let's go to that other town. All of these things are so heavy
   with money.
They'll weigh us down for sure.
We'll be lost."
"Uhuh," said the girl, "you will give the orders now." "Me? I
   can't give orders."
"Who are you afraid of? You're not afraid of anyone. Didn't you
   kill my father?
Now you have no fear."
"Well, okay, but we have to leave this town.
We won't take even one penny," he said.
"Okay."
They left the town.
They left it ALL there. They closed up all of the houses full of
   MONEY.
Well, they started out to the town. They started out to that
   other town.
Well, boy, when I passed by there this morning,
they were sitting together in their house,
VERY HAPPY.
That's how that small story ends.

6. THE MILPA STORY

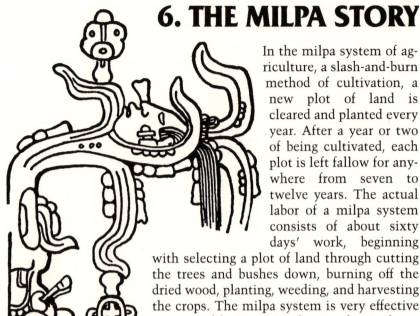

In the milpa system of agriculture, a slash-and-burn method of cultivation, a new plot of land is cleared and planted every year. After a year or two of being cultivated, each plot is left fallow for anywhere from seven to twelve years. The actual labor of a milpa system consists of about sixty days' work, beginning with selecting a plot of land through cutting the trees and bushes down, burning off the dried wood, planting, weeding, and harvesting the crops. The milpa system is very effective in an area like Yucatán where surface soils are very shallow and most nutrients are located in the growth above ground. By bringing the nutrients down to the soil, slash-and-burn agriculture allows for spectacular crops on land with sometimes no more than a few inches of topsoil.

The milpa system is more than a way of growing crops, however. It is an ethnic identifier, separating Yucatec Mayan people from others. The Maya farm milpas with a sense of religious zeal; to a non-Mayan person milpa agriculture is just a peasant occupation. Milpa agriculture is something even urban Maya look upon as being truly Mayan. A prominent shoemaker in the capital city of Mérida once remarked that, when he retires, he plans to move out to the country and make a small milpa. A non-Mayan would not make a milpa, nor would he or she think of retiring to the idealized life of a milpa agriculturalist.

Growing corn, *santo gracia* or "sacred grace" in Mayan language and thought, is an activity that connotes religiosity. Every stage of milpa production is bound by ritual celebrations to the guardians of the forest, and every ear of corn is harvested with an attitude of reverence and prayer. The tools of a *milpero* and the corn are important to maintaining health and well-being. For example, the small tote sack or *paawo'* that a *milpero* carries to the fields, filled with corn and other seeds of the milpa, is an important element in Yucatec Mayan traditional medicine. The sack can be boiled with herbs to cure life-threatening illnesses. Our nine-month-old daughter once caught an intestinal disease for which we could find no cure. We took her to several physicians in Mérida and tried as best we could to keep her from dehydrating. Finally, after three long weeks of our attempts to cure her with modern pharmaceutical drugs, antibiotics, and elixirs, Doña Severina Orozco, a close friend and confidant, suggested that we try a traditional cure. Doña Severina diagnosed the case as an accidental and unfortunate case of envy or *mal de ojo*. It was her opinion that a pregnant woman had seen our daughter in public when the baby was not properly covered with a shawl. The unknown woman probably wanted to touch or hold the child. When this desire was not fulfilled, our daughter became sick. The cure that Doña Severina performed included an herbal soup for the baby as well as a bath in water that had been boiled through a *milpero*'s *paawo'*. The child became better within a week of the cure.

The Story of the Milpa

"The Story of the Milpa" was an experimental narrative. I had noticed that many stories in Yucatec Mayan had begun with the phrase "there was a *milpero*" or a variation of it. Since a nameless and faceless *milpero* seemed to be a key character in so many examples of Mayan oral literature, I asked Alonzo if he could tell a story about the milpa. He proceeded to perform the following narrative. Although he was intimately familiar with all the details of the making of a milpa, Alonzo did not tell an autobiographical story. His story is highly stylized along traditional lines and is a cultural, not a personal, narrative.

A *MILPERO*

Well,
it will be completed. There is a
milpero.
•   •
The milpero
is a man of the fields.
•   •   •

He has to go and make a milpa a long ways off.
Well, he has to make his food
so he can go into the fields.

•

The day has arrived for him to find a little forest to cut down.
Good forest.
Well, he has to make a little food to take into the fields for one
      WEEK.

•   •   •

Well, he wakes up on Monday.
Well, a little food is prepared. He starts to go to the fields.

•   •   •

He goes to the fields.
He arrives in the fields during the day like that.

•   •

Well, he rests.

•   •

After he rests there in the hut,

•   •

then
he drinks a little CORN DRINK.[1]
After he drinks a little CORN, then
he wakes up the next day. He says, "I'm going to see if I can
      find a little bit of forest to cut down,
somewhere that looks good to me, so I can see where I'll make
      a milpa. On the side of last year's milpa, I'll find another."

•   •

Well, the man
goes.

•   •

He climbs over the old fence, goes into the forest, into the
      forest where he went, he goes to find out how much forest
      remains.
He walks around to see how it is, whether there is much
      forest left.

•   •

After he goes around to see how the forest is: if a lot of virgin
      land is left, open land,
if it looks GOOD,
"Well," he says, "it has to be opened up."
Then he walks around it like that.

---

1. I have translated *keeyem*, "pozole," as "corn drink" in order to emphasize just what this food is made of. It is limited to use when one travels or when one goes to the fields to work, as in this narrative.

There is one part of the forest he walks around,
"GOOD BROWN LAND."[2]

•   •

Then he walks around the "good brown land" like that. Then
    he walks around another part like that,
that which is called "GREEN LAND."
It is for "old corn," that "brown land" is for
"little corn."[3]
Then a path is cut like that.

•   •

He comes to where
a corner will be, where he will think to begin the path.
Then he prepares . . . he finds four little sticks.
Then he cleans up a little of the ground, so he can see where he
    will square off the land,
how he will make a straight path, so he can cut the path.
Then,
he puts the little sticks end to end. He squares off the little
    sticks.

•   •

Then he sees if he will make a straight path. The sticks mark
    off the square.

•   •

Then, if he sees that it isn't straight, he can change the path a
    little.
He can change the direction a little, so he can see how he will
    cut the path.
After he sees that it is well squared off, well squared, then he
    begins to cut the path. He cuts the path. HAALAH he goes
    cutting.
He cuts about
six or seven hundred yards,
as much as he thinks he will use. If the milpa will be four
    thousand yards square, he goes on cutting.
He cuts about seven hundred or six hundred yards,
then he cuts another path.
To the
south.

•   •

He goes on cutting a path.
After he has cut a path all the way around,

2. "Good brown land" is *kanka e'lu'um*, recognized as much by the flora as by
the geology of the soil. It is more common than "green land," *ya'ax kaax*, which denotes uncultivated land.
    3. "Little corn": *mehen nal.*

he returns to the beginning. He begins measuring how much
    there is,
he measures how much land to see how he will use it, perhaps
    up to four thousand square yards
or a little more.
He is then able to cut down the trees.
The land is marked off in two parts, one part for "little corn"—
    "*good brown land.*"
There among beec trees, among boxcatzim trees, among
    xtziwuche' trees, among be'eb trees, among xputzcitam
    trees.[4]
  •   •

All of those things like that show that it is for
planting "little corn."
The other part of the land, then,
isn't the same.
The land is called
"green land," it is for "old corn."[5]
It is good forest.
The "brown land" isn't good forest;
the trees are intertwined. The work is a little harder.
The other part of the land,
for the milpa,
that "yellow land," is good forest; the work isn't so bad.
Then,
  •   •

after it is all measured to see how much land he thinks to cut,
he thinks of the cutting.
Then he begins to measure it by units, by "sides."
  •   •

He measures, he begins to measure it by units.
He measures all of it for the six hundred yards by units.
  •

A "unit" is a side,
how many sides it will give.
Then, after it is all measured, after he sees how much land
    there will be,
after he measures, he sees then how much milpa will be
    squared off—a little more than four thousand square yards.
Then he says,
"However much more it will give, I will cut."
Then,

---

4. *Beec* is an oak, *Ehretia tinifolia*; boxcatzim is *Acacia* species; *xtziwuche'* is
unknown to me; *be'eb* is *Pisonia acleata*, a bramble or cockspur; *xputzcitam* (*citam-che?*) is probably *Caesalpinia* species, a brazilwood.
    5. "Old corn": *xnuuc nal.*

he goes back to the hut.
The LAND has a path around it.
During those days,
on the next day,

   •   •

another milpero arrives. The two of them are together.
His friend says, "Have you finished the path around the land?"
    —"It's finished."
"How much did the land you've marked off give?"
"Well, it gave a little more than four thousand yards."

   •   •

"Good.
Will there be any left for me?"—"Why not? There will be . . .
    aren't we making a milpa together?"
"Together." "Okay, there's a milpa for you, there's a milpa for
    me. Together, equal parts."
"Fine then . . ." "Tomorrow,

   •   •

we'll go again to see how the land is."
"Okay." Another day comes,
(*quietly*) he goes walking in the forest. The man says
to his friend,
(*with surprise*) "Jesus, man, you've marked off really GOOD
    LAND. REALLY GOOD 'brown land,' REAL 'brown land,'
    good 'yellow-brown land.'
Look at those trees! Look at those trees!
Look at the saccatzim, the boxcatzim, the be'eb, the canche
    trees![6]
GOOD LAND FOR THE
MILPA, for the 'little corn.' GOOD for planting things.
For planting TOMATOES, for SQUASH, REALLY GOOD
    LAND: EVEN FOR TOBACCO.

   •   •

Well, good. You've marked it off."
"Well, perhaps next week we'll return
to see where to begin the cutting."
"Okay, then."
Then,
they begin to leave the field, because it is Saturday.

   •   •

They come home.
He says to his wife,
"Wife, if you can believe it,

   •   •   •

---

6. *Kanche: Conocarpus erecta.*

I've found a little forest to cut down. Since we have a few
       bones to eat these days, well, I guess I'll make a milpa. We
       have a little corn left, about fifty sacks of corn. We have
       bones to eat.
The thing is,
I'm going to see if I can find three men
to help us with the cutting.
It remains to be seen if the cutting will be done,
because the land I've found is a little difficult to work.
Well, I have to find someone to help us, so it can be seen if it
       will be completed."
(*with enthusiasm*) "That's fine, my husband. It's better if you
       finish it all at once, so when the time comes for burning,
it will have dried. The trees will look good. Perhaps True God
       will throw us a blessing, if it looks good."
"Well, that would be good."
"That's how I'm thinking, just like that, dear. That's how I'm
       thinking."
    •   •

"Well, tomorrow, dear, since it's Sunday today, we came home
       Saturday . . .
well, since it is Saturday today,
put a little corn to soak for my food.
I need a lot of food. I need about two pounds of tortillas,
two pounds of corn drink, enough food for a WEEK.
Would you buy me about two and a half pounds of beans,
would you buy me about a pound of salted meat,
a pound of sugar, about twenty cents' worth of coffee for the
       week?
    •   •

As I'll be there a full week, well,
I have to have something to eat."
"Okay, dear."
Well,
at dawn
    •   •

the woman puts corn on the fire to make the corn drink.
Then when the corn is soaked, she washes it.
She carries it off to be ground at midday. She goes to have the
       corn ground for her husband. She sits to make tortillas for
       her husband.
She makes the food
GOOD, especially for
a milpero, because you don't make the food "half-cooked."
You always make the food "WELL COOKED."
Well cooked inside. Durable. Instead of STICKY—WELL
       DONE.

A woman who knows how to work,
her husband is a milpero,
she ought to learn to do things right—not make bad tortillas.
A woman who doesn't know how to make tortillas, to make
    food for her husband . . .
within two days, STICKY—they can't be eaten.
A woman knows how to do all of the things for the work of the
    milpa, how the milpa work is done.
Then,

•   •

"Well, my husband, I've made your corn drink, I've made your
    food, I've made all of your food.
Your food. Meat, to make a little 'beefsteak' to carry with you
    tomorrow.
I bought you a few beans, two and a half pounds of beans I've
    bought. A pound of sugar, twenty cents' worth of coffee. I
    bought you a little salted meat to carry and eat. When you
    get there you'll have a little meat.
It's for 'beefsteak.'"
"That's good.
Did you make a little ground pumpkin seed for me to carry for
    the first meal tomorrow?" "Why not? I put it there, I've
    ground a few seeds
for your breakfast. It will be ready in half an hour.
Well, there is pumpkin seed for you to eat
so that you can make a taco or a roll to eat."
"That's fine, dear, that's good."
Well, he wakes up on Monday.
The man gets up at five
in the morning.
He goes and passes by to get his friend.
(*louder*) "Let's go, friend. The time has come. Let's go to the
    field."
"Let's go, then. How about the others?"
"They're waiting for us at the edge of town. I told them to wait
    for us at the edge of town." "How many did you find?" "I
    found four, how about you?" "I found three." "Well, with
    that, man, there are enough."
"Let's go."
"Okay."
They come to the edge of town. The seven men are there,
    the milperos.
Well, they leave.

•

As the milpa
where they are going is more than ten miles
DISTANT from the town,

they go on.
They come to the milpa
around . . . around noon, I suppose.

•   •

They arrive and take a rest.
After they've rested
he says,

•   •

"Let's go find some water at the hollow rock
so we can drink a little corn drink.
There is some water left in the water gourds,
but it isn't enough."

•   •   •

"Hey, that's fine." They go to find water. They come with a
    container.
They go to find the water at the big hollow in the rocks.

•   •

They come to the large water hole.

•

They carry two containers.
They enter by the rocks there, they fill the container.
They draw it out. They fill the other, they draw it out.
They leave after that and then go to the hut.
They arrive. He says, "Well, let's drink a little corn drink then.
    We're hungry." They drink, each of them has a cup of corn
    drink
with a little CHILE and a little SALT. They chew the chile,
    drink the corn drink afterward.

•   •

That's how the day ends.
Around,
around four o'clock, I suppose,
he says, "Well, let's eat, men, let's eat."
(*higher*) "Let's."
They . . . "Pile up wood on the fire. Put a lot of branches on
    the fire so there'll be enough embers
to toast tortillas on to eat."
(*higher*) "Okay."
They pile up the branches on the fire, they put firewood, lots of
    firewood on it. It burns up so that in a little while,
there are enough embers
to toast the tortillas.
The embers are spread out like that—they begin to spread out
    tortillas.
The tortillas are done.
They eat. Some bring "beefsteak," some bring fried eggs, some
    bring ground pumpkin seeds, some bring intestines, some

bring . . . well, all sorts of things. Each one brings his
favorite food to eat in the fields.

•   •

Then, after eating, around . . .
around four,
"Well,
let's take a rest.
Afterward, let's go and find a few branches
for the morning."
They don't rest more than a short time. Around five,
they go to find a few branches and bring them
to the house, to the hut.
Well,

•   •

around six or
six-thirty

•   •

in the evening like that, someone says,
"Let's go and drink a little COFFEE."
A little water is put on the fire. Water is put on the fire.
A little coffee is made to be drunk.
Ground pumpkin seeds are EATEN.
After the seeds have been eaten,
drunk, after drinking, well, they LIE DOWN
to sleep.
Well, as they begin to sleep like that, JOKES are told.
There is someone who tells a tale . . .
well, they relax like that there in that house there in the
        FOREST;
they tell TALES, they tell STORIES,
they laugh; they're happy
(*quietly*) in the milpa.
Because a milpero, if there are many of them,
they tell STORIES, they are telling TALES, happy like that
        before they fall asleep.
Well, the SUN RISES.
Well,

•   •

"Let's go, friends, there to where we'll begin the felling.
I'll show you where we'll begin the felling."
Well, they have drunk food early. They get up, drink like that.
        After drinking,
eating like that, all have eaten, drunk, finished like that,
well, they get up, they go to be shown
where the milpa will be cut. He shows them where the felling
        will begin.
Then,

"Well, here's the milpa; here the cutting will begin."
(*higher*) "Okay, then, old man, okay."
Then they each take a twenty-yard section of the milpa,
(*quietly*) they begin to cut down the trees.
•   •

Well, the milpa is begun.
It is said that
•   •

within three weeks,
they've cut down the larger trees.
•   •

Four thousand five hundred square yards of milpa.
•   •

Because four thousand yards have been measured, but there is
      more. Five hundred yards more are measured too.
Well, all of the four thousand five hundred yards, all of the
      "green forest," "brown land," all . . . all of it,
they say that within three weeks it is done.
Well, the man who is making the milpa is happy.
Well, at the end of three weeks,
they go home.
Because they don't go home every week. They don't go home
      weekly because it is a long trip. Ten miles DISTANT.
Well, after the cutting, they go home.
Then they return home.
The men are paid for the work by the man who makes the
      milpa.
Then his wife says to him, "Did you finish the cutting, my
      husband?"—"Ay, dear, the cutting is FINISHED,
      completed. The felling is DONE.
The thing we wait for now is a little dryness
so it can be burned."
"Ahah, that's good."
Then he waits for a little TI—ME, about three weeks.
Because the milpa he makes,
the milpa made in the month . . .
the month of DECEMBER,
they say the cutting is completed at the beginning of January.
Because during the month of December, the wood isn't
      HARD—it's so—ft because there is a little ra—in.
Well, they say in the month of January,
in the time of PREDICTION,[7]
well, the felling is completed before the leaves have fallen.

7. For explanations of the *xoc kin* or days of prediction, see chapter 2 and Robert Redfield and Alfonso Villa Rojas (1962: 132).

Because when the leaves fall,
the wood is left hard, DURABLE.
•   •

Well, in the time of prediction, well, there are leaves.
It is good, it isn't hard.
But if it is left until the month of March, until the month of
     March, April—HARD WOOD.
There aren't any leaves.
Well, it's better to cut down a milpa in DECEMBER OR
     JANUARY.
The wood is ready.
Then the milpa is left
until the end of three months, to the month of April, the end of
     April.
Then the man says, "Well, dear,
•   •

we have to clean up around the fallen trees.
The day is coming for the burning.
The milpa has to be burned.
The sun has shone well, the trees are already dry, really DRIED
     OUT."
"Okay, dear, that's good."
"I have to go and tell my friend: 'Well, what do you say
if it's okay, let's go Monday.'"
"Fine then."
Well, the man goes to tell his FRIEND then.
•   •   •

He comes to the house of his friend.
He knocks.
The door is opened.
"I just came to tell you,
my friend,
•   •

we have to go Monday and clean up around the fallen trees.
We have to find two people to help us, because it's a long way
     around the trees. It's a large milpa.
We need to find two people to help us so we can sweep up
     around it, so that the trees can be cut back."
•   •

"Okay, then. If it needs to be done like that, let's go."
"Fine. We'll go tomorrow, Monday. I have to have some food
     made ready for me." "Me too."
"Right now I'll have some made for me too. Some corn will be
     put on the fire too. So some food can be made ready too."
•

(*quietly*) Well, the food was made on Sunday.

The others are going along too.
Well, then,

•   •

early on Monday,
they begin to go.
HALLAH they go to the milpa.
They arrive in the milpa about . . . about noon, I suppose.
Then they take a little rest.
They rest.
Rest.
He says to them,
"Let's get a little water at the HOLLOW ROCK."
Because there is a large water hole there in the deep forest, it
    never dries up.
(*aside*) The old days weren't like today.
Then, they go to find the water there at the water hole.
They bring two containers of water.
They drink corn drink.
They take a little rest.
Then, after resting, around three or four, he says,
"Let's eat."
Then the fire is BURNED so that EMBERS are left so that they
    can EAT.
After the embers are spread out, then the tortillas are spread
    out on the fire.
The tortillas are TOASTED. They EAT.
After eating, well, they lie down again.
Then the SUN RISES.
The man says,
"Well, let's go to the edge of the milpa to see what we'll do."
(*higher*) "Okay, then, old man, let's go."
They go into the field.
They come to the big field.
He says, "Well, here we'll begin to work.

•   •

Here we'll begin to sweep."
"Okay, then." They begin to sweep back leaves from the field.
The field is swept back. The branches are cut back, even those
    high on the trees are cut off like that.
It is left clear, because the field is swept back
FOR A YARD AND A HALF. It is measured all the way
    around.
Then
they work
for a week like that. When it is all swept clear around the
    felled trees, really CLEAR,

then it is left to be burned. All of the dry trees are swept clear.
All of the piles of tinder must be made. All of the overhanging
 branches must be cut.
The tinder is piled up. All of the leaves are swept back.
All . . . all around the edge of the dry trees, there the leaves are
 swept to be put in piles so that the field can be burned.
 •   •

Then,
they return home on Saturday like that.
Then, "What did you do, dear?
(*higher*) Are you finished?" "All done, dear, all done.
Everything is cleaned up from around the field. Next week will
 be the time that we'll have to go and burn the field.
 •   •

We'll go on Monday, I guess.
To see if we'll burn the field because it's April. It's almost the
 end of April. The month of May
IS COMING."
"That's good."
Then on Monday,
they leave town.
 •   •   •

He says,
"How are we going to do it?" "What do you mean? We'll just do
 it. We'll burn it between the two of us."
"Okay, then." "Anyway, another milpero will help us."
They go. They arrive in the milpa again.
It is already afternoon.
Well, he says,
"It's around noon. When we arrive, let's drink a little corn
 drink."
 •   •

"Let's."
There is some water left in the container.
They drink a little corn drink.
There is a man, a neighbor in his milpa.
"Let's listen to see if he'll come and help us with the burning."
"Okay." Then they go and ask that neighbor, that milpero,
if he will come and help them with the burning.
 •   •

Then he says, "Well, let's go, friend, why not? I'll come and
 help you with the burning.
After yours is burned, then we can burn mine too.
We'll do them together."
"That's good."
Then they come,

they arrive at the edge of the field. Then they go to find the
torches.
After finding the torches like that, just saccatzim or boxcatzim
trees, because those are the only trees needed for lighting
the fire.
Sac or boxcatzim. The other kinds of trees won't work.
Well, one finds boxcatzim. Another finds saccatzim.
Just straight, smooth limbs
to be split, to cut
for the lighting.
Then, after they have all returned from finding the torches,
they go to the edge of the field like that.
Then they begin to split the ends. Split the ends.
The torches are left . . . they are left . . . well, they are left split
at the ends for lighting the fire.
Then, after all of the torches have been split,
then he says, "Let's do it, I guess."
They are lit. The man who makes the milpa says,
(*formally*) "In the name of God, my Wonderful True God, here
I light the milpa in your presence.
Perhaps it will happen that you will throw down your blessing
so the milpa will burn. So it will be left for me to see if I
can plant it too."
•   •

Well, he asks True God if he can go and light the milpa. He
seeks permission like that.
Then,
The torches are lit like that. Then after the torches are lit, then
they split up.
Two go to the south and two go to the NORTH.
The one who goes to the NORTH has to turn at the corner to
the WEST.
The one who goes SOUTH will make a turn, too, to go WEST
also.
Then there to the west, there they will meet and pass by.
Then EAST and SOUTH and NORTH. The burning will be
finished at the WEST end.
The lighting will begin in the east. The lighting will go to the
south and to the north.
The lighting will end in the west.
(*quietly*) Then they begin to go lighting it.
After it is all lit, it is all lit around the field,
then,
the fire rises up and burns.
The fire RISES UP since it's such a la—rge milpa.
Well, the fire rise up; it's a big thing.

The fire comes making a NOISE at a DISTANCE. You can see
    the redness.
Then they leave running.
They go into the forest, a WAYS away.
Then (*quietly*) they begin to watch the burning of the milpa
    . . . the burning of the milpa.
Then
after
  • •

the milpa has burned,
he says, "*Jesus,*" he says, "look how beautiful the milpa burns!
The milpa burns well. Look how beautiful!"
  • •

"JESUS," the man just says,
"that measuring stick there, it . . . it didn't burn!
The one that measured the field." "That one?"
"Ahah. That's good."
He grabs the measuring stick like that. He throws it into the
    bush. "It won't burn like that."
It is called a "measuring stick" because it is used to measure
    off the milpa.
  • •

The "measuring stick" is TWO ARM LENGTHS AND TWO
    FINGERS long.
A "measuring stick" is TWO ARM LENGTHS AND TWO
    FINGERS long.
A "measuring stick" is for measuring the field.
Then he pulls it to the edge like that.
It didn't burn.
A "measuring stick" is for measuring the field.
It is called a "standing stick"; its name is "measuring stick,"
    for measuring the field.
It can be called a "measuring stick"; it can be called a
    "standing stick."
Then the milpa is left.
The field has burned like that. Well, they leave the field, they
    go to the HUT.
Then he says,
"The milpa has burned. It burned well. Now what we await,
WATER:
that a storm would come, so we could see if we could plant 450
    as well.
What we'll do,
since we're here, let's prepare the EARS."
Then they go to where the corn bin is. They bring out the ears.
The ears are brought out like that.

They begin to remove the husks
of the ears . . .
of what is known as SEEDS.
Then, they begin to husk it.
They husk it like that.
They make up one part of "LITTLE CORN," the "little corn"
        of two and a half:
two months and a half, that "little corn."
After they make up the "little corn," all of the unusable grains,
ALL of the little kernels like that, they take out all of them;
        separated for planting.
THEY SELECT the ones to be used as seeds.
Then after all of the seeds of the "little corn" are brought
        together,
then another part is made ready, the
"OLD CORN."
Then after it is all made up then, they make ready
the "old corn."
The seeds are done.
Two sacks.
The seeds are done because soon the rain will come.
The seeds are ready to be planted.
The seeds of WATER GOURDS are prepared. Water gourd
        seeds, round gourd seeds,
TOMATO SEEDS,
cucumber, watermelon, cantaloupe,
ALL . . . all are prepared. Because all of these are found in a
        milpa.
Even manioc is found in a milpa,
yams . . . there is jicama;
there are all kinds of things in a milpa.
They are prepared.
Then,
they leave the field.
Everything is ready; they leave the field one day.
They return to town, to the town like that.
Then, at the end of a week,
a storm rises up, but A REAL STORM. IT'S A HARD RAIN.
•   •
Then
the man says . . .
he says, "Until another storm comes . . . until it is seconded by
        another storm,
then IT WILL BE PLANTED."
Well,
then, just three days later,

another storm comes,
A REAL STORM.
Then, (*quickly*) "Let's go, then." Then they go like that;
on a TUESDAY they go.

•   •

Six helpers are found;
the other man found FIVE.
There are enough planters to be sure of planting quickly.
(*quietly*) Then they go. They come to the field
on a TUESDAY.
They rest. I guess they arrived around noon or one o'clock in
    the fields.
They go to get water to drink
at the water hole.
Then all of the water is carried back.
They drink CORN DRINK.
After drinking, they take a little rest.
They're tired as they came with loads on their backs.
Then, about four, he says,
"Jesus, I'm a little hungry," he says. "Me too, I feel hungry."
"Let's eat."
"Why wait any longer," they say, "let's eat."
Then they BUILD UP THE FIRE,
it burns
like this . . .
then the embers are SPREAD,
they are spread out. The tortillas are SPREAD OUT then.
There is one of them who roasts SALTED MEAT, there is one
    who roasts tomatoes,
tomatoes to be toasted and ground. "Ground tomato with
    chile"
and SALTED MEAT.
They make it then. "Let's make a dinner then. Bring me a cup,
    that large bowl there."
(*higher*) "What are we going to make?" (*normal voice*) "A
    'xtorocaapu.'" "Okay." The large bowl is brought like
    that . . .
that large one is brought.
Water is put in, hot water.
Then lemon is squeezed into it.
Garlic is put in, salt is put in, chile is put in.
Onion and cilantro are made ready for the "xtorocaapu."
It is to accompany the salted meat and the "tomato and chile."
Then they eat it.
(*quietly*) It is eaten like that, (*quieter still*) eaten.
After it is eaten like that,

•   •

after it is eaten like that,
well,
they . . . lie down after eating like that. He says,
around six, "Do you want to drink some coffee with
the other ground pumpkin seeds or the rest of the 'tomato and
   chile'?"
"Well, let's eat it."
"Okay, then."

•   •

Well, around six at night, "Well, let's drink it then; put the
   water on the fire." (*higher*) "Okay." He gets up, puts a pot
   of water on the fire.
The water boils; a little coffee is made like that.
Then, after it is drunk, "Toast the tortillas to be eaten with the
   ground pumpkin seeds."
It is eaten like that,
even the ground tomato.
Then
some "xpapadzul" is eaten;
it is eaten.
Then . . .
then

•   •   •

they begin to eat and drink like that.
Then one of them says, "Tsk, there's something I brought to
   eat." (*higher*) "What?"[8]
"I brought to eat
some really good food."
(*higher*) "What good food?"
"Ha! You don't know what it is."
(*higher*) "What is it then?"

•   •

"It's *powdered beefsteak.*"
(*higher*) "What did you say? What's 'powdered beefsteak'?"
"Here it is . . ."
(*higher*) "Is it really good?"
"Hmmm . . . a really good thing, man."
(*higher*) "What did you say? What's 'powdered beefsteak'?"
"Here it is . . ."
(*higher*) "Is it really good?"
"Hmmm . . . a really good thing, man."
(*higher*) "Where is it?" (*normal voice*) "Here it is."
(*lower*) "Ha! Man, look what it is, by God. Ground cucumber
   seeds."
"Let's eat them. Let's finish them."

8. This is an extended joke.

Then they eat the "xpapadzul."
That "powdered beefsteak" was GROUND CUCUMBER
    SEEDS stuck to the paper they were wrapped in.
Then they begin to eat.
They drink coffee.
When they've finished,
they rest. They rest like that, they sleep.

•

Then, as they begin to go to sleep, they begin to tell STORIES,
they tell STORIES.
"If there are any to converse,
tell us a tale here, man.
Do you know any tales?"
"Well . . ."
(*higher*) "Tell a tale for us to hear."
"All right.
The only thing is, the tale I will tell . . .
that I will begin—is a long tale.
Anyone who falls asleep listening to the tale before it is ended
will have his face painted.
Straightened out."
Well, then,
the man told a tale.
A long tale.
Well, there was one who sle—pt.
He was seen falling asleep. His mouth was open.
Just the whites of his eyes were visible.
Well, the man says,

• •

"Let's paint his face. Paint his face."
"Okay."
The men get up,
the ashes of the embers of the fire are taken and prepared.
The man's face is painted like that
because he fell asleep.
Well,
the tale was finished around eleven at night.
Then they SLEPT.
(*quietly*) They stretched out and slept.
Well, they awoke around four. "Let's get up; it's time to get
    up."
They got up at four in the morning like that.
Then it was said,
"Let's drink." "Let's."
"Put water on the fire."
Well, they put water on the fire.
He placed water on the fire. The water BOILED.

They made their breakfast.
They ate, they ate the rest of the PUMPKIN SEEDS.
They mixed another TOMATO with another CHILE. They
    began to EAT.
They ate breakfast. They made it like that.
Then he said, "Let's go then; let's go plant.
PREPARE the planting gourds, the DIGGING STICKS."
They carried the MAIZE.
The CORN had to be carried to the field. One SACKFUL.
They came to the field,
they took two small sacks,
they POURED OUT the corn.
THEY POURED OUT the squash seeds.
They mixed the
   •   •

"little squash" and the "big squash" which are called "big
    pumpkins."
"Little squash"—"little pumpkins."
They MIXED THEM UP like that.
The seeds of . . . of
BEANS.
Black beans, small beans;
they were MIXED TOGETHER like that. The planting was
    begun.
While they plant, they are left without any water.
He said, "Jesus,
we don't have any water today; how will we make it?"
(*higher*) "Well, don't ask—let's see how
we are going to get water." They go to get water at the water
    hole.
The water hole is already dry.
Not only that, but there aren't any other water holes.
There isn't any way to make food:
they aren't going home this week—not until the next week do
    they leave.
They have to be there at least two weeks
so that the planting can be finished.
They go and get water.
Then, they make a BIN, just like a corn bin.
After it is made, they put DIRT INTO IT.
They fill it with DIRT.
Then as
there isn't enough water for them, they want to bathe—there
    isn't any water.
   •

Well, since it is FAR to where there is any water, where else
    can they get water—the water from the water hole barely
    trickles out.

"Well, the water that has already served us,
after
washing the corn like that,
instead of throwing it out,
POUR IT into the bin. The bin will serve as a FILTER. Then
     below, a pail will be placed for the water to drip into.
The water that will drip through will serve us another day."
It's difficult to be a MILPERO.
THERE ISN'T ANY WATER while they work.
Well, within about THREE DAYS, while they are going along
     without any water like that, planting like that,
a storm RISES UP, but a REAL STORM. A real storm.
When the sun rises another day, the water hole is filled.
They are happy because of the water.
THREE DAYS have passed without any water. They didn't
     bathe:
STICKY FEELING.
They had been there almost a week without bathing—without
     water.[9]
Then they were happy. They continued planting.
They went about planting in the SO—FT earth.
The milperos planted in
SO—FT EARTH.
(*quickly*) "Chicin chicin chicin" they went planting.
Well, it was all planted, all of the four thousand five hundred
     square yards of the milpa.
One part was planted with "little corn."
The "little corn" was planted apart.
The "large corn" is planted quickly.
Well, the "little corn,"
well, there is other seed which is put with the "little corn":
just "little squash" goes in with it.
Then all of the milpa was planted with the things in the "little
     corn."
In the "yellow-brown land."
Then it was left.
•   •

Then the man, after finishing the planting, left for town.
The man will return in a week.
Then he says,
"Man, I'm going to find some yams to transplant. There is a
     section, a large section—a wide, smooth section of land.
     There I . . .
there I will plant jicama."

---

9. Bathing and cleanliness in Yucatán were often commented on by earlier
writers. See Diego de Landa (1978) or Ralph Roys (1933).

He planted forty square yards of jicama.
He planted a section and a half
of white yams.

•   •

He planted one section
of MANIOC.
Then he planted other things . . . sweet potatoes;
in all of the "brown land" he planted sweet potatoes.
Then one piece of the land was left for BLACK BEANS,
for those "little beans,"
"climbing beans" they are called.
Then, after all these things have been planted like that,
he begins to find small sticks to place next to the beans, next
    to those that are called "climbing beans."
Then, it is said at the end of one month, the beans SPROUT.
They rise up beautifully, a little twisted.
WATERMELON is planted, CANTALOUPE, CUCUMBER,
    CHILE, RED CHILE.
All of these things are mixed up in the milpa. Everything
    needed is there.
This is why it is said everything is
in a milpa.
When the harvest comes for a milpero
all sorts of good things are there.
It is a gift from True God.
Then, when the harvest of the watermelon, the harvest of
    cucumber, the harvest of jicama come . . .
all of these,
then he takes them down to sell, to find a few cents.
He sells a few.
Then that "yellow-brown land,"
when the time comes to plant tobacco,
it is the month of AUGUST.

•   •

Around then.
Sixty yards are
cleaned up
within that . . .
that field
among the stalks like that.
All of the stalks are cut down so that it is left clean.
Tobacco is scattered.
The tobacco is thrown around.
They already begin to sprout up,
just like little buttons.
Then
all of the stalks have to be taken out

so that it is left CLEAN.
It is left CLEAN; all of the stalks have to be taken out
so that it is left clean all around.
The only thing you see is tobacco there.
Then, they say at the end of January,
the tobacco is ready.
The time for the "little corn," by God,
it is said within two months and a half
the ears appear.
Among the ears, a few are yellow.
The "large corn" is done in the month of October.
In September
a few ears are fully grown.
They begin to ripen
and break at the joint,
that Sacred Corn.
Then, it is said at the end of December, the corn is all yellow.
Yellow and ripe.
A few are ready.
Then, there are things for the man to eat.
He begins his work again. There are things to eat.
Then, it is finished like that.
In January or February the TOBACCO is harvested.
In MARCH another harvest is made.
A little corn is harvested.
A bin is made
for BEATING the corn.
A lot of people are brought for the HARVEST,
to help in the
harvest of the milpa.
Since it is a large milpa, it is done like this:
the corn is piled up and a bin is made.
Then the Sacred Corn is beaten.
The grains fall through.
The grains fall through into a cart.
The maize is brought into TOWN.
Then, the man's milpa is finished.
There is something left for the man.
There is corn for him, there are all things.
Well, this man,
a milpero,
when the harvest is complete, he has his way.
All of his life comes from the milpa.
•   •

(*quietly*) Because the life of a milpero
is like that.

7. WORDPLAY

Plays on words, riddles, and other short forms of verbal art are common in everyday conversations. Wordplay spices up conversational exchanges, even if the double meanings and slightly off-color references have been used many times before. Some wordplay goes back to a time before the Spaniards came to Yucatán. Plays on the names of towns and cities, for example, seem to have been common among the writers of the *Chilam Balam of Chumayel*; riddles are a common form of the "Chapter of Questions" in the same book of Chilam Balam (Roys 1933: 73, 125).

Some wordplay is reserved for ritual contexts. Riddles can be heard during wakes, for example. In small villages it is common to prepare a funeral dinner for the departed person and then set up a table outside his or her house where men can play dominoes and tell riddles. Women tend to remain in the house to comfort the women of the family. The games that go on outside the house are played in earnest. One funeral that I attended was in a house at the outskirts of a small village. There was no electricity; the only illumination was provided by a number of candles placed around the outside of the house and a kerosene lamp in the house. When my friend and I arrived, we were poured a ritual drink of liquor and then shown the body of the man, who had died of snakebite. After we went back outside, we were asked to play another two men in a game of dominoes.

Since I was an outsider, many of the people there assumed that I was an expert domino player. While I was able to play an adequate game under more illuminated and less ritually charged circumstances, the evening's game proved to be a disaster for our team. The other team was highly skilled; they threw the dominoes down without hesitation. I was unable to even hold the dominoes correctly, as the darkness and the unsteady table precluded placing the pieces down. They had to be held in one's hands, four in one and three in the other. After a few minutes of play, I asked a neighbor to take my place at the table and I went over and sat with another friend. He gave me a drink before he took one, then used a formula to signify the opening of a riddle event: "Kill the turkey, I tell you. What does the riddle mean?" He then asked me a few riddles which I did not know the answers for, but I was able to ask him one I had learned earlier: "Goes in hungry, comes out full." The answer was a bucket used to get the water from a well.

I can only speculate on the reasons why riddles are told at wakes. When I asked people, I was told that there was nothing else to do. I found that riddles are also told on certain other ritual occasions, such as the harvest feast, the "dinner of the milpa," *haanli col.* At that ceremony there are long periods of time when food is cooking in an earth oven and a ritual specialist is saying prayers in front of an altar. During that time, people sit around, sometimes weaving animals out of palm leaves, sometimes telling riddles. Perhaps riddles are told under ritual circumstances to clarify and open the minds of participants—the riddles strike at the heart of the everyday referential use of language and cause no one to question the surety of the significance normally given to words. In this sense, riddles may function as a kind of humor which Barbara Tedlock (1975: 115) has suggested clears one's mind for the important messages of ritual events.

Jokes, short narratives with a humorous ending, were found only in villages with much Spanish culture. The term for jokes itself was the Spanish *bolada*, which suggests that the form has been borrowed from Old World verbal art. Humorous narratives were told in the villages around X-cacal, but they were in the form of "Ahau" in chapter 5, a story with several funny incidents, rather than in the form of a very short anecdote.

In addition to riddles and jokes, short forms of verbal art include ditties or songs, bird lore, and definitions. Yucatec Mayan people do not retain an elaborate musical tradition, although ceremonial musicians still play at the shrine center of X-cacal. Many people know short songs, however, some of which are modeled on the dominant Mexican style of the region, the *jarana*. Bird lore is an important genre of verbal art. In chapter 2 several stories were presented which described how particular birds ended up with the songs or other characteristics that they have today. Short anecdotes or descriptions of other birds are a common form of verbal art. Some of the bird lore can be strung together onto other narratives, so that the story of the birth of corn (see chapter 2) can be extended with several short narratives about other birds, making the story more about birds than about corn.

Alonzo Gonzales Mó produced a notebook of definitions for common things in the Mayan world. This notebook included items that he dictated to me as well as those which he himself composed after he had been taught to write in Yucatec Mayan. As such, these definitions are more didactic in their intent than artistic. Alonzo told me how things were in the Mayan world so that I could learn Yucatec Mayan. What is striking is that the definitions are more than simple references or descriptions. They are highly stylized poems which show a different way of thinking about the world than one might expect. Some of the definitions are in narrative form while others are exercises in rhythm and word juxtaposition. Like the words of Aztec priests that Sahagún was able to record in the Florentine Codex, Alonzo's definitions are imbued with the meaning of life in the New World.

Riddles

Some riddles are connected to one another. The riddle mentioned at the beginning of this chapter is an example of wordplay that has a vaguely obscene reference (to sexual intercourse) and also a reference to a paired riddle.

> *Statement:* Goes in hungry, comes out full.
> *Response:* A bucket.

> *Statement:* Goes in full, comes out hungry.
> *Response:* A skyrocket.

Other riddles take note of the conception of the world as being divided into a daytime and a nighttime universe, as did the narrator in the story of the hunchbacks when he described forty days and forty nights of rain as eighty days.

> *Statement:* There is a tree. It has twenty-four flowers: twelve
>   black and twelve white. What does it mean?
> *Response:* The world. [Twelve months of darkness and twelve
>   of daylight.]

Some riddles depend on visual referents for their meaning.

> *Statement:* There's a hen turkey with her children under her
>   feathers.
> *Response:* A house. [A Mayan house with its thatched roof
>   looks like a turkey.]

> *Statement:* An old mule eats you so very beautifully.

Response: A house. [The door of a house looks like the mouth of a mule.]

Statement: At night it's full, in the day it's hungry.
Response: A hammock.

Statement: There are two blacks guarded by sentinels.
Response: Eyes. [The sentinels are eyelashes.]

Statement: There is a big thing. It drinks up a lot of people.
   When it is full, it goes. It opens its mouth and people go in.
Response: A bus.

Statement: There it is! There it is! There it is! [Riddler points
   in different directions.]
Response: Your hand.

Statement: San Francisco goes headfirst down to hell.
Response: You drink your beverage.

Statement: There is a rich girl that you kiss every day.
Response: A water gourd. [Water gourds are hourglass-shaped.]

Statement: A plate of your grandma's vagina.
Response: Scrambled eggs.

Statement: The bucket goes first, in the middle goes the drum,
   in back goes the brush.
Response: A horse.

Statement: A prince goes walking on the horns of a bull.
Response: An ant. [This riddle refers to a thorn bush whose
   thorns resemble bull horns. The bush often has ants on it.]

Statement: When it leaves it's a hen, when it returns it's a
   rooster.
Response: Leaf-cutting ants. [Leaf-cutting ants go out in the
   morning and return later carrying bits of leaves.]

Statement: The tumpline of a lazy person is stretching out in
   the country.
Response: A vine.

Statement: The point is drying out while the trunk is getting
   wet.
Response: A cigarette.

Statement: It comes to your ass, it comes to my ass.
Response: A chair.

Statement: You grab it, I grab it.
Response: Air.

Statement: You just glance at a big valley and your mouth
   wrinkles.
Response: Your armpit. [This riddle refers to the odor of
   perspiration.]

Statement: You just look out in the ocean and see a prince.
Response: A mirror.

Statement: Every year you love three blacks.
Response: The hearth. [A Mayan hearth consists of three
   stones. During the cool months of winter people gather
   around the hearth for warmth.]

Statement: It takes five soldiers to pull out the prize.
Response: A prick.

Statement: It is being born, it is being baptized.
Response: Defecating and urinating at the same time.

Statement: You see it but you can't grab it. It goes with you but
   you can't grab it.
Response: A shadow.

Statement: There is an American who is going out all the
   time. There are twenty-four guards watching the door. He
   gets bit if he is discovered.
Response: A person's tongue.

Statement: You hear it hum, it hits you, but you don't see it.
Response: The wind.

Statement: You hear it leave but you don't see it.
Response: A fart.

Statement: Silver on the outside, gold on the inside.
Response: An egg.

Some riddles depend more on sound than on sight for their
meaning.

Statement: Chichice, yuyuce, hahaale. [Rattle it, shake it, dig
   it.]
Response: Chi'ic, yuc, haale'. [The animals: a coati, a brocket
   deer, and an agouti.]

Statement: Its voice is heard a mile away. It has a beard of skin.
Response: A rooster.

Statement: Its voice is heard a half mile away. It has no guts.
Response: A bugle.

Statement: At every corner it farts.
Response: A car.

Statement: Your sister is shouting every time you hear it.
Response: A pulley at the well. [Pulleys without oil squeak.]

Some riddles are more philosophical than visual or aural.

Statement: Letters are coming, letters are being sent off.
Response: Thoughts.

A Song

The following is a popular little ditty that is known throughout most of Yucatán. Alonzo dictated this version to me.

THE ARMADILLO

Recete brecon, brecon tu breco, brecon tu breco brec.
Lorito's a parrot, cen cen cen.
Your head is light, your ass is heavy.
The armadillo's shell
is the rich man's purse.
The armadillo's shell
is the rich man's purse.
The armadillo's tail
is the rich man's cane.
The armadillo's tail
is the rich man's cane.
The armadillo's head
is the rich man's cheese soup.
The armadillo's head
is the rich man's cheese soup.
The armadillo's nose
is the rich man's pipe.
The armadillo's nose
is the rich man's pipe.
The armadillo's ears
are the rich man's spoon.
The armadillo's ears
are the rich man's spoon.
Tzurun tzun tzun, Lorito's a parrot.
Cen cen cen, your head is light, your ass is heavy.
The armadillo's guts
are the rich woman's rosary.
The armadillo's guts
are the rich woman's rosary.
The armadillo's claws
are the rich man's fork.

The armadillo's claws
are the rich man's fork.
The armadillo's asshole
is the rich man's ring.
The armadillo's asshole
is the rich man's ring.

Jokes

Mayan people are not prudish. Jokes with strong sexual content are
told, although scatalogical humor is not very common. In several of
the stories presented in this volume, sexual content has been a
source of humor. "Ahau" depends on double entendre for its success,
and the story of San Antonio begins with a possible case of adultery.
The only humor involving other body functions occurred in the
story of the man and the vulture, in which the old man was expected
to eat excrement. The following three jokes were told by Alonzo
Gonzales Mó in Ticul.

THE JOKE ABOUT THE ANNIVERSARY

A woman talks like this:
"It's already time to celebrate the anniversary of the funeral.
I'm so poor, I don't have any money to make the celebration."
That's what she says like that, "How can I make the
    celebration?"
Like this: "Well, in place of making the food, I'll put the table
    up,
because my poor husband has already been dead a year.
In place of offering some sweets, well, I'll get up on the table.
I'll take off my clothes so when my husband comes,
in place of eating chicken,
well, when he sees me lying like that on the table,
when he comes,
I'll open my legs.
When the spirit comes, he'll eat me."

THE JOKE ABOUT THE WOMAN AND HER CHILDREN

Well, this old lady had a lot of children.
She was ninety-seven years old and had twelve.
The woman was an elder.
Well, the elder woman got sick and was put in her hammock.
The mother of the children.

Well, for a long time she hung there in her hammock in agony.
She says, "Oh God, I have a lot of sins."
She says that to God because she's paying for what she did here
    on earth.
Well, because the woman got worse, her daughter said,
"Ay mama, is there anything you want to eat?"
"Oh daughter, I can't eat."
"Why?"
"Because I have no appetite," she says.
"Daughter, you can bring me a chicken to eat,
bring me lots of food to eat,
but the thing I want to eat most of all is a head."
"Ay mama, what kind of head do you want to eat?
A head of a pig or a head of a cow or a head of a chicken or a
    head of a turkey or a head of a deer?
Whatever you want, we'll make it. Any food made from a head,
    we'll make.
But mama, tell me what head it is you want to eat."
"Ay daughter, the head that I want is so tasty,
there isn't any other kind of head like it that is
as sweet as the sweetest head on earth.
Ay the head, ay the head that I want so bad to eat . . ."
"Ay mama, what head is that?"
"Ay daughter, it is the head of a prick that is the sweetest in
    the world."

THE JOKE ABOUT AN OLD MAN WHO WENT TO MÉRIDA FOR A YEAR

There is a man called Don Sandiego Fulano.
He went to Mérida.
He was there for a year.
When he came back here he went to his house.
When he woke up a rooster was singing, "T'en t'eresey."
That old man said, "Hey, woman, what's singing?"
"A rooster."
"Oh a looser is fishing."[1]
"Not a looser fishing, a rooster is singing."
"Oh, an 'ooster, 'ooster, 'ooster."
"Not 'ooster, not 'ooster, rooster."
Well, then, some ducks came by.

---

1. The old man's first mistake in sound is the deletion of a glottalized feature in the beginning consonants of the two words. The word for "rooster" is *thel*, which he pronounces as *tel*, a meaningless word in Mayan. The word for "sing" is *kay*, which he pronounces as *cay*, "fish."

"What's coming, woman?"
"You mean you don't recognize ducks, husband?"
"No, I didn't recognize them. Oh docks, docks."[2]
"Not docks, little fart, ducks."
Well, he left to take a walk to buy some tobacco.
"Here I am, sir."
"What do you want, Don San?"
"Do you have some turkey for me to buy?"[3]
"Yes, Don San, I have a turkey."
He brings it out, "Here it is, Don San. You're lucky; they just
      brought this turkey in yesterday."
"Hey, friend, I don't want turkey, that's not what I want."
"You went away to Mérida for one year, Don San," he says.
"Now you don't know Mayan. You forgot your Mayan.
You asked for tobacco, you little runt, not turkey, tobacco.
You forgot how to talk in Mayan."
Well, he left.
He came to a corner and said,
"María Santísima, here comes a shout. Here comes a shout."[4]
"Not a shout, you little fart, not a shout, an auto."
"Oh I didn't know how to say it because I forgot how to speak
      Mayan."

Bird Lore

The jungles of Yucatán contain a wide variety of birds, from orioles
to parrots. Yucatec Mayan people enjoy birds and often keep them in
homemade cages close to their houses. A gift of a bird is special, particularly the gift of a parrot. The following short forms of verbal art
are examples of anecdotes told about birds. The first two were told
by Paulino, the rest by Alonzo. The occasions for talk of this type
include a journey through the jungle, when many bird calls can be
heard, or the telling of stories that have bird characters in them.

---

2. The Mayan word for "ducks" is a borrowed Spanish word with an elongated
middle vowel, *paato'ob*. The old man pronounces it as *pahtico'ob*, a word that is
close to a verb form meaning "is able."
3. The word for "tobacco," *kuutz*, and the word for "turkey," *cuutz*, differ only
in that the first word has a glottalized consonant which is missing from the second.
4. The Yucatec Mayan word for "shout" is *awat*, whereas the word for the vehicle should have been *auto*.

THE SACRED MOCKINGBIRDS

The Sacred MOCKINGBIRD,[5]
of A—LL of the birds, just that one *steals*—steals songs.
•

Of all of the people, so GOOD, so BEAUTIFUL their clothing,
    like the larger birds, like the CURASSOW, like the
    TURKEY, like the GUAN,[6]
A—LL
of the birds with BEAUTIFUL clothing,
like the CHACHALACA,[7] were taught . . . were taught to sing,
to sing as youngsters
at the time they were born.
•

(*quietly*) Well, not one learned it.
THEN WHO TAUGHT THE MOCKINGBIRD?
The mockingbird wasn't taught, it just steals.
Why does it learn songs like that?
•

Well, for this reason: at the time the corn is little,
(*quietly*) at the very time the corn is little, (*normal voice*) the
    Sacred Mockingbirds make a BUZZING song.
•

They sing because they're, (*quietly*) they're the GUARDians of
    the Sacred Corn. The Sacred Mockingbird is the
    GUARDIAN of the Sacred Beautiful Corn.
It was ordered by the Wonderful True God
that it sing for the little children
all over, at the time of the little corn,
A—LL over, the Sacred Mockingbird sings.
•

But the important ONES, the first ones who were taught, like
    the CURASSOWS, *turkeys*, *guans*, A—LL of the birds,
•

with GOOD clothes,
(*higher*) just sing mixed up.
Their songs are without reason; it can't be understood just
    what they are singing.
The . . . the little children aren't calmed down, (*quieter*) the
    little children. But the Sacred Mockingbird
is the GUARDIAN of the little Sacred Corn.

5. This is *Mimus gilvus*, the Tropical Mockingbird.
    6. The Great Curassow is *Crax rubra*; the Ocellated Turkey is *Meleagris ocellata*; the Crested Guan is *Penelope purpurascens*.
    7. The Plain Chachalaca is *Ortalis vetula*.

That one . . . that one distracts the Sacred Corn. That one
  calms the Sacred Corn down, the Sacred *Mockingbirds.*

TASAPATAN

The Tasapatan[8] is like that too.
A—LL of the large Sacred BI—RDS, like the CURASSOWS,
like the GUANS, like
•

BLUE JAYS, MAGPIES,[9] like A—LL of the birds that are large,
  they bring the nest of the little Tasapatan.
The Tasapatan, it
doesn't make its nest.
(*aside*) Let's say it then.
(*higher*) Well, I guess it's the king of the birds. Why? Its song is
  heard.
It's so
small.
Its nest is so large,
the Sapatan's nest is so VERY large.
The name of that . . . that bird . . .
it just says its name, (*higher and sung*) "Tah sapatan . . . tah
  sapatan . . . tah sapatan," *its song.*[10]
It . . . it . . . it is saying like that: "Let it be a house," it is
  saying.
•

Well, that's why A—LL of the birds, the large ones, the ones
  with strength,
they bring the nest of Sapatan. It is finished with large thorns.
  Just thorns, its *nest.*

A DOVE

"Here comes a bad storm," says the squirrel.
The poor dove[11] goes to its house.
The squirrel says, "Well, if you can believe it, a bad storm is
  rising up today, this very day."
"What will I do with my children?
Where will I put them?

8. I was unable to identify the Tasapatan.
9. Blue jay: *Cissilopha yucatanica*, the Yucatán Jay; magpie: *Psilorhinus morio*, the Brown Jay.
10. The song can also be interpreted as "*taaseh, ppaatah tan*" or "bring it, a house is left."
11. I was unable to identify this bird as being anything other than a dove, *paloma.*

What will happen when the wind comes?"
"Why are you talking like this? Here comes a tornado.
You have to throw the eggs out over the edge.
Then you have to go so you won't be killed."
"Okay, I'll have to do it."
The dove throws the eggs over and leaves.
But a tornado doesn't come.
The dove says, "The squirrel tricked me, the storm didn't
    come."
The dove says it very sadly.
The squirrel says, "I did it, I don't feel bad."
Well, you see, the song of the dove is very sad.
It sings, "Uuh, uuh, the squirrel tricked me."

THE WOODPECKER ·

That woodpecker[12] is going to make a nest.
It finds a smooth tree. It makes a hole.
There it will make a nest to put its eggs there.
That's where the young will be.
A person comes and gets close to the tree and shakes it.
He listens to hear if there are any small woodpeckers in it.
He takes a stone or a stick and makes a hole in the nest.
Then he puts something there so the birds can't see.
When the woodpecker comes and sees that the hole has been
    enlarged where the children were, it flies away.
Then it comes back with twigs to cover the hole.
When the hole is covered up the tree is cut down and the xe'[13]
    twigs are in the hole.
Then the small birds are gone.
The man takes the little xe' twigs for medicine.
That's a truth.

THE THRUSH

The thrush goes to a nest.
It drinks the eggs of that bird.
Then it puts its eggs there to be nurtured.
Then it goes.
The poor bird has to nurture those little birds.
They come out as little black birds.

12. Woodpecker: *Phloeoceastes guatemalensis*, the Pale-billed Woodpecker.
13. I was unable to identify the plant named here.

THE CARDINAL

That cardinal was taught long ago by True God.
It is a beautiful bird, it has a beautiful coat.
It has a crown.
The poor robin feels bad because it has a dark brown coat.
That's how it grew up.
The poor robin was taught how to sing.
It always came last because it had such ugly feathers.
So the cardinal taught it all of the songs.
He heard the song of the cardinal, so Beautiful True God said,
"You will learn more songs."
That's why the robin is the one that learns the songs.

Definitions

The following definitions were either written down by Alonzo or
dictated to me. They are experimental forms of verbal art in that
they were created in order to teach me how to speak Mayan. They
can also make up parts of natural conversations where such wordplay is appreciated. The form of these definitions may well be an ancient one, however, as seen in the books of Chilam Balam (Roys
1933) and the eleventh book of the Florentine Codex of the Aztecs,
which contains similar items (Sahagún 1963).

HO, CUL, UXMAL

You know, long ago people started to make things.
There weren't huge buildings cut from stone long ago.
There weren't any like there are today.
They were all made.
They thought up the idea in their minds to make a huge
        building in Ho, Cul, and Uxmal.[14]
It was said that whoever finished at midnight would ring a bell
        at midnight.
Then the huge building would be finished like that.
This was all the work of the Hunchbacks long ago.
Well, when the morning came,
the building was complete like that by the Hunchbacks.
That's how it came to be long ago.
Like "Ho"—"Pulled out"—was the name it was given.
That's how "Cul"—"Sat down"—got its name.

14. Ho is Mérida, Cul is Ticul.

"Uxmal" wasn't completed, it was just "One-third built." It
    wasn't finished, so it was left like that.

TABI

That Tabi,[15] long ago in the time of slavery.
There were so many things that were hard then.
They whipped you in the old days,
in the time of the Rich People long ago.
They put your name on the list too.
If you answered to your name or if you didn't—
if you weren't there and didn't answer,
you were whipped by the Big Man.
They grabbed you and took you away with the people who
    worked with you.
They threw you over the sacks of corn,
took off your shirt.
If you had done something really wrong,
they gave you twenty-five lashes.

ODOR

The thing there is smelling.
Because it has begun to have an odor.
The vultures arrive because the thing has begun to rot.
A horse or a cow.
They all die like that.
They are carried to the edge of town and thrown out
to become food for the vultures too.
The thing there has a good smell,
like the flower of a tree like that.
They are all smelling good like that.
Like the things that women put on.
The thing they buy to put on themselves.
What a sweet smell it has: perfume.

PATH

One path,
when it's made there,
it is slashed open.
Afterward the trees are cut back too.
They throw the trees aside as they are out like that.

15. Tabi was once one of the large henequen plantations in Yucatán. It was the
home of Alonzo before the Second World War.

The jungle is opened about six yards wide;
the path is the width of a measuring rod.
It isn't the work of just one person,
a lot of people work there at the road
so that it can be finished in a hurry.
When it is finished like that,
the path is left like that.
It is for the people of the milpa to travel on.
It is for the carts to travel.
It is for bringing the corn from the fields.

THINGS

When they say, "There is a thing."
It is a thing lying on the ground.
Or a thing comes down the road,
noise.
One might say it is a snake
or a beast
or a thing someone will show you.
You feel like this,
"What will he show me?"
Well, who knows what he will show me?
Perhaps what he will show me,
perhaps palm
or gold.
Perhaps he will show me
things of the house.
Perhaps a thing, too.
Perhaps a cunt.
Perhaps a cockroach, too.
Or a small cockroach,
or an iguana,
or a scorpion,
or a tarantula,
or a centipede,
or a small iguana,
or a large iguana,
or a large centipede,
or a woman
embracing.
She is kissing a man.
Lonely street,
fence near the road.
Or a thing one will ask of you.
The thing he asks of you,

a person asks of you,
a thing to buy.
You answer,
"There is that thing
I will sell, also."
We are waiting for a thing
to carry us.
As we leave it appears.
A bus.
Let's get on.

HAIL

The day arrives of its falling.
After the time of dryness has come.
Those hot days like that.
Then a cloud rises,
reddish.
Then a wind begins,
a strong wind with hail.
Corn hail falls.
Then the other, large hail, falls.
It is eaten by some.
Given that, who makes it,
who puts it,
who does it,
whose work is it?
The work of God.
Where is he?
There in the sky.
No man knows him here,
in the world here.

RAINBOW

What is it made of?
Of water.
The rainbow, it stands still.
The water is like that because
when a storm, a big storm, rises up
the water really comes.
The rainbow comes out, it is seen.
Then the rain won't come.
Because the rainbow,
because the rainbow
is the vapor of the earth.

There it comes out.
Because the rainbow is the fart of the devil.
Where it comes out,
the vapor is a fart of the devil.
When a man passes,
the rainbow smells.

ANTEATER

Anteater is an animal of the country.
What does it eat?
It finds ants to eat.
It lives in the country.
When it comes to an anthill, it digs.
Then it draws its tongue where it has dug.
It loads its tongue.
It puts its tongue in its mouth, it pulls it through its mouth.
It eats like that.
It makes its living like that in the country,
the anteater.
It is the priest of the country.
Its hair is black, its collar white,
as those of a priest, just as they wear.
The anteater is like this: a large nose, a mustache, a large tail,
    long fingernails.
It has intestines, it has heart, it has lungs.
It has throat, it has windpipe, it has liver, it has belly.
It has penis, where it pisses.
It has asshole, where it shits.

SHADE

Where does a horse shade itself?
Under the shade of a tree.
Shade.
Where do cattle shade themselves?
Under the shade of a tree.
Shade.
Where do chickens, turkeys, ducks shade themselves?
Under the shade of a tree.
Shade.
Where do deer shade themselves?
By a fence,
under the shade of a tree.
Shade.
Where do wild boars shade themselves?

Under the shade of a tree.
Shade.
Where do birds shade themselves?
Under the shade of a tree.
That is the reason for shade.
For all animals, even for people.
Shade.

PERHAPS

Perhaps, maybe, we'll see how the world ends.
Perhaps the day will come of hunger.
There are those who will see what will come to pass on the
   earth.
Perhaps we'll die too. We don't know what day.
Perhaps we'll go to Mérida or another town.
Perhaps I'll come to visit your house or home too.
Perhaps I'll buy what I need.
Perhaps soon I'll have money too
with the little that I'll sell.
Perhaps soon I'll have a woman too,
to marry.
Perhaps soon I'll have land to work,
to build a house to live in.
Perhaps I'll go far away too,
to know places.
Perhaps soon I'll have a cow, a horse, a milpa.

8. THE FEATHERED SERPENT

The Feathered Serpent has occupied the center of Mayan religious thought since Olmec times some three thousand years ago. The Feathered Serpent in Quiche Mayan mythology is Huruacan, one of the creators of the world. In Yucatán the Feathered Serpent is called Cuculcan (*kukul*, "feathered," and *can*, "snake"), although more often Mayan people refer simply to the Nohoch Can, the Large Snake. The Feathered Serpent is an awesome creature in contemporary Mayan thought, where it is considered more of a primeval force than a deity. In the story of the man who goes to the underworld in search of his lost wife, given in chapter 4, the Feathered Serpent is encountered only when the deepest level of the underworld is reached. Once when Alonzo and I visited the ruins of Uxmal, he pointed out the large rattlesnake motifs on one of the sculptured walls. Alonzo noted at that time that the Noboch Can even lived in the days of the hunchbacks who had built the ruins.

All snakes are related to the Feathered Serpent in Mayan thought. During one outing to Paulino Yamá's cornfields to harvest the first or "green" corn of the year for a ceremony, Paulino pulled out his long machete, handed it to me, and said, "*He'ele can, ciinse!*" ("There's a snake, kill it!"). Paulino had very poor eyesight, so I took the machete and began cutting through the underbrush. After a time I succeeded in killing a large, noisy snake. Paulino took the machete back, cleaned off the blade with a leaf, and then looked at the snake. "Oh," he said, "it was only a boa, it wouldn't have killed us." I asked him why we had killed it if it wasn't dangerous. "All snakes are dangerous," he said, "we kill them all." This attitude makes good sense in Yucatán, since many poisonous snakes can be found in the jungle, including several pit vipers.

The Feathered Serpent in contemporary Mayan thought is not a horrible monster or a fierce dragon that is feared. The creature is powerful, but its power derives from its size, not its disposition. It is not an active evildoer but something of a power or force that can cause catastrophes because of its size.

The Last Story of the Feathered Serpent

Our last visit to Yucatán occurred during the summer. As always I wanted to pay a visit to Alonzo. In Mérida we spent a few days with friends, who said that they had seen Alonzo when they were in Ticul but had heard that he had been ill. We were told that his grown children did not know how to take care of him, a remark which could be interpreted as a bit of gossip about the family or as a pointed comment by Doña Severina about her own grown children. When we came to Ticul, I stopped at the store where Alonzo's brother-in-law kept his market produce. Alonzo had been working for his brother-in-law for the past ten years, doing odd jobs around the market—carrying produce, washing vegetables, and cleaning up the stall after the market closed. He had been very weak and unable to work in the milpa fields; working for his brother-in-law was the only employment he could find, as he was now sixty years old. Alonzo's brother-in-law was pleased to see us but was noncommittal when I asked about Alonzo. He hadn't seen him lately and didn't know what he was doing.

I went to Alonzo's house. It was hard to find as it was almost dusk and the street seemed different to me. Alonzo usually met me at his gate whenever I came to visit. He often remarked that he had known of my coming through some sign, because the cooking fire had sputtered and popped, just like the car I drove did, or because he had dreamed of talking with me the night before. These common kinds of divination by perception guaranteed that welcomes would always be understated, never surprising. On this visit, though, Alonzo was not at the gate. His house was dark and I had to ask some neighbors if indeed he still lived there. At his gate I called out a traditional greeting, "*Hei, cin tah te'elo,*" "Hey, here I come there." There was no answer, so I called out again. Alonzo's ten-year-old son, Jemuel, came around the side of the building and opened the gate for us.

Alonzo wasn't in his main house; he was in a small house on one side of his yard. His wife, Elba, invited us in. Alonzo was in a hammock. He apologized for his appearance and said he had been taking a nap. He related how he had been quite ill and unable to work for the past several months. Doña Elba said that her brother had not helped out at all. Alonzo had worked for him for years and he didn't help him one bit. Alonzo said he had "something" on the back of his head. He had had an attack and had lain in a hammock for a week as if he were dead. Doña Elba said that she had thought he was dead. But then he got well enough to see a doctor, who said that he needed an operation. The doctor gave Alonzo some medication and he had been at home ever since, unable to do any work except help Doña Elba with the chickens and other domestic animals that she keeps.

Alonzo's eyes were bloodshot and his face drawn, but he was pleased that I had come. We talked for a while about some of the experiences we had had together over the years. He called Jemuel in and the two of them told me that they had found a chacmol, a stone jaguar, in a cave Alonzo and I had once visited in the Puuc Hills. The eyes of the jaguar were precious stones that glowed in the dark. Alonzo wanted to take me to see it the next day, but we were leaving to go back to the United States so I declined. Near the end of our visit, Alonzo and Elba talked to us about our journey, asking in a rhetorical way whether we would ever see each other again. I realized that we had slowly entered into a kind of interaction that was similar to the leave-taking ceremony we had experienced almost ten years previously in Quintana Roo. Alonzo said that he had a story for us, one he had told me before but that I had not been able to record. I had a tape recorder with me, so I took it out and put it on a small stool in front of his hammock. He said he would tell me the story of Colas, the Feathered Serpent. When the story was over, we took formal leave of Alonzo and his family and left Ticul.

The story is about a boy who was born a snake and his older sister. As the boy snake grows larger and larger, it becomes apparent that it is a Feathered Serpent. Finally, it flies out of the cave in which it was living and creates an earthquake. The return of the Feathered Serpent is signaled every year in the middle of July by an earthquake. That is how the older sister of the Feathered Serpent knows that it is still alive.

Alonzo's grave illness and the other circumstances surrounding the telling of the narrative made it more than an entertaining performance. The story of Colas encapsulated much of what I had learned from Alonzo and other narrators about Yucatec Mayan tradition. The cyclical conception of time and activities is contained in the recurrence of Colas every year. The fact that the narrative was told at the beginning of July, just before Colas was due to be heard from again, brought the story into the reality of the time of our visit. The wistful Feathered Serpent, harmful but not malevolent, captured the sense of fatalism that had been expressed in both humorous and serious tones in many of the narratives. The annual coming of the Serpent, its cyclical return from the sea, is analogous to the round of stories that arise in Mayan conversations, giving everyday occurrences and people a mythic backdrop before which life is played.

COLAS

Well, the story of
•   •   •
Colas,
Nicolás.
•
WELL,
•   •
LONG AGO there was a person.
•   •   •
Two children
were born.
The old man
was Don Nicolás.
That was the name of the children's father.
Well, then,
THAT ONE, the first child, was a GIRL.
The first child was a girl. *Her name was Juanita.*
Then, after two years
•   •

another was born, another child, a son.
He was big.
Colas, Nicolás.
•   •

Well, THAT LITTLE BOY THERE WAS
A SERPENT!
A boa . . . a boa . . . a boa . . .
a HUMAN BEING.
It was really on the day . . .
the day . . . the day of July 15 that the boy was born.
Then
that boy there . . .
they saw that it was a serpent.
When the boy was born, the mother DIED.
•

The mother died.
Then
that little,
that little boy . . . that SERPENT
•

was seen by the SISTER, Juanita.
"Jesus!" she said, "my little brother is a serpent.
I've got to FEED HIM."
Then she found him a BOX.
•   •

COLAS

Entonces, le cuento ti'e
•   •   •
Colas,
Nicolaso.
•
HA'ALIBE,
•   •
cah yan huntul maac UUCHE.
•   •   •
Cah aahi'e
ca'atul u pa'alo'o.
Le nohoch maaco,
don Nicolas u kaaba.
U kaaba u taata u pa'alo'obo.
Entonces,
LE TI'E TUNE, le ti'e yax pa'alo, humppe XCHHUUPAL.
Xchhuupal yax pa'ala. *Juanita u kaaba.*
Entonces, ti tu buelta dos añose
•   •
la' tun, u la' tusiihile, u la' huntul, u hijo.
Puro nohoch.
Colas, u Nicolaso.
•   •
Entonces, LE'A HUNTUL U CHAMPATZILO
CAN!
Hun boe . . . boe . . . humppe boe . . .
CRISTIANO.
Hach tune kiin . . .
le kiine . . . le ti'a kiine quince de Julio cah siihe champalo.
Entonces
le tune chambalo . . .
cah ilah ti teh caan.
Es que cah siihe chambalo, u mama CIIMI.
•
Ciim u mama.
Entonces
le ti tune chan
le chamac le . . . le CAN
•
cah tiyalah u CIICE, Juanita.
"Tu Magis!" dzi'ce, "in wiitzima caan.
Yan in TZEENTIC."
Entonces cay tu caxitic humppe BUUL.
•   •

The serpent
was put in there.
He was put into the box so he could be fed.
Then she found things to feed him, like MEAT.
She gave him things to eat.
He was given things to eat,
  •   •

like deer, mice,
  •   •

birds.
He ate everything that he was given to eat.
She saw that he was getting big.
Then LATER the serpent,
the little Nicolás,
was getting big.
He got big.
When his sister, Juanita, saw him
he had really BROKEN OUT.
She said, "Well, what will I do?
My little brother has GROWN LARGE."
Then she found a stone, a larger . . .
a larger
POT, a pot that was
larger.
She put him in there.
Well, she began to feed him again.
She fed him, she fed him.
She found him meat, she found him chicken, she found him
        large . . . well, things to eat,
like mice, like rabbits, well, she found him things to eat.
As a result he grew larger.
Well, the serpent got big, he grew larger.
Meanwhile, it could be seen that he had,
he had grown large and BROKEN OUT of the box again.
She said, "Well, what can I do?
How can I GIVE him things?
He's grown into a large thing;
he's filled up his house."
  •   •

She said, "*Well, it doesn't matter how I will do it.*"
She took him where she found a cave, then,
a large cave.
Then she put the younger brother in there.
Well, since they were poor, they didn't have anything,
what else could she give him?
She couldn't buy meat; he ate a lot.

Cah tu tzahi
le caano.
U tzah teh buulo yo' lu le u paa' tutzeentic.
Entonces tu caxtu ba'alu tzeentic, BAK.
Cah tu tzic u ba'al u haante.
Cah tu tzic ba'alo'obo u haante,

• •

can ceh, chhop,

• •

chhiichh.
Le humppe u tzeentic u ha'ante.
Cah tu wilic u le nohochbah.
Entonces ti le HE'ELO le caane,
le u chan Nicolaso,
dzubin nohochtahah.
Dzu nohochtahah.
Le cah tutzila le ciico, u Juanita'i
le puro so'obo XIICIC.
Cah tyalah, "Pues, bix tun cininbeetic?
In wiitzin, dzu NOHOCHTAHAH."
Entonces, cah tun u caxtic humppe tunich, mas nohoch . . .
mas nohoch
TINAJA, humppe tinaja
mas nohoch.
Le tutzahi.
Entonces, cah tu tzeentic tu ca'aten.
Tu tzeentic, tu tzeentic.
U caxtic bak, u caxtic caax, u caxtic nucuch . . . bueno, ba'alo
    u haanta,
e chho, e thuul, bueno, u caxtic ba'al u tzeentic.
Cu paatic u nohochcintic.
Ha'alibe, tu nohoch tun u caan, le u nohochtahah.
Ti'e'elo, cah tzileh dzo'ocu
dzo'ocu nohoch, dzu XIHIC le tinaja tu ca'aten.
Cah tyalah, "Pues, bix tun cininbeeteh?
Bix cininTZA?
Dzunohochba'altah;
chuc u nah cucaha."

• •

Cah tyalah, *"Pues nimodos, bix tun cininbeeteh."*
Cah tu bisah xaxteh humppe sahca tune,
nohoch sahca.
Cah tun u dzah le tune yiitzin beyo.
Pues, como mina'an, otzilo'obe,
pues ba'an mas u tzicti'e?
Ma tu paa tu manic bak; ya'a u ha'ante.

She couldn't go on. She couldn't feed him.
Well, then, she found grass,
plants.
WHATEVER she found she fed to that
younger brother.

•   •

Well, he was there in the cave, eating every hour.
If she found deer or things like that, she fed him.
If there WEREN'T ANY, she fed him plants or GRASS.
She fed him grass . . . fed him grass there in the cave.
(*higher*) The serpent ate it all.

•

He ate cows or whatever . . . whatever could be found she fed
    him.
But because they were poor, he ate grass; there was no meat to
    give him to eat.
One day when the serpent was finished growing, when it was
    big,
she said, "I'll have to put him somewhere.
(*quietly*) What can I do? My poor younger brother
(*quietly*) has grown up.
(*quietly*) He's overgrown.
(*quietly*) He's, well, he's all
beginning to come out of the cave.
It's all,
it's all FILLED UP.
He's grown up, he's filled it up.
He's a big thing, a large serpent.
BRISTLES are coming out."
The bristles were the
hair, what's called "pelo."
Well, she said, "What can I do?
He's really filled up the cave."

•   •

Then
the poor Juanita
said,
"My younger brother's grown up as a
MONSTER!
He eats people.
What can I do?"
(*quietly*) But she couldn't do anything to help.
(*quietly*) Well, she brought her younger brother something to
    eat. He ate things like grass, she gave grass to her brother
    to eat.
Well, one day like that,

Ma tu paa'tu ya'ati. Ma'tu paa'tu tzeentic.
Pues cah entonces, cah tu caxtic su'uc,
xiu.
Le cu BA'AH yan u caxce, yan u paa'tu tzeece le ti'e
yiitzino.

• •

Entonces, tiyan teh sahcabo pues le ora cutocare.
U caxtic wa ceh, wa ba'ah beyo, u tzic ti'e.
We MINA'ANE, u tzictic xiu, puro SU'UC.
Tu tzic su'uci . . . utzic su'uc ti'e sahcabo.
(*higher*) Le ti caan cu haantic xan.

•

Tu haantic waacxo wa ba'ax . . . wa ba'ah pahtali tu tzic ti.
Pero puro su'uc tumen otzi; mina'an bak u tzatic u haantic.
Humppe kiin beyo dzunohochtah le caano, dzunohochchaha,
cah tyalah beya, "Pues minin chha'ic.
(*quietly*) Bix tun ceninbeete? Otzi in wiitzina
(*quietly*) tu nohochchaha.
(*quietly*) Dzu cub ich.
(*quietly*) Dzu, bueno, dzu lah
ho'opu lu calcula'atah te lu sahcabo.
Tu dzo'ocu lah
dzu lah CHHUPIC.
Nohochtaha, tzu chhupic.
Nohoch ba'alche, nohoch caan.
Dzu ho'ol u SUUC."
Es que tu suuc le u
tzo'otzil u pelo, bix u ya'ale u "pelo."
Entonces, ciya'ice, "Pues bix tun ceninbeeteh?
Dzu seten chhup le sahcabo."

• •

Ha'alibe,
cya'ice le otzi
Juanita,
"Dzo'ocu nohochtah in wiitzin
BA'ABAL!
U haantic maace ti.
Bix tun cininbeeteh?"
(*quietly*) Pero le ma tu beetah mixba'ah ti.
(*quietly*) Ha'alibe, tah tu taas humppe ba'al tu haantic u
   yiitzin. Tu haantic ba'alu su'uc, u dza su'uc u yiitzin tu
   haantic.
Ha'alibe, ti humppe kiin beyo,

he said this,
"Well,
SISTER

•   •

JUANA,
I guess I'll be going.
The day has come for me TO LEAVE."

•

"But younger brother, where are you going?"
"Well, I've got to go where I'm going, sister.
You can't FEED ME. I EAT A LOT.
So I'm going.
I have to leave you.

•

My mother is dead;
I love my dead mother.
My father's the only one alive.
Just you *and father* were left to feed me.

•

Well, I've got to go.
I'm going to tell you something, though, sister:
the day I come out to leave,
go far away. Get far away from me
because when I come out I might harm you as I leave."
"Where are you going, brother?"
"I'M GOING TO GO INTO,
INTO THE WATER,
I'm going INTO THE OCEAN."

•

"Really? Okay."
"Well, when I BEGIN TO LEAVE,
that day that I'll leave . . . the day I leave
will be the fifteenth of July.
(*quietly*) I'll leave then."
"Okay."
Well, the morning of the next day, "Well, sister . . .
good-bye, my sister.
You'll be okay here when I go
and you go too.
I'm really going. I won't be able to ever
SEE YOU AGAIN,
see your face. You too won't see my face again.
I'm going.
Whenever you hear me
on the fifteenth of July . . .
when I SHAKE MYSELF,

ciya'ic beya,
"Ha'alibe este,
CIIC
•   •
JUANA,
bin in cahal wale.
Dzo'ocuchtu kiin IN BIN."

•

"Pero iitzin, tu'ux ca bin?"
"Pues, inca'a tu'ux in bin, ciic.
Ma tu pa'atah TZENCEN. YA'AB TIN HAANAH.
Entonces tene, yan in bin.
Yan in ppaatcech.

•

Tac in mama'i, dzuciimi;
in wolah ciin mama'i.
Chen papa cuxa'an.
Es que chen tech ppaatech a tzencen *yete papa.*

•

Pues, yan in bin.
Chen ba'ax in wa'ictech, ciic:
le cah ho'ocen binbale,
cah chan xiicech naach. Naach cuntubahten
tumen cah ho'ocene ma xan in beetch loobi."
"Tu'un ca bin beya, iitzin?"
"BIN CIN IN BEET ICH,
ICH HA,
NUUCUCH KA'NA'O ken in bin."

•

"Haah. Ma'alo."
"Ha'alibe, cah LE CAH XIICENE,
tal dia cah xiicen . . . tal kiin cah xiicen
uti'alu quince de Julio'i.
(*quietly*) Cah xiicen."
"Ma'alo."
Ha'alibe, le cah saastah tu la kiin, "Ha'alibe, ciic . . .
adiosech, wale ciic.
U tzic tech wey tech u pul in bin
yete a bin xan.
Tin bin ten. Bin cen in beetah mix bikiin tu ca'aten
A WICEN,
a pac in wiich. Bey xan ten xan, dzoka'an in pac a wich xan.
Bin cin in beetaten.
Le can a wu'eh
la quince de Julio'i . . .
cen in TIITIN BAY,

when I SHAKE MYSELF, then you know that I'm alive!
I'll be alive, I won't be dead. I'LL BE ALIVE, not dead.

•

I'll be going again."
One of those days then he said,
"Sister, I've got to go on my journey; I'm going now."

•   •

When the sister had gone far, far away,
she heard, (*very loud*) "YI—IN . . ."
Even the trees shook.
Everything shook as he went.
He went on, that thing went on.
That Serpent went on.
When it had flown up through the sky it came back again to
      the sea.

•

Then the sister was left
so
SAD, SHE CRIED.
HER YOUNGER BROTHER had gone away.
Then, a year later

•

she heard HIM RISING UP.
It was her younger brother.
She said, "It's true; my younger brother's alive!"
He rose up on the fifteenth of July!
He began in July and then stopped on the twenty-fourth of
      August.
He finished then.
Every . . . every year like that,
every year
he rises up.
Well, *the sister was left very sad.*
When I passed by there the sister
was THINKING,
thinking of her younger brother.
There it is left; there it ends.

Cen in TIITINBA'O, es que a wohe tzin cuxa'anen!
Cin cuxtah, ma ciimene. CUXA'ANEN, ma ciimene.

Es que bin cen in beeteh."
Iche humppc kiin tun beya can tyah tune,
"Ah ciic, humppe beh wale in cahal; bin cen in beeteh."

Le cah luc u ciic ubeh naach, naache,
cah tyuce, (*very loud*) "YI—IN . . ."
Tac bine le che'o tu bo'otu.
Ba'ah tu ba'atu uch u bino.
Bin tu beeta, bin tu beetah le ba'alo.
Bin tu beetah le Caano.
Caancha'ah tune, cah sunactubah bine ich ha.

Entonces cah ppaat u ciic
hach
TRISTE, hach OTZIYIICH.
Mina'an bin u YIITZIN.
Entonces, tu buelta humppe ha'ab.

cah tyubah tune TU LILCUBAH tune.
Tun u yiitzina.
Cah tyalah, "Haah, cuxa'an in wiitzin!"
Le cu lilcubah humppel quince de Julio!
Cu caaxah de Julio, ha'alibe teh cu dzo'oc le venticuatro de
    Agosto.
Cu dzo'oc ba'ah beyo.
Hasta cada . . . cada ha'ab beyo,
cada humppe ha'abe
cu lilscubah.
Entonces, cah pah tu *ciice, otzi, triste.*
Le cah maanene u ciice
u TUUCUL,
u ticlic u yiitzin.
Le ppaatico; le dzo'ocico.

9. DISCUSSION

Yucatec Mayan oral literature contains humor, pathos, macabre events, and catastrophic predictions. The tradition is kept alive by all adults who are familiar with the cultural details of the stories. The common opening line "There was a person of the milpa," for example, brings to mind all the experiences of milpa farming as told in chapter 6. Mayan narrators assume that their audiences can and will fill in the details of stories in their minds; this is in contrast to European and North American prose writers, who supply intricate details and character descriptions in the written tradition. Where those of us who are attuned to the Western written tradition of prose stories might expect the story of Colas to include an elaborate description of the effects of the earthquake engendered by the Feathered Serpent, such detail is the responsibility of the audience members in the Mayan tradition.

The oral tradition is still a strong force in the lives of Mayan people in Yucatán. The tradition embraces themes and characters from the remote past of the Classic Mayan world, and it also embraces the changes and issues of the world of today. The stories are a rich repository of cultural knowledge and belief, but they should not be mistaken for antiquarian curiosities. The oral tradition is a means through which Mayan people can engage in speculation about the nature of the world and the course of current events. It serves as a system of narrative logic that can be put to use to argue a point or to bring cultural significance to things that might easily be overlooked.

A casual tourist visiting the ruins of the Classic Mayan civilization in Yucatán is often so enamored of the majesty of the architecture that the stone troughs lying about are easily overlooked. To a Mayan observer, however, these troughs are visible evidence of the story of the hunchbacks. The troughs remind one that the last world creation ended in catastrophic floods and that the present world may likewise end in tragedy. While the troughs remind Mayan observers that too much water was responsible for the demise of the hunch-backs, they also remind them of the predictions for the end of the present age, an end that will come about because of lack of water.

Yucatec Mayan oral literature is also used in arguments. The counsels, secrets, and other forms of verbal art are active statements that are molded through conversations to fit changing social conditions. The stories are not thought of as ancient truths that are un-bending in their form or content. Instead, the narratives are linked with present issues, conflicts, and interests so as to function as rhetorical devices. The use of my own statements about the evaporation of water into clouds that was mentioned in chapter 3 is a good example of this process. When I was unable to state clearly just how the water vapor in the air turned into raindrops, Paulino was able to link the concept of the rain gods, the Caste War, and my presence into a counsel for the children and adults in the sacred temple to hear (see "Signs, II" in chapter 3).

The logic of narration can be seen in any of several dimensions of the Yucatec Mayan oral tradition. If a historical dimension is examined, many of the narratives can be understood as repeating a paradigm of destruction and tragedy from earliest times through the present and on into the future. The narratives of the second chapter about the origin of corn tell of a time when people awoke every day dying of hunger. This theme of destruction is repeated in "The Story of the Hunchbacks" in chapter 2 also. When the Spanish colonization of the New World is chronicled in chapter 3, hunger and catastrophe again arise, this time expressed in the race for food between the Spaniards and the Maya. The Spaniards send a horse to fetch the hot tortillas, while the Maya send a squirrel. Although the Mayan squirrel wins, the people disappear from the face of the earth. The Caste War of the nineteenth and twentieth centuries is also remembered in counsels as a time of death and destruction, as exemplified by the narrative about Venancio Puc in chapter 3 where some 550 innocent people are slaughtered. Narratives about the present time, such as the recollection of the visit with Sylvanus Morley or the message to President Nixon, tell of the loss of Mayan resources to the nation of Mexico. The narratives that predict the future also contain this paradigm of destruction. The references to the Chilam Balam in chapter 2 are concerned with the end of the world, when the "Old Lady of Mani" will require a baby boy as the price for a single cup of water. The story of the Feathered Serpent in chapter 8 suggests that earthquakes will also be felt at the end of this age, when the Nohoch Can arises out of its home in the sea.

The logic of the oral tradition can also be seen in some of the shortest examples of verbal art. Narration is a frame within which Mayan people give significance to almost everything in their lives. One of the definitions that Alonzo dictated to me captures this use of narration to make sense out of the world. I had asked Alonzo to tell me about armadillos. He might have given me a simple dictionary description, had he not been a Mayan storyteller. Instead, he related the following macabre story:

> That Motmot and the Armadillo.
> There is a man who catches armadillos.
> He went and caught an armadillo.
> After he caught the armadillo,
> he began to take the armadillo home along with a friend.
> There were two people like that.
> As they are walking along he says to him,
> "Careful, that armadillo can do you wrong."
> So he says to him, "No, it can't do wrong."
> While he's talking like that,
> a Motmot comes along and says, *"Tocti, tocti, tocti!"*[1]
> That's how the Motmot talks to them.
> So the man says, "How can I leave it?
> I have it right here."
> The man says, "Well, things that are mine are mine,
> whether God likes it or God doesn't like it."
> The thing rips open his stomach,
> out come his guts.
> The man says, "Look what happened to you!"
> The Motmot says again, "Tocti, tocti, tocti!"
> The man says, "What can he leave?
> He's already dead."

Narrative logic can also be understood by looking at the nature of verbal art performance. The tradition has great strength and resiliency because it arises out of conversation. Stories, secret knowledge, and ancient conversations are all subsumed in Mayan thought under the term "conversation." Good narration arises out of the engagement of people in good conversations. Because of this, the oral tradition is used as a constant reference in conversations. Allusions to mythic events and figures, excerpts from stories about animals and tricksters, and references to the powers of the winds are brought into discussions so that the everyday world is always connected to the world of narrative. When a skillful narrator is present and the setting is relaxed enough to allow for stories, these allusions and ref-

---

1. "Leave it, leave it, leave it."

erences are picked up and elaborated into more complete narratives, like the short vignette about armadillos given above or the longer chains of narratives given in earlier chapters. As attuned to the sound of good voices and the nuances of wordplay and vocal mannerisms as Yucatec Mayan people are, narrative performance does not need to be signaled by a stage or a loud announcement. Performance cues include the subtle shift of conversation into a dialogue between two people and an understated opening line.

The grounding of Mayan storytelling in conversation insures that the tradition will continue—it cannot be easily forgotten because of the constant references to the tradition made in conversation. While expert narrators are recognized, they are not storytellers by profession and so will not die out in times of economic hardship or political strife. The oral tradition is still found among the three hundred thousand Yucatec Mayan speakers going about their daily lives. As a narrator might say at the end of a story, "When I passed by there earlier, they were conversing with stories."

WORKS CITED

Adams, Richard
  1977   Foreword. In George E. Stuart and Gene S. Stuart, *The Mysterious Maya*. Washington, D.C.: National Geographic Society.
Andrade, Manuel J.
  1957   *A Grammar of Modern Yucatec*. Chicago: University of Chicago Library.
Barrera Vásquez, Alfredo
  1946   La lengua maya de Yucatán. Mérida, Yucatán: Enciclopedia Yucatanense.
Barrera Vásquez, Alfredo, and Sylvanus G. Morley
  1949   *The Maya Chronicles*. Publication 585 of the Carnegie Institution of Washington. Washington, D.C.
Barrera Vásquez, Alfredo, and Silvia Rendón
  1948   *El libro de los libros de Chilam Balam*. Mexico City: Fondo de Cultura Económica.
Bauman, Richard
  1977   *Verbal Art as Performance*. Rowley, Mass.: Newbury House.
Bauman, Richard, and Joel Sherzer
  1974   *Explorations in the Ethnography of Speaking*. New York: Cambridge University Press.
Blair, Robert, and Refugio Vermont-Salas
  1971   *Spoken Yucatec Maya*. Vols. 1 and 2. Chicago: University of Chicago Library.
Bolles, David, and Alejandra Kim de Bolles
  1973   *A Grammar of Yucatecan Maya: Mayan Folk Tales*. Komchhen, Yucatán.
Bricker, Victoria Reifler
  1977   The Caste War of Yucatán: The History of a Myth and the Myth of History. In Grant D. Jones, ed., *Anthropology and History in Yucatán*. Austin: University of Texas Press.
  1979   Yucatec Maya Text. In Louanna Furbee-Losee, ed., *Mayan Texts II*. International Journal of American Linguistics Native American Texts Series. Chicago: University of Chicago.
Brinton, Daniel
  1883   The Folklore of Yucatán. *Folklore Journal* 1: 224–256.
Brunhouse, Robert L.
  1971   *Sylvanus G. Morley and the World of the Ancient Mayas*. Norman: University of Oklahoma Press.
Burns, Allan F.
  1973   Pattern in Yucatec Mayan Narrative Performance. Ph.D. dissertation. Seattle: University of Washington Department of Anthropology.
  1977   The Caste War in the 1970's: Present-Day Accounts from Village

Quintana Roo. In Grant D. Jones, ed., *Anthropology and History in Yucatán.* Austin: University of Texas Press.

1980   Interactive Features in Yucatec Mayan Narratives. *Language in Society* 9: 307–319.

Coe, Michael D.

1966   *The Maya.* New York: Frederick A. Praeger.

de Angulo, Jaime

1973   *Coyote Man and Old Doctor Loon.* San Francisco: Turtle Island Foundation.

Dundes, Alan

1972   Seeing Is Believing. *Natural History* 81 (2): 8.

Edmonson, Munro S.

1971   *The Book of Counsel: The Popol Vuh of the Quiche Maya of Guatemala.* Publication 35 of the Middle American Research Institute. New Orleans: Tulane University.

Elmendorf, Mary

1976   *Nine Mayan Women.* New York: Schenkman Publishing Co.

Gleason, H. A.

1961   *An Introduction to Descriptive Linguistics.* Rev. ed. New York: Holt, Rinehart and Winston.

Goetz, Delia, and Sylvanus G. Morley

1950   *Popol Vuh: The Sacred Book of the Ancient Quiche Maya.* Norman: University of Oklahoma Press.

Goldman-Eisler, Frieda

1964   Discussion and Further Comments. In Eric Lenneberg, ed., *New Directions in the Study of Language.* Cambridge, Mass.: MIT Press.

Gossen, Gary H.

1974   *Chamulas in the World of the Sun: Time and Space in a Maya Oral Tradition.* Cambridge, Mass.: Harvard University Press.

Gumperz, John

1978   The Conversational Analysis of Interethnic Communication. In E. Lamar Ross, ed., *Interethnic Communication.* Southern Anthropological Society Proceedings 12. Athens: University of Georgia Press.

Hymes, Dell

1972   Models of the Interaction of Language and Social Life. In John Gumperz and Dell Hymes, eds., *Directions in Sociolinguistics: The Ethnography of Communication.* New York: Holt, Rinehart and Winston.

Isbell, Billie Jean, and Freddy Roncalla Fernandez

1977   The Ontogenesis of Metaphor: Riddle Games among Quechua Speakers Seen as Cognitive Discovery Procedures. *Journal of Latin American Lore* 3 (1): 19–49.

Jacobs, Melville

1959   *The Content and Style of an Oral Literature.* Chicago: University of Chicago Press.

Jones, Grant D.

1974 Revolution and Continuity in Santa Cruz Maya Society. *American Ethnologist* 1 (4): 79–109.

Landa, Fray Diego de

1978 *Yucatan before and after the Conquest.* Translated with notes by William Gates. New York: Dover Publications. First published as Publication 20 of the Maya Society, Baltimore, in 1937.

Lord, Albert

1960 *The Singer of Tales.* Cambridge, Mass.: Harvard University Press.

McQuown, Norman

1979 A Modern Yucatec Maya Text. In Louanna Furbee-Losee, ed., *Mayan Texts II.* International Journal of American Linguistics Native American Texts Series. Chicago: University of Chicago.

Pacheco Cruz, Santiago

1958 *Diccionario de la fauna yucateca.* Mérida, Yucatán: Pecho Cruz.

1970 *Compendio del idioma maya.* 7th ed. Mérida, Yucatán: Imprenta Manlio.

Paynter, Raymond A.

1955 *The Ornithogeography of the Yucatan Peninsula.* Peabody Museum of Natural History Bulletin 9. New Haven: Yale University Press.

Redfield, Margaret Park

1935 *The Folk Literature of a Yucatecan Town.* Publication 456 of the Carnegie Institution of Washington. Washington, D.C.

Redfield, Robert

1941 *The Folk Culture of Yucatan.* Chicago: University of Chicago Press.

1950 *A Village That Chose Progress: Chan Kom Revisited.* Chicago: University of Chicago Press.

Redfield, Robert, and Alfonso Villa Rojas

1934 *Chan Kom: A Maya Village.* Publication 488 of the Carnegie Institution of Washington. Washington, D.C. Rev. ed., 1962, University of Chicago Press.

Reed, Nelson

1964 *The Caste War of Yucatan.* Stanford: Stanford University Press.

Rothenberg, Jerome

1972 *Shaking the Pumpkin: Traditional Poetry of the Indian North Americas.* Garden City, N.Y.: Doubleday.

Roys, Ralph L.

1931 *The Ethno-Botany of the Maya.* Publication 2 of the Middle American Research Institute. New Orleans: Tulane University.

1933 *The Book of Chilam Balam of Chumayel.* Publication 438 of the Carnegie Institution of Washington. Washington, D.C.

1965 *Ritual of the Bacabs.* Norman: University of Oklahoma Press.

Rubel, Arthur J.

1965 Prognosticative Calendar Systems. *American Anthropologist* 67: 107–110.

Sahagún, Bernardino de
  1963   *Florentine Codex: General History of the Things of New Spain.*
         Trans. Charles E. Dibble and Arthur J. Anderson. Salt Lake City:
         University of Utah Press.
Samarin, William
  1965   The Language of Silence. *Practical Anthropology* 12: 115–119.
Stross, Brian
  1973   Reconstructed Humor in a Tzeltal Ritual Formula. *International
         Journal of American Linguistics* 39 (1): 32–44.
Stuart, George E., and Gene S. Stuart
  1977   *The Mysterious Maya.* Washington, D.C.: National Geographic
         Society.
Tedlock, Barbara
  1975   The Clown's Way. In Dennis Tedlock and Barbara Tedlock, eds.,
         *Teachings from the American Earth: Indian Religion and Phi-
         losophy.* New York: Liveright.
Tedlock, Dennis
  1972   *Finding the Center: Narrative Poetry of the Zuñi Indians.* New
         York: Dial Press.
  1980a *Las formas del verso quiche, de la paleografía a la grabadora.* Ed.
         Robert Carmack. Actas del I Congreso sobre el Popol Vuh (1979).
         Guatemala City: Piedra Santa.
  1980b A New World Classic: The Light from across the Sea. *Bostonia
         Magazine* 54 (5): 39–47.
Thompson, J. E. S.
  1970   *Maya History and Religion.* Norman: University of Oklahoma
         Press.
  1972   *A Commentary on the Dresden Codex: A Maya Hieroglyphic
         Book.* Philadelphia: American Philosophical Society.
Thompson, Richard
  1974   *The Winds of Tomorrow.* Chicago: University of Chicago Press.
Tozzer, Alfred M.
  1921   *A Maya Grammar.* Vol. 9 of the Papers of the Peabody Museum of
         American Archaeology and Ethnology. Cambridge, Mass.: Har-
         vard University.
Villa Rojas, Alfonso
  1945   *The Maya of East Central Quintana Roo.* Publication 559 of the
         Carnegie Institution of Washington. Washington, D.C.
  1969   The Maya of Yucatan. In Robert Wauchope, ed., *Handbook of
         Middle American Indians,* vol. 7: *Ethnology.* Austin: University
         of Texas Press.